Backpacker Magazine's
Guide to the
APPALACHIAN
TRAIL

Backpacker Magazine's
Guide to the
APPALACHIAN
TRAIL

The diamond Trail marker is a registered
servicemark of the Appalachian Trail
Conference. All rights reserved.

Jim Chase

Stackpole Books

Published by
STACKPOLE BOOKS
Cameron and Kelker Streets
P.O. Box 1831
Harrisburg, PA 17105

Printed in the United States of America

10   9

Cover design by Tracy Patterson
Cover photo by Les Holmes, courtesy of the Appalachian Trail Conference
Interior design by Ellen C. Dawson

Library of Congress Cataloging-in-Publication Data

Chase, Jim.
    Backpacker magazine's guide to the Appalachian Trail / by Jim
Chase.
        p.   cm.
    Includes index.
    ISBN 0-8117-2237-6
    1. Backpacking—Appalachian Trail.   2. Appalachian Trail—
Description and travel.   I. Title.   II. Title: Guide to the
Appalachian Trail.
GV199.42.A68C46   1989
796.5'1'0974—dc19   88-28258
                                                               CIP

Contents

Acknowledgments

ACKNOWLEDGMENTS MUST start with my wife, Barbara, for her help, encouragement, and amusing our son Charles when I needed to write, as well as for her endless reading of my accounts of places she has never seen and for her superb comments on those accounts. Also to Charles himself, for understanding why Daddy couldn't go bike riding. Thanks, too, to my parents for instilling in me the love of wild places and the urge to preserve them, and especially to my father for teaching me to backpack before it was in fashion.

I am grateful to the following people: David Startzell, Executive Director of the Appalachian Trail Conference; Jean Cashin, Information Specialist, Appalachian Trail Conference; Anne Bennett, Appalachian Trail Conference; Brian King, Public Affairs Director, Appalachian Trail Conference; Bill Witter, thru-hiker; Potomac Appalachian Trail Club; Michael A. Hurley, Publisher, *Backpacker* Magazine, for his support and encouragement; John A. Delves III, *Backpacker* Magazine, for his getting me into all this in the first place; Kathy Bobseine of the Piedmont Appalachian Trail Hikers; Rachel Schneider of the Chattahoochee National Forest; Garry Friend of the Natural Bridge Appalachian Trail Club; John Giacalone of the Kanawha Appalachian Trail Club; John Morgan of the Maine Appalachian Trail Club; Kay Wood of the Massachusetts Chapter, Appalachian Mountain Club, who wrote from her thru-hike to help; Martha Makosky of the Dartmouth Outing Club; Leona C. Collyer of the Potomac Appalachian Trail Club; M. Virginia Musser of the Keystone Trails Association/Allentown Hiking Club; Joseph F. Cook of the Green Mountain Club; Dick Blake of the Connecticut Chapter, Appalachian Mountain Club; Mark DiMiceli ("Second Wind"); Marianne Skeen of the Georgia Appalachian Trail Club;

Kay Coriell of the Nantahala Appalachian Trail Club; Pat Robinson of the United States Forest Service, Asheville, North Carolina; Dave Sherman of the National Park Service, for advice, counsel, and that beer we haven't yet had the chance to share; Chris Kounkel, Forest Ranger, Shenandoah National Park.

And special thanks to the late Dr. Jean Stephenson of the Appalachian Trail Conference, for making sure that it all got written down.

To Irv Rockwood, super neighbor.

To Myron Avery for making it happen.

And above all, homage to Benton MacKaye for his vision.

The Publisher wishes to acknowledge the invaluable assistance of the staff of *Backpacker* Magazine in the preparation of this book. Subscription information and assistance for *Backpacker* Magazine may be obtained from the magazine offices at 33 East Minor Street, Emmaus, Pennsylvania 18098, telephone number (215) 967-5171.

Introduction: The World's First Linear Park

BEGINNINGS

The project is one for a series of recreational communities throughout the Appalachian chain of mountains from New England to Georgia, these to be connected by a walking trail.

THUS WROTE Benton MacKaye (muh-KYE) in 1921, in what was to become the unofficial manifesto of the Appalachian Trail. "Its purpose is to establish a base for a more extensive and systematic development of outdoor community life," he continued. "It is a project in housing and community architecture."

Clearly, this wasn't merely a simple desire to see a long footpath blazed along the crest of the Appalachian Mountains. MacKaye had more in mind—much more.

THE START OF THE TRAIL

It surprises most people that the Appalachian Trail is not an old pathway of the Native Americans who lived in the region long before the European immigration. Others think of it as a trade route for the settlers, or at the very least a compendium of avenues for early pioneers, traders, Revolutionary armies, or what-have-you, tacked together at logical points by dedicated volunteers.

The volunteers part is true enough. And the Trail does in places use byways of our Native American and colonial forebears, although not in any consistent or organized way. However, Native Americans and settlers alike tended to do the bulk of their travel in valleys, not along ridge lines. The Appalachian Trail as it exists is a creation whose birth is well within the recollection of many people. It was blazed, and is maintained, by the aforementioned dedicated volunteers, who are the sole reason for its existence.

The Trail was first given life in the mind of a single person: E. Benton MacKaye, a civil servant who worked for the federal government. MacKaye published his manifesto, "An Appalachian Trail, A Project in Regional Planning," in the October 1921 issue of *Journal of the American Institute of Architects.* Having long recognized the beneficial effect of trips to the wilderness on increasingly citified Americans, MacKaye was proposing nothing less than a linear park along the crest of the great Appalachian ranges, from Mt. Mitchell in North Carolina to Mt. Washington in New Hampshire.

WILDERNESS NOSTALGIA

America in 1921 was ready, even eager, for the idea. After three hundred years of mortal combat against the "howling wilderness," the last frontiers had been subdued in the nineteenth century. A change, at first subtle and then pronounced, had taken place in the American conception of wilderness. Faced with the extinction of the central influence in the formation of the solid, self-sufficient American character, a romanticism appeared in the late nineteenth century that was to picture wilderness not as threatening, but rather as untamed and pure. Here flowered the romantic "noble savage" ideal of James Fenimore Cooper. America in 1921 was in perhaps the heyday of a great nostalgia, heralded a hundred years before in the more civilized eastern states by such writers as Cooper, Henry David Thoreau, and Ralph Waldo Emerson. It was a yearning for the vanished American frontier, a sentiment that was to produce, among other things, the Wild West show, the Hudson River School, the Boy Scouts and Girl Scouts, the National Parks system, and the Buntline dime novel.

By 1921, this yearning had ripened considerably. The horrors of World War I had served to suggest to the war-weary

United States that perhaps civilization (as represented by the jaded, immoral Old World) wasn't all it was cracked up to be, and that what America needed was a healthy dose of what had made it great in the first place: wilderness, and those people of character who had tamed it. "Without parks and outdoor life," exclaimed Colorado mountain guide Enos Mills in 1917, "all that is best in civilization will be smothered."

The world that MacKaye faced seemed to bear out that notion. Postwar unemployment was at its height, for the first time population in the cities was exceeding that in the country, and the pace of life in general was accelerating. MacKaye hit upon the idea of wilderness camps as an escape for world-weary workers from the cities, people of all classes.

There was a real problem to be solved. Urban workers in America and elsewhere were exhibiting an alienation from the workplace that would have been unthinkable just a few years before by their agrarian predecessors. That is, they didn't like their jobs—or their lives.

Faced with a legion of workers who were falling inexorably into the workaday humdrum of industrial-age living, MacKaye proposed to put a little adventure into their lives, to give them the chance to prove themselves *to* themselves. Rather than live out the rat race all of their days, they could breathe more freely and function as they wished. They could become the heroes of their own life stories. Nature and wilderness would be their teacher, their companion, their friend. In wilderness, modern people could, in the words of Clarence Stein's introduction to MacKaye's seminal article, *re-create* themselves. (Stein was a friend of MacKaye's, a member of the Association of Architects and an early Trail backer.)

Wilderness romanticism had already demonstrated its effects in 1921. John Muir had done battle in the West to preserve the wildlands of the Sierra Nevada. Aldo Leopold had gone far to develop the theories of ecology, beginning the process of convincing Americans and the world that there was a natural balance to be preserved. Bob Marshall would, just a few years later, burst forth from the Adirondacks to propel—in cahoots with MacKaye and others—thousands of square miles of wilderness into federal protection.

It was into this ideological stew that MacKaye dropped,

The backbone of the Appalachian Trail: volunteers build up the cairn on Katahdin in the 1920s. (Photograph courtesy of the Appalachian Trail Conference)

almost casually, his idea for a park that would run the length of the Eastern Seaboard. People latched onto his idea with a firmness that surprised even MacKaye, nowhere more strongly than in the industrial areas of the Northeast, and within a couple of years the Trail's first sections were blazed. The volunteer corps that would be the lifeblood and driving force of the Trail had begun forming. And the Appalachian Trail (AT) as we know it was born.

WHY TWO THOUSAND MILES?

In a year's time, the number of people who hike the entire Trail from end to end usually totals less than two hundred. Compare that with the untold thousands who ramble it for short stretches, and a logical question might be: What does it matter that the Trail is a 2000-mile, unbroken link? And, logically, it doesn't matter. Not a particle. Because the spirit of the Trail is not a matter of reason. There is no good, explainable reason why a hiker gets a special feeling when he or she knows that the trail under his or her feet is the Appalachian Trail. But hikers *do* get that feeling. It's a conviction inside that they're part of something.

As the Georgia Appalachian Trail Club puts it in their motto, it may be the "fellowship of the trail." It's a shared experience, a sense of kinship, a binding of like-minded people. And it shows in a variety of ways: in the powerful drive of local Appalachian Trail clubs to maintain their sections of the Trail in order to preserve the unbroken link; in the tendency of hikers to "go for a hike on the AT," when there are other trails around, just as good; and in the sheer pride a community takes in having the great Trail pass within its boundaries. They are all part of something special, a part of the rugged, self-sufficient American character.

ON THRU-HIKERS

Much of the literature devoted to the Appalachian Trail is centered on the thru-hikers. These are the several hundred people who, each year, start at one end of the Trail or the other—usually in Georgia—and hike until they reach the opposite end. They come from all walks of life and hike in all kinds of ways.

Thru-hikers are not on the trail for the same reason the rest of us are. That's not to say that theirs is the better reason or the more compelling or even the deeper—although it's a

The first of many, Earl Shaffer completed the end-to-end hike of the AT in 1948. (Photograph courtesy of the Appalachian Trail Conference)

pretty profound experience for most of them. It's just that, where the average need for wilderness, be it for renewal, beauty, or sheer physical exertion, can be satisfied in a week or a weekend, theirs can only be satisfied by a total commitment. And you can take that notion to the bank because it takes six months to hike the entire Appalachian Trail, and those without total commitment simply don't make it.

If you meet thru-hikers on the Trail, chances are they will be polite but a bit distant. The fact is, they tend to regard us day hikers as tourists and themselves as the true natives of the Trail community. Don't let it bother you. It's just that, engaged as they are in such a major undertaking, they tend to be a bit detached from the world the rest of us live in.

There are probably as many reasons why a person thru-hikes as there are thru-hikers, but among those I've met, two general themes stand out. The first reminds me eerily of the rite of passage common to many cultures around the world that I'll call the Vision Quest. In Native American culture it would often take the form of a young adult leaving home for the wilderness in search of enlightenment. He or she would fast for long periods of time, exerting to the physical and mental limits, and suffering any number of privations. And often visions would come, sometimes powerful ones, ones that might influence the spirit for the rest of the seeker's life.

If you want to see what I mean, read the trail registers in the shelters along the route, especially in the summer months when most of the thru-hikers are passing by. While many thru-hikers in their entries comment on the weather and cravings for ice cream and steaks, others will often pour their souls onto the pages, describing what's going on in their minds and spirits. Many are very much within themselves.

The second motive is the spirit of adventure. It's much closer to the reasons we all escape to the wilderness from time to time. Closely allied is the "flow experience." It's a motive not unlike what one finds in mountaineers, polar explorers, or anyone who embarks upon an intensive personal effort of that order.

The seductive quality of such endeavors lies for many people in the elimination of extraneous stimuli. Gone are the honking car horns, the sticky elevator doors, the demanding bosses. All that's left is the Trail and the necessity of walking it. The challenges, though they may be formidable, are simple: get up the hill, pitch the tent, get in from the storm. What you do is all part of a *flow,* a simpler, more reassuring reality. Your benchmark is the measure of how well you can do it: how comfortable you can be in the storm, how many miles you can put in, how self-sufficient you can make yourself. It's you and the Trail, *mano a mano.* Your success is easily measured, your satisfaction easy to enjoy without second thoughts. In describing their flow experiences, mountaineers say that they don't really think about danger or glory or anything else. Rather, they think simply about the task at hand, and about overcoming the obstacles in their drive for the summit. That's where they get their satisfaction. One thing I have *never* encountered is a thru-hiker who walks the Trail for recognition, although some of them write books afterward.

Thru-hikers typically embark from the southern terminus at Springer Mountain in the early spring—frequently in March, usually in April. This is to take advantage of the warm southern weather and get a jump on the season (Katahdin is usually inhospitable at that time of year). April and May see them through the Carolinas and into Virginia. June and July find them passing Harpers Ferry and the Pennsylvania line. By late July and early August many will have crossed New Jersey and New York and headed due north in New England. The rest of the month they will be in the highlands of Vermont and New Hampshire, fortified for the effort by all the conditioning they've gotten to that point.

In September they're usually zeroing in on Katahdin, trying to beat the blasts of winter on their way to the wire. Often, they will take the ferry across the Kennebec River and then have to wait several days for Pamola, the spirit of the summit, to decide to let them up and allow the fall storms to clear. Then they make their way up to The Greatest Mountain and the finish. What goes on in their minds has been the subject of countless articles and interviews. I'm not sure I've ever heard what sounded like the whole story. I'm not sure that can be told.

Several of the thru-hikers I've met have gone back a year, or two or three, later to do it all again. Many say "I'm not going to rush it this time." They declare "This time is for enjoyment, to look at the scenery." Perhaps that's true. On the other hand, perhaps they'll do it again even faster. It doesn't matter. For each one, there's something in the experience that's almost like a drug. It's a fine addiction.

Benton MacKaye, speaking of the Trail in the last years of his life, said, "The ultimate purpose? There are three things: 1) to walk; 2) to see; 3) to *see* what you see. . . . Some people like to record how speedily they can traverse the length of the trail, but I would give a prize for the ones who took the longest time."

Still, I hate to think that MacKaye would object to the true speedsters, the thru-hikers, keeping up their pace of 11 miles per day, or 14 or 21. They're *seeing* as well, only for them the seeing is within. A different wind blows in their faces, but it comes from another kind of re-creation. It's perhaps unlike the one that the rest of us enjoy and to which MacKaye was referring. But it's one that only the Appalachian Trail can provide.

THE TRAIL GUIDES

Individual-trail-description chapters follow the divisions of the ten trail guides that are published periodically by the Appalachian Trail Conference (ATC) and its local member clubs. That's on purpose, so that you can read up on a section of the Trail, perhaps decide on a destination, and then check the trail guide for the ground-level information it gives so well. The trail guides, in order, are:

1. Maine
2. New Hampshire and Vermont
3. Massachusetts and Connecticut
4. New York and New Jersey
5. Pennsylvania
6. Maryland and northern Virginia
7. Shenandoah National Park, Virginia
8. Central and southwest Virginia
9. North Carolina and Tennessee (including the Great Smokies)
10. North Carolina and Georgia (including the Great Smokies)

For each of these sections there is a specific trail guide,

which comes with the appropriate topographic maps. Some have been revised more recently than others, and they each have unique features. The New Hampshire/Vermont guide, for example, has the best section on geology. The recently redone Maine guide introduces an interesting new concept in trail guide layout; rather than including all of the detailed trail information in the book itself, the Maine guide prints it on the back of its maps and the guide itself includes information on the history of the Trail, helpful hints, and general trail-mileage listings. It gives the hiker the choice of carrying the whole package out onto the trail or of leaving the book at home and saving weight by carrying just the appropriate maps.

Information common to all trail guides includes:

1. How to use the guide
2. Maps
3. The hiker's responsibilities
4. Transportation to the Trail
5. Description of shelters and campgrounds
6. Advice and precautions about things like weather, pests, getting lost, trail relocations
7. Trail markings
8. The Appalachian Trail, including general information on the route, the Appalachian Trail Conference, and the history of the Trail
9. Detailed trail descriptions—where the best views are, what the trail is like

This last item constitutes the preponderance of information contained in any given guide. It is usually detailed to the point of giving mileage markers to tenths or even hundredths of a mile, and descriptions on the order of: "At mile 5.83, you will find a potable spring rising behind a large rock." This information is the latest available at press time, collected by the same local people who maintain and watch over that section of the Trail. I have seldom found this information to be inaccurate.

The only time it isn't accurate is when the Trail is relocated for one reason or another. That's why the trail guides have to be revised every so often, and it's a major source of frustration to the ATC's publications folks; even as they're going to press on any given edition they know it may be outdated by the time it hits the stands. The best way to keep up on relocations is to join the Appalachian Trail Conference. Their bimonthly magazine, the *Appalachian Trailway News,* gives authoritative updates on relocations, in addition to a lot of other interesting and useful information.

The only other route-finding suggestion I would make, beyond the trail guides, is to get U.S. Geological Survey (USGS) maps for certain sections. Be advised, however, that the AT route may be out of date on some of them.

SIGNIFICANT MINUTIAE

"The Appalachian Trail" being rather a long monicker, I will use two shorthand references in ensuing pages. The Appalachian Trail is known affectionately to hikers as "The A.T." I will shorten that further to "AT," both in deference to common usage and as a kind of tribute to the symbol of the Trail: the "AT" with the two letters sharing crossbars, the A over the T. (It's a great symbol, but not easy to explain.)

You may have noticed the spelling of "thru-hiker." That is the common way to spell it, instead of the more proper "through-hiker." Remember, the name of the game here is to travel light.

In addition, I will capitalize the word "Trail" in reference to the Appalachian Trail, and use lowercase "trail" in reference to other trails or to trails in general.

Got it? Let's go.

A truly unsung heroine, Dr. Jean Stephenson was the founding editor of the Appalachian Trailway News, *the magazine of the Appalachian Trail Conference. As secretary of the ATC, she kept in touch with the many member clubs through the delicate formative years and into the 1960s. Without her tireless and totally voluntary efforts, most of the wonderful stories of the early Trail days would have been lost. (Photograph courtesy of the Appalachian Trail Conference)*

1

The Bones of the Appalachians

GENERAL GEOLOGY OF THE AT*

THE FIRST thing to understand about a trail like the Appalachian is its setting. Benton MacKaye intended that the stage upon which he set his refuge for beleaguered urbanites be the long spine of the East Coast of North America. In "An Appalachian Trail, A Project in Regional Planning," he envisioned a giant marching south down the central ridges of the Appalachians, and what that giant would see. Everywhere, as he stood high in his wilderness refuge, the giant would see nearby cities and industrial centers. It was this kind of proximity that Mac-Kaye sought. His trail could only happen in the Appalachian range.

A mountain range is a combination of many characteristics. Its flesh and blood are forests and fields, wildlife and weather, and the people who live and work in them. But its bones are the very rocks upon which it is founded. They are rocks that may have come from deep within the earth, or that may once have been laid down on the bottom of a sea so ancient that our minds cannot comprehend its age. These rocks were then hurled high into the air to form the mountain range. And the story of what these rocks are, how they came to be where they are and why they are, has a profound effect on the Trail and the hiking experience.

---

* A geological glossary is provided at the end of this chapter.

The mountain ranges that are variously classified as Appalachian begin in northeast Alabama, run up through Georgia, North Carolina, Tennessee, Virginia, West Virginia, Maryland, Pennsylvania, New Jersey, New York, Connecticut, Massachusetts, Vermont, New Hampshire, and Maine. They continue into Canada and up through Newfoundland. From there occurs a gap for the Atlantic Ocean and the chain continues over the Caledonian highlands of Scotland, the rugged mountains of western Norway, and ends (some say) on the islands of Spitsbergen. The distance all told (minus interruptions for oceans) is over 4000 miles. These ranges form one of the longest cordilleras on record. At one time they may have been nearly 50,000 feet high in places—20,000 feet higher than Mt. Everest!

To understand how this can be, you have to know a bit about these marvelous mountains. They have been uplifted and worn down a number of times; they are perhaps the most orderly, perfectly formed series of folded mountains in the world; the mountains we see today are the result of one of the greatest slow-motion cataclysms since the earth began: the Appalachian Revolution.

But, first of all, geological time is seldom cast in bronze. Geologists have only glimpses of the whole picture with which to work in creating their ingenious scenarios of what happened a billion years ago; and opinions of actual time will differ from scientist to scientist. So will the various scenarios themselves. I've had to interpret several different theories, and often my unscientific mind has chosen the one that seems most correct to me.

Here's what seems to have happened. In the dim early millennia of life, near the beginning of the Cambrian period (about 570 million years ago) and in the first period of the Paleozoic ("old life") era, the eastern section of what is now North America was pretty flat. Some geologists say that conditions were much like those you'll find in the Atlantic Gulf Coast area today—low, flat land gradually descending into an extensive continental shelf. Mountains had existed there before, and their bones lay buried under the flatlands, perhaps rising inland into a gentle mountain range, much like today. In what is now New York state, the Adirondacks, already ancient in that era, lay inland, a mass of low, rolling hills.

To say that these flats existed in eastern North America is perhaps a bit misleading. Nobody really knows for certain what part of the globe these primordial layers of sand and mud occupied; the world, as we have since realized, is not a very stable place, particularly in geological terms. Some scientists suggest that the East Coast might actually have run along an east/west axis, near the equator. Many things have changed in all those years.

It would be more accurate to say that the area where the Appalachian Mountains rose could be found toward the edge of the forerunner of today's North American plate. And therein lies a tale.

PLATE TECTONICS

It has been a century or more since it was first noticed that the shape of the eastern edge of South America bore a striking similarity to that of the west edge of Africa. The conclusion was easy, if controversial: the two continents had indeed been welded to each other at some point in the distant past. Perhaps it was *too* simple, because for decades, few people gave the proposition serious thought.

But on reflection, in the mid-twentieth century, geologists found that the theory that became known as "Plate Tectonics" could, in fact, answer many troubling questions. Why, for example, were fossils found in northeastern North America also found in northern Europe? Why did mountain ranges seem to continue from one continent to another—right down to the structure of the ridges and the composition of the rock? And why were there earthquake zones at the edges of these hypothetical "plates," and what did it all mean?

The theory also answered more important concerns, such as why mountains form in the first place. Such concerns had always been a fatal weakness of conventional geology: Who could seriously believe that the crust of the earth would buckle and fold or fault without some other agency crunching it together?

And so a theory developed and gained increasing—and lately nearly universal—acceptance. It said this: The earth's surface is composed almost entirely of plates—hardened surfaces that float atop the molten rock below. Thick plates form land-masses. Thinner plates are covered by ocean.

These plates are in constant motion. The Pacific Coast of North America, for example, has lately been the scene of a sideswipe maneuver by the Pacific plate. To the north, another plate has been slowly diving—or *subducting*—underneath the landmass. The results are numerous: the San Andreas Fault, where a sizable chunk of Southern California is heading for Northern California; Yosemite National Park, where spectacular rock domes have been formed of cooled magma that bubbled toward the surface as *plutons,* released by the sea plate diving underground; or the chain of volcanoes in the Cascades.

In the beginning of the Paleozoic era, the situation in the east was this: the remains of an earlier round of mountain-building had been worn down essentially to nothing. This in-comprehensibly ancient mountain-building was the *Grenville Event,* an only dimly understood episode that occurred some-where between 1.4 and 1.1 billion years ago, and that (after millions of years of erosion) left rugged crystalline rock that formed a foundation for what was to come. The only known remnants of Grenville mountains are the Adirondacks and other smaller ranges, and they survived only because they were reju-venated by later uplifting. They are easily some of the oldest mountains in the world.

At the start of the Grenville Event, North America was much smaller than it is now. It covered perhaps half to two-thirds of the continent as it exists today, and was surrounded by a continental shelf and volcanic islands similar to those of Japan and the Philippines. The landmass evidently consisted of all three kinds of rock: igneous, sedimentary, and metamorphic. The sediments confirmed what we could have guessed: The rocks formed and molded by the Grenville Event were com-posed, in part, of the eroded remains of even older rocks from mountain-building that we will never know anything about; its history is lost forever in the inconceivable time-abyss of the earth's formation. So, the Grenville Event had almost certainly not been the first uplift in the neighborhood.

The plates began to close in together. Some other conti-nental mass—maybe Europe and Africa, maybe not—moved in on the East Coast, and the North American plate began to crumple. By the time the two continents crashed into each other, probably around 1300 million years ago, a range of mountains, probably much like the present-day Appalachians, had formed.

It wasn't until perhaps 700 million years ago that the two plates began to part. As they did, a new round of vulcanism began, filling around, and in some cases over, the remains of the Grenville mountains—by that time worn down to stumps seldom over 1000 feet tall. As is typical of such activity when continents separate, the volcanoes emitted basalt, a flowing hard form of lava much different from the more explosive ash-pumice types found where continents come together. A present-day example of the former would be the fast-flowing lava of Hawaii, and of the latter would be the ashy, cindery spume of Mount St. Helens. The basalt of these eruptions, metamorphosed during the uplift of the present-day Appalachians, is visible as the greenstone atop the Blue Ridge in Shenandoah National Park. The proto-Atlantic Ocean—called *Iapetus* by some scientists—was formed.

Grenville rock will be encountered later, in certain sections of the Trail, where it has been raised and uncovered. The changes to the landscape that the Event unleashed (those we can still identify) form some of the most interesting sections of the Trail.

Which all brings us, in a roundabout way, to our gentle coastal plain of 570 million years ago. *Iapetus* had been getting wider for millions of years, and was finally reaching its widest point. As it expanded, lava flowing up in the middle of the ocean formed a thin ocean plate between shores. It eventually reached its widest point some 500 to 600 million years ago. From there, the ocean started to contract again. Geologists disagree as to

All was quiet 550 million years ago. The proto-Atlantic, which some geologists call Iapetus, *was at its widest point, and the North American coast* (left) *consisted of a coastal plain, a continental shelf, and the remains of old mountains, perhaps the Adirondacks, built during the Grenville Event 1.1 billion years ago.*

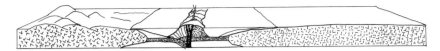

Continents approach, and the first round of mountain-building, the Taconic Orogeny, begins 450 million years ago. As Europe and/or Africa approaches, one scenario has the North American side of the ocean floor (left) diving under, or subducting, the Eurafrican side, which builds mountains by shoveling ocean sediment and releasing volcanic action. These mountains will later become the Green Mountains of Vermont, the Taconics, the Hudson Highlands, and the Reading Prong. An arc of volcanic islands (not shown) forms offshore. An inland sea forms to the left of the new mountains.

how wide the proto-Atlantic was—thousands of kilometers, or merely hundreds.

As other plates (Europe and Africa) homed in on North America, one side of the thin ocean floor began to dive under the other. This was common, as other, thinner, plates often went under (or "subducted"), to be remelted into magma. Offshore, volcanic islands formed. The stage was set for the first great uplift in the formation of the Appalachian range: the Taconic Orogeny, 450 million years ago.

As the approaching continent neared, mountains began to be uplifted near the outer edge of the continental shelf, forming the Green Mountains of Vermont, the Berkshires of Massachusetts, the Taconics of New York, the Hudson Highlands, and the Reading Prong through northern New Jersey into Pennsylvania. Inland, as the coastline uplifted, a shallow sea extended in places all the way to Minnesota, rimmed to the "east" (whichever direction it really was is open to conjecture) by mountains. Offshore, an ocean-floor trench was probably formed at the point of the ocean plate's subduction.

Then, for 100 million years, things quieted down. The European and African plates were still coming, but instead of the sea floor being forced under North America, it was diving under Africa, relieving the pressure on the North American coast.

The second great episode in the forming of the Appalachians was the Acadian Orogeny, which happened 100 million years later, as northern Europe swept across the ocean floor, crashing into the northeast corner of North America. At the time, the coast in New England ran roughly down the Connecticut River valley.

As Europe approached, it pushed the ocean floor ahead of it, crushing volcanic ocean islands and ocean-floor sediment onto the coast, in many cases thrusting the material right over on top of the existing landmass. There is an entire zone of *metavolcanics*, including a number of identifiable vol-

Crunch! The two plates (the one at the right may have been Europe) collide. The result is the uplifting of the Blue Ridge and related ranges, and the welding of the offshore volcanic islands into the center of New England. The shallow inland sea, filled with eroded sediment of the new mountains, survives this, the Acadian Orogeny, 350 million years ago but will be uplifted in the later Alleghany Orogeny, 230 to 250 million years ago, as the African plate plows into the lower East Coast.

canic island formations, up and down the Connecticut valley. Swamps formed on either side of the suture line, leaving coal deposits from Pennsylvania to Wales and beyond.

This went on until around 230 million years ago. The situation at that time was this: Europe and North America had welded together down to around the Connecticut/New York border. Below that, the much smaller *Iapetus* was still open. That set the stage for the final cataclysm.

And what a crunch it was! Until about 450 million years ago, the African plate had been rubbing up against Antarctica and other land plates off to the side somewhere, some say forming a supercontinent geologists call *Gondwanaland*. At that point, however, it had started a 200-million-year-long march to join Europe and America. And 230 million years ago it arrived, bulldozing enormous amounts of ocean floor right up over the existing land formations. So great was the impact of this, the Alleghany Orogeny (some geologists spell it Allegh*any* and the mountains themselves Allegh*eny*), that it uplifted all that sediment that had been accumulating in the inland sea for all those millions of years and then folded the inland lowlands into washboard mountains, forming first the Allegheny plateau and the Catskill plateau, and then the Allegheny Mountains and the side ranges in Virginia and the lower Appalachians.

The result was a vast supercontinent that geologists call *Pangaea*. But for every action there is an equal and opposite reaction. Geologic history since then is said to consist mostly of

The continents separated 200 million years ago. Some geologists say that a portion of the European plate (center) *remained welded to the North American plate to become eastern New England. Plutonic activity bubbles near the surface, especially in the White Mountains of New Hampshire. The Atlantic Ocean is reborn.*

the breakup of that merging of major landmasses on the Paleozoic globe, because no sooner had they merged than Europe and Africa headed back across the newly reopened Atlantic. To this day, the Atlantic is still widening, the new ocean plate expanding from the middle as lava oozes out at the Mid-Atlantic Ridge.

But the big story in the Appalachians is weathering. What had been built up was being broken down. Actually, the erosion of the mountains had started even while they were being up-lifted. The Acadian Orogeny, for example, uplifted the eroded rock dust of the Taconic; the Acadian's own waste was thrust up by the Alleghanian. But 200 million years ago, with Europe and Africa going back across the Atlantic Ocean, the uplifting ended and the story from there on is one of wearing away.

As the European and African plates inched off, though, an exchange may have been taking place. Parts of Newfound-land and lands north seem to have been broken off and became parts of the British Isles, northern Europe, and Scandinavia. Parts of western Europe stayed, becoming eastern New Eng-land, east of the former coast at the Connecticut River valley. (Until Europe hit the coast the route of the Appalachian Trail would have reached the ocean near Norwich, Vermont.)

The actual appearance of the Appalachians as they exist today, then, isn't so much the result of mountain building as it is of erosion. Their configuration is the result of different layers of rock weathering at different rates.

The principle is simple: Some rocks don't resist weather-ing very well; others hold up through most anything. Examples abound: Niagara Falls, for example, is a precipitous drop rather than rubble and rapids because its capping layer of extra-hard dolomite wears away much more slowly than does the softer rock underneath. Likewise, the Grand Canyon has sheer vertical walls because of a hard caprock layer of dolomite.

A typical Appalachian scenario starts with an enormous

folded ridge—some will say the size of Mt. Everest, while most will only say at least 15,000 feet. As it weathers away, erosion eats down through the layers. Depending on the hardness of the various layers, a number of things can happen. If the inner layers are soft and the outer ones hard, the center of the ridge will be worn away, leaving two lower ridges held up by the harder layers. If, on the other hand, it is the inner rock that is the harder, the outer layers will strip away, leaving the harder, often igneous or hard metamorphic, core.

There are, in places, variables. For example, where the Trail crosses the Hudson River, the rocks are exceedingly old. Some of the rounded summits that hikers see there are billion-year-old plutons—bubbles of molten rock that melted their way up through the strata above until they came close enough to the surface to harden. They were eventually exposed by weathering. Old Rag Mountain, in Shenandoah National Park, is totally different in structure from the rest of the ridge. It is also an exceedingly old Precambrian pluton, once lying underneath the sedimentary layers but tilted up by later folding. The white Barre granite in eastern Vermont is of more recent plutonic origin, forming during the Appalachian Revolution.

THE SHAPE OF THE RANGE

The Appalachians are so orderly that some features extend for hundreds of miles. For example, there are three basic provinces of the range: 1. the eastern ranges, from Maine down through the White Mountains of New Hampshire and the Green Mountains of Vermont, the Taconics, and Hudson Highlands of New York, and the Reading Prong into central Pennsylvania, down to South Mountain in Maryland, which will become the Blue Ridge of Virginia, North Carolina, and Georgia; 2. the Great Valley, extending from southern Vermont across central New York, down through the Susquehanna and Cumberland valleys, through the famous Shenandoah Valley all the way to Tennessee; and 3. the western ridges, mostly designated as the Alleghenies, extending from the Shawangunks in eastern New York down through the Kittatinnies of New Jersey, Blue Mountain in Pennsylvania, and on through West Virginia and Kentucky into Tennessee.

Each ridge and mountain has its own story within the context of the dramatic origins of the Appalachian ranges. These are better left for later, when we're discussing individual sections of the Trail.

But be aware, as you walk, that you're on some of the most interesting ground on earth—ground where continents once collided.

A NOTE ON METAMORPHISM

Whenever there is vigorous mountain-building, as there was during the various orogenies that formed the Appalachians, the rock strata that are uplifted are likely to undergo metamorphism, or change into a different form or rock. This happens because of crushing, bending, and the extreme heat that usually accompanies the process.

Heat is especially likely to make changes. As rocks cool, the minerals within them tend to separate and harden into recognizable crystals. The faster the rock hardens, the smaller the crystals will be; conversely, the slower the cooling process, the larger. Sedimentary rocks, of course, have no chance at all to form crystals because they are not formed with heat.

Add heat to already-formed rocks, though, and the process of crystallization can begin again. What was once merely sandstone, for example, can be forged into translucent crystalline quartzite. Even shale can form crystals and become a glittering mica-laden schist. And in some cases a rock may melt again and harden as something igneous.

In many, if not most, areas through which the Trail passes, the vast majority of the rocks will have been metamorphosed by the forces that created the mountains. It's one reason the mountains have endured for, in some places, 450 million years: metamorphic rocks tend to be harder than the often sedimentary ones from which they were formed.

A BRIEF GLOSSARY OF GEOLOGICAL TERMS

Anticline.   An upward fold in the rock strata.

Appalachian Revolution.   The sequence of mountain-building episodes, or orogenies, that formed the Appalachian ranges.

Basalt.   Hardened lava.

Batholith.   A large mass—at least 40 square miles—of coarse-grained, intrusive igneous rock that has been exposed by erosion.

Clastic sediments.   Deposits formed of broken-up bits of older rock.

Cordillera.   A chain of mountains, usually continental in proportions.

Dolomite.   Sedimentary rock formed of the mineral *dolomite*, a calcium and magnesium carbonate deposited in shallow seas.

Equigranular.   Formed of different kinds of mineral crystals that are of approximately the same size.

Erratic.   Typically, a boulder left by a glacier and not of the same type as the local bedrocks.

Fault.   A break in the rock strata.

Fold.   A bend of rock strata by pressure, usually horizontal.

Geosyncline.   A huge basin in the earth's crust, within which vast amounts of sediments accumulate.

Gneiss.   Metamorphosed rock, frequently from granite, often characterized by a banded appearance.

Granite.   A crystalline igneous rock composed chiefly of quartz and feldspar.

Graywacke.   A very common form of "dirty" sandstone, composed of sand mixed with rock fragments and often with clay.

Grenville Event (*or* Orogeny).   The original uplift of the eastern edge of the North American plate, which occurred between 1.4 billion and 1.1 billion years ago. Crystalline Grenville rocks lie under virtually the entire Appalachian range. Grenville mountains were probably completely eroded away (except the Adirondacks) when the existing ranges were uplifted. Named for Grenville, Ontario.

Iapetus Ocean.   Name used by some geologists to refer to the proto-Atlantic Ocean prior to the Appalachian Revolution and the formation of the *Pangaea* supercontinent.

Igneous rock.   Rock composed of hardened molten rock.

Klippe.   A part of a thrust-slab isolated later by erosion. Plural: *klippen.*

Limestone.   A sedimentary rock composed mostly of the mineral calcite.

Marble.   Metamorphosed limestone or dolomite.

Metamorphic rock.   Sedimentary or igneous rock, the composition of which has been changed by extreme heat and pressure.

Monadnock.   A solitary, usually domed, mountain, often formed by plutonic action.

Moraine.   A buildup of sand, gravel, and rounded boulders left by a glacier at its mouth and edges.

Orogeny.   The process of mountain formation, particularly by folding or faulting of the earth's crust.

Pangaea.   A supercontinent formed by the collision of Europe, Africa, and the Americas during the Acadian and Alleghany Orogenies.

Plate.   A hardened section of the earth's crust, floating on molten rock below the surface.

Pluton.   A large blob of igneous rock formed by a bubble of molten rock rising toward the earth's surface through the strata until it cools.

Quartzite.   Metamorphosed sandstone or conglomerate. Very hard.

Sandstone.   A sedimentary rock composed of sand cemented together.

Schist.   A metamorphic rock that can be formed from anything from shale to basalt. Characterized by crystalline structure (indicative of a greater degree of heat pressure) and often distinct fracture layers.

Sedimentary rock.   Hardened layers of material deposited on the surface or under water.

Shale.   A sedimentary rock composed of hardened mud.

Slate.   Metamorphosed shale. Characterized by sharply defined horizontal fracturing.

Strata.   Layers of rock.

Subduction.   In plate tectonics, the process, during the impact of two plates, of one plate descending beneath the other to be melted in the magma beneath.

Syncline.   A downward fold in the rock strata.

Water gap.   A sharp division through a ridge through which a river flows. Often, the ridge was uplifted under the river, which wore its pass through the rock as the uplift occurred.

	Geological Time	Age in Millions	
C		Present	
E			
N	Quaternary Period	Holocene Epoch	(10,000 yrs)
O		*Last Ice Age*	
Z		Pleistocene Epoch	2
O		Pliocene Epoch	5
I		Miocene Epoch	24
C	Tertiary Period	Oligocene Epoch	38
E		Eocene Epoch	55
R			
A		Paleocene Epoch	63

	Geological Time		Age in Millions
M **E** **S** **O** **Z** **O** **I** **C**	Cretaceous Period	(Late Cretaceous Epoch)	96
		(Early Cretaceous Epoch	138
	Jurassic Period		205
	Triassic Period	*Pangaea Breaks Up*	~240
P **A** **L** **E** **O** **Z** **O** **I** **C** **E** **R** **A**	Permian Period	*Alleghany Orogeny*	290
	Carboniferous	(Pennsylvanian Period)	~330
	Periods	(Mississippian Period) *Acadian Orogeny*	360
	Devonian Period		410
	Silurian Period		435
	Ordovician Period	*Taconic Orogeny*	500
	Cambrian Period		~570
P **R** **E** **C** **A** **M** **B** **R** **I** **A** **N**	*Breakup of Grenville Continent—volcanic activity forms lava flows*		700
	PROTEROZOIC ERA	*Grenville Event*	1200 2500
	ARCHAEOZOIC ERA		3600

2

Appalachian Forests

IT IS said that when European settlers arrived in North America four hundred years ago, a squirrel (granted, a highly motivated one) could have traveled from the Gulf of Mexico to the Canadian border and beyond without once touching its feet to the ground, so great was the enormous forest in the Appalachian ranges. The woodlands through which the Appalachian Trail passes are the remnants of forests that once had a profound effect on the lives and minds of those settlers. They provided a seemingly unlimited source of fuel and building materials.

Indeed, the frame and post-and-beam structures familiar in American architecture were relatively unknown in Europe outside Scandinavia (the log cabin in America was perfected by Swedish settlers in Virginia). To this day, while we Americans blithely raise our roofs on walls of wood, Europeans regard such methods as foolish—inefficient and expensive beyond reason. For their own situation, they're right.

But in this country wood made—makes—perfect sense. It was not merely easily and cheaply available; it had to be harvested in order to make room for growing food. Therein lay the rub.

It may seem strange to outdoorspeople today, but for the first three centuries of European rule in America, the forest was considered an adversary. And it did present real challenges. Trees had to be chopped and their stumps pulled before a tillable field emerged. The endless woods blocked expansion by their ruggedness and sheer size.

A perceived malice took on symbolic form over the years; a perceived enmity and danger presented to the settlers by the wilds took on unreal proportions. Settlers and city dwellers alike began to believe that the forests harbored danger in the form of hostile animals and people. This was especially bad in the East, where there were no great mountain ranges above tree line. It was difficult to get an overview of where you were. Travelers easily became lost; one valley looked much like another, especially when the most you could see was about 50 yards at ground level. The woods were no place to be. They had to be tamed.

Small wonder that early European-Americans became positively obsessed with the idea of the "howling wilderness." For better or worse, European domination of North America was founded in large part on an *idée fixe* that the wilderness had to be tamed and made useful to humanity. And thus was born the idea of "harvesting" the forests and using the "resources" of the earth. Anyone who has ever walked through the clear-cuts of the Carolinas or the strip mines of Pennsylvania knows the rest.

By its location on the very ridge line of the East, the Appalachian Trail passes through the best of what remains of that incomprehensibly vast forest—in its day perhaps the greatest forest in the world. Fortunately, attitudes changed just in time to save this small stretch of America's heritage.

LIFE ZONES

Forests are differentiated by type. The categories are dictated mostly by climate: how cold it gets, how long the growing season is. The entire type gamut is found in the space, be it narrow or wide, between tropic zone and tree line.

Tree line is that division beyond which no tree can grow: the conditions are too harsh, the temperature is too cold, the growing season too short. It is dictated by one or both of two factors: latitude and elevation.

In the southern Appalachians there is no tree line. There is no place in the entire region where trees do not grow because it is too harsh for them; both the latitude and elevation are too low. You have to travel hundreds of miles north—and then climb up into the Appalachians—for that.

As you travel north from the gulf plain, the first zone through which you pass is southern pineland. As you climb uphill to the Trail, pines gradually mix with hardwoods until you reach the southern Appalachian forest. As you pass through lower zones where the logging of centuries past has altered the interaction of the various species (but not always the feel of the Appalachian woods), you approach the real thing: world-famous woods where hundreds of species vie with one another to be the most magnificent.

Between the lowest and highest levels of the southern Appalachians rises a mile of mountain. By the time the hiker reaches the 6000-plus-foot summits, practically all the life zones in the East have been traversed, up to the boreal forests that are the stunted last stop before virtual tundra—tree line. There is some disagreement whether that exists in the South: Some experts theorize that the famous "balds" of the southern ranges might be semialpine remnants of the summit tundra left by the Ice Age.

As the Trail moves north, it encounters type after type, from the spruce summits of the high Smokies to the more open oak and hickory woods through the Appalachians of North Carolina and Virginia. As it winds through the northern states the route travels the hard, shattered, Precambrian rock stripped bare by the last Ice Age, which retreated a mere ten thousand years ago. Here, summits are increasingly boreal, full of hardy conifers and blast-proof hardwoods like birch, aspen, and red oak. In the valleys, one passes through northern transition forest—home to the giant sugar maples and beeches that turn to flame every fall. Finally, the boreal forest takes over, except for the summits of the White Mountains. There is true tundra, home only to grasses, lichens, mosses, and the small bushes and flowers that can handle the hurricane winds and short growing season.

North of Katahdin—itself an alpine summit—the life zones span out across the face of the continent until the ultimate tree line is reached, where the tundra extends right down to sea level and all the way up to the Arctic sea.

Starting at the Trail's terminus on the alpine slopes of Katahdin, the life of the forests will become more vigorous as one moves south to Springer Mountain. Each zone has its own story, and its own charm.

Alpine summit. This is life at a minimum. Plants that

thrive here do so by rigid adherence to a single axiom: Waste not, want not. Nothing grows very tall, mainly to present a smaller target to the cold and wind, to offer less surface area for evaporation of precious water, and in recognition of the simple fact that there isn't very much soil in which to grow. Flowers have mastered the trick of sprouting, blossoming, and going to seed in a matter of a few weeks, which is about all the growing season they get. Dominant plants are lichens and mosses, many of which represent species that can only be found at lower elevations if one goes hundreds and thousands of miles to the north. Going downhill, the hiker gradually enters the upper reaches of the boreal forest, usually starting first with stunted balsam firs and spruces.

Boreal forest.   The dominant species here share one thing with the alpine varieties and with one another: they're survivors.

Conifers predominate simply because they're efficient. Their needles give them two advantages: they allow much less evaporation than broad leaves, and they don't waste the tree's energy and nutrients by falling off each year.

The most common deciduous trees are the hardy birches and aspens. These are the first to grow after cataclysms like fire and landslide (and chainsaw) have destroyed the lower transition forest, and they are the first to appear higher up, mixed with the boreal evergreens where the maples and beeches refuse to grow. Farther down, oaks and tamaracks blend in.

Also characteristic of boreal forests are bogs, in many places features left by the glaciers. The wide band of subarctic forest is largely covered by lakes and streams. As a lake fills in with soil and vegetable matter, a bog is formed.

Bogs are notable for their wide variety of specialized plants like sedges and water lilies. As the tangle of tree roots and plants crowds in around the edges of a bog, a living mat of plants may form, creating a "quaking bog": a seemingly solid surface that is actually floating over water. Spruces may figure in this mat, and their roots in this easily accessible state were once used to lace up birchbark canoes.

On the mat of vegetation you may find other, even stranger, plants. The nitrogen-poorness of bogs often opens a niche for species that take nitrogen from other sources, such as animals. Carnivorous pitcher plants and sundews are common in northern bogs.

Boreal forests strike a delicate balance. Lately, they have been particularly susceptible to pollution—the thin soil offers much less buffer to harsh chemicals than does the deeper soil of the lowlands, and the mists and rains of higher elevations bring more pollution with them. Acid deposition ("acid rain") has in recent years decimated the red spruce and balsam fir on eastern mountaintops and the destruction may only abate when the trees are all gone or the pollution is stopped.

Boreal forest, which covers the landscape through much of Canada and the northern United States, continues southward at gradually higher elevations. A forest type that is universal at 2500 feet in New Hampshire might be pushed up to above 4000 feet in North Carolina, but it's still there.

Maples and beeches.   As the Trail moves out of the true boreal forest it gradually enters the northern reaches of the mixed deciduous forest. Unlike the forests of the West, where the dividing lines are sharply defined, the change in the East is gradual, probably due to increased moisture acting as a buffer to temperature extremes.

As the forest moves into the northern lowlands the forest type is increasingly dominated by maples and beeches. They are by no means the only species, however. Even this far north the great variety of the Appalachian deciduous forest is evident. Interspersed with the maples are pines and hemlocks (the latter are especially fond of moist stream valleys). In places, the first oak-hickory forests, so characteristic of southern ridges, will be found—this is especially true in the Hudson Highlands.

The stately American chestnut, once a major presence in these parts, is gone, destroyed by a fungus blight introduced by accident in New York City in 1904. The chestnut is represented only by spindly shoots that grow from existing roots, and die when they reach a diameter of two or three inches. In some places along the Trail huge chestnut logs—too rot-resistant to decay—have lain through the woods like jackstraws for a half-century or more, witness to the ecological disaster that befell them decades ago.

SOUTHERN APPALACHIAN FOREST

Beneath the boreal and transitional forests of the southern Blue Ridge and the Great Smokies in North Carolina, Tennessee, and Georgia, one finds not the maple-beech forests that dominate in the North, but a spectacularly rich forest type characteristic only of that region. Growing on terrain that has never been stripped bare by glaciers, the incredibly diverse and vigorous southern forests offer a greater variety of plant life than occurs anywhere else on the continent.

The reasons are many. Not only has the soil not been carried away by millenia of glaciation but the climate is milder and moister than in the North. Then, too, the position of these forests in a "periglacial" region also made for diversity. In the frequent warming and cooling trends of the lands in the shadow of the great ice sheets to the north, a variety of species must have taken hold.

Southern Appalachian forests, which lie between the lowlands and the boreal forests above 4000 feet, are dominated only by diversity. Huge tulip trees (yellow poplar), sugar maples, yellow birch, hickory, and oak stand side by side, with redbud, dogwood, and mountain laurel underneath. As the forest progresses uphill it becomes more and more open, tending toward the oaks and red maples, with pines mixed in. The richness of the plant life is incredible. Water trickles everywhere, moss and lichens cover the rocks, hemlocks and firs crowd into the protected, wet stream gullies.

It is said that a short car drive from the lowlands to the high-elevation boreal forest is the same in botanical terms as a drive of several days from the South up into Canada. In a way, that's true. You pass through a similar number of forest types into a boreal forest not unlike those you'd find up North. But the forests aren't shaped just by the climate. History and geology do their parts, too. In the southern Appalachians the characteristics of the forests you see today have as much or more to do with humans and their axes and the fact that the glaciers didn't quite reach the region, than they do with the actual climate.

A NOTE ON ACID RAIN

Professor Hubert Vogelmann of the University of Vermont, one of the foremost experts on the effects of pollution on plant life, once said, "To say that acid deposition kills trees is kind of like saying that cigarettes cause cancer. Scientifically speaking, you can't say either."

He's not begging the question. Nor is he expressing an opinion that there's no harm in acid rain. What he means is that it's not within the realm of scientific inquiry to prove empirically that the obvious tree death in the forests of the East is due to pollution. You can't actually see it happening.

Which leaves us with an argument. Even scientists who are terrified by what's happening to our forests won't say for sure that it's pollution from Ohio Valley power plants or auto exhaust that's doing it—even though the preponderance of evidence points that way. There still remains the possibility that it's something else. True, most scientists don't believe that, but the scientific method isn't majority rule.

What they can say is that trees are dying, as are fish in mountain ponds, lakes, and streams. They can also say that rain, snow, and mist, especially at high elevations, are becoming increasingly acidic. They know, too, that tree rings show that growth in trees has slowed down since the late 1950s—just about the time that the amount of sulfur dioxide emissions from Ohio Valley power plants underwent a sharp increase. They know that in lab conditions, trees that are subjected to acid typical of pollution conditions tend to die quickly in just the ways they're dying in the wild.

From there, it's speculation. Does the acid get into the tree itself and kill it outright? Or does it release heavy metals like aluminum from the rocks and soil and let them do the job? Does acid damage the root hairs of the plants, causing them to die of thirst? Which does the actual damage: power plant emission, or auto exhaust? If it's a combination of the two, which is worse? Exactly what happens?

There are scientists who refuse to say absolutely that pollution damages trees. Faced with obvious damage, they offer a dozen or more possible reasons—most if not all caused by pollution—but won't take the last step of concluding that acid deposition is the culprit after all. It's not wrong—it's just the way they work.

Unfortunately, this opens the door for special-interest groups who oppose acid deposition control and block any action to solve the problem. As long as scientists are unwilling or unable to draw ironclad conclusions, opponents of action can always call for "More Studies!" In 1984 one Ohio congressman, whose district enjoys some of the lowest electrical power rates in the East, blocked an acid rain control bill in the House of Representatives. Two years later an industry group supported by industrial coal users launched a million-dollar campaign of disinformation and letter writing and succeeded in defeating another acid rain bill.

But the trees and the fish keep dying. You'll see the results from Maine to Georgia. If you want to do something, get hold of your senators and representatives.

3

History Along the Trail

AS I walk along the Trail I always enjoy looking out over the hills and valleys below and imagining what went on there over the years. Most people feel some kinship for their American forebears when they stand on the spot where something important happened in history.

It's interesting, for example, to stand on the middle of the Bear Mountain Bridge span in New York and look out over the valley that was the scene of so much struggle during the American Revolution and before—especially since so much of what went on occurred right in view of the bridge site!

Or look out over the French Broad River at Hot Springs, North Carolina, and pretend that you're there in 1540 watching DeSoto and his train of hundreds of Spanish warriors—and literally thousands of pigs—cross the gap, looking for gold. You can pretend as you walk up South Mountain in Maryland that you're there in the 1850s, guiding slaves along the Underground Railroad to Canada and freedom.

In each trail-section chapter I will offer some of the specific historical events that occurred along the Trail route. Here, though, are some of the events and movements of national—and at times continental or even hemispheric, importance: the fabric of Appalachian history, if you will.

ON NATIVE AMERICANS

The land was, of course, occupied long before Europeans arrived to settle it. It must be with a mixture of amusement and resentment that Native Americans read or hear about the "first settlers in Virginia," or "the first to sail up the Hudson." We should try to keep a lid on absurdity of that magnitude.

It's very difficult to fix exactly where a given tribe or nation might have lived. Even the most authoritative works on the subject have to plead a certain amount of uncertainty about where the boundaries actually were. There are several reasons for this: First, even as the European settlers moved in, they were pushing Native American peoples off their traditional lands. It is hard, then, to know where the nations originally lived, since by the time Europeans got close to them they may already have moved.

Also, in places, the arrival of white settlers was preceded by their diseases, which in some cases nearly exterminated whole villages before white settlers got there. These maladies may have been brought by traders or fishermen who stopped along the coast. One famous example confronted the Pilgrims. When they reached Plymouth in 1620, Chief Massasoit's Wampanoags had already been decimated by some plague, brought by traders or explorers, which had run rampant through the peoples of the Massachusetts coast around 1617. They may have lost as many as two-thirds to *three-quarters* of their number! No wonder Massasoit was so friendly; he had no warriors left with which to fight.

Then, too, tribes tended to move about. There were lots of reasons for this, ranging from the need to get *to* an area where living was better to the need to get *away* from an area where a more powerful enemy was pushing in. The Iroquois, for example, having finally banded together to prevent powerful neighbors from bullying *them,* managed to push the Mahicans out of eastern New York state into Vermont and Massachusetts. Things got so rough for the Mahicans that one whole division moved out and muscled into Connecticut and Rhode Island between neighboring tribes, becoming known as the Pequots. The process repeated itself. The Pequots in turn, having pushed their way into their new home, became so hated for their bullying that the Puritans eventually manufactured an excuse to exterminate them, but not before *another* group, known as the Mohegans, split off due to some internal dispute. This tribe, under the leadership of its chief, Uncas, would later become one of the inspirations for James Fenimore Cooper's famous novel *The*

Last of the Mohicans.

Finally, territorial limits are hard to pinpoint due to the Native-American habit of not setting them formally. They had their villages, which many nations would move from time to time; they had their hunting territories, which they would hold against their neighbors by a combination of peaceful agreement, implied threat, and, on occasion, out-and-out warfare; and there were lands that were not strongly under anyone's sphere. Native Americans had little conception that land could be *owned.* It simply was.

This was further complicated by the sparseness of the native population: In the entire area traversed by the Appalachian Trail there were probably fewer than 175,000 people. In all that great big land you could walk a far piece without seeing a soul. That made it very hard to figure who the proprietors were in any given place.

We do know certain things. We know, for example, that the route that became known to white settlers as The Great War Path ran practically the length of the Great Valley of the Appalachians, from Pennsylvania or even from up in New York, all the way to Tennessee and Alabama. It was one of the major avenues of the day for both raiding and trading, a preferred trail of the Iroquois Confederacy for regular attacks on their favorite targets, the Creeks and the Catawbas of the South. For extra-secretive passages, war parties of any stripe may have taken to the ridge lines to avoid detection, running along the actual route of the AT. So, for a sizable part of its length, the AT runs parallel to an actual historical path.

There is also a certain amount of oral tradition to be reckoned with (the accuracy of oral accounts is fast becoming legendary). The Iroquois Nations, for example, have stories of the days when they came east from the Mississippi valley. How many hundreds—or even thousands—of years ago we can only guess. Oral accounts have been used by scholars to fix the location of territorial boundaries that no longer exist.

But for the purposes of this book, turf limits must in many cases be approximate. In most events this will take the form of a description of who lived in a certain place when European settlers arrived; in others, such as in Cherokee territory, Native Americans did establish formal borders when faced by

European expansion; in still others, like the Shenandoah Valley, there were for some reason no resident tribes when the white settlers first took notice of the area.

EUROPEANS IN THE APPALACHIANS

The role of the Appalachian ranges in European settlement is better known, simply because those who participated in it kept written records. The mountains were the barrier, the limits of the known world. The history of cities on the coast was profoundly influenced by their proximity to the Appalachians or, more appropriately, to passages through them. The early history of the North American continent was in great measure controlled by anyone who could control those passages.

In the beginning of the nineteenth century, two hundred years after the first settlement of North America by Europeans, the limit of truly known land still hadn't extended much beyond the coastal plain and the Piedmont. The way West was barred, both physically and psychologically, by the range of mountains, running north to south, that stood in the way. Territory beyond the Appalachians was largely unknown and unmapped—the dense forests, unknown and presumably hostile peoples, and the maze of ridges and mountains made the prospect of crossing the range daunting to say the least.

As early as the 1700s, the growth of cities was being determined by the way West. New York, for example, not only had a fine harbor, but also stood at the mouth of the vast Hudson/Mohawk river basin, which led deep into the western reaches of what is today New York state. Already fueling expansion in the 1700s, the route, once hooked up with Lake Erie via the Erie Canal in the 1820s, constituted the finest route west available in the United States and assured the growth and prosperity of New York. Similarly, Philadelphia and Baltimore stood at the beginnings of fine water routes that gave access to the rich interior valleys of the Shenandoah and Ohio rivers.

But the Hudson was not the most influential passage in the early centuries of European settlement—the St. Lawrence was. It was inevitable that the first explorers in the West would come not from the territory that is now the United States, but rather from the area of the great waterway of the St. Lawrence and the Great Lakes, which offered an effective end run around the mountains. And that was just how it happened: That area's political control was held by France, and they had the honor of exploring the Lakes, the Ohio and Mississippi basins, and the beginnings of the great American West. It was only later, when the English had defeated the French and Indians in the 1760s and pushed over the Appalachians, that the English settlers and their descendants finally made their way across the great mountain chain.

It wasn't long before the areas around the route of the AT became sites of many battles in many wars. This is especially true where there are rivers: the Potomac, for example, was hotly contested in the American Civil War; it was a vital route in the struggles of the French and Indian War. The Civil War notwithstanding, the Hudson, once the football of the English and Dutch, then the French and English, and later the English and Continentals, was the focus of more battles than practically any other waterway in America.

Since those times the situation of the great coastal cities has become a mixed blessing. Placed as they were along the transportation routes inland, they were the natural sites for the Industrial Revolution to take hold in. Raw materials could move down from the heartland, and they did: Timber was cut for charcoal and holes dug into the ground for iron ore and both were shipped to the cities for smelting; fields were cleared and the crops grown on them taken to urban markets; coal and oil were taken from the ground. Because the cities were on the coast, finished products could be loaded on ships for trade. The coastal cities (and those along the Great Lakes later, as transportation became more sophisticated along that sea lane) grew and developed into the envy of the industrial world.

And again, the Appalachians acted as a barrier. Immigrants arrived and stayed in the coastal areas. For years, few ventured away from the ocean front to the inland areas. So many stayed that in the early twentieth century industrial workers outnumbered farmers and the Appalachians remained mostly wild.

The result was the opportunity Benton MacKaye would address with his proposal for an Appalachian Trail: A wilderness mountain range within a day's travel of half the people in America, ideal for the respite from city life that modern industrial workers so desperately needed.

HIKERS IN THE APPALACHIANS
How the Appalachian Trail Came to Be

The major history that interests us, however, is of the Trail itself. How did it get there? Who did the work and why? This is an easier story to tell.

The Appalachian Trail can be traced to a very specific point in time: October of 1921. It was then that E. Benton Mac-Kaye published his work, "An Appalachian Trail, A Project in Regional Planning," in the *Journal of the American Institute of Architects.* The Trail started from there.

MacKaye's whole idea was not just to create a trail. On the contrary—a trail was just the method he chose to do a larger, greater job.

MacKaye was a thinker, an idea man. During his years in government service, first with the Forest Service in its early years, and later with the Department of Labor, he had become concerned with the impact of industrialization on workers, and on ways in which government and human resources could be marshaled to ease the stress. Like many outdoorsmen, he had become convinced that recreation time in the wilderness was a surefire way of restoring the spirits and energy of people who were able to spend the 1921 equivalent of "quality time" there.

Earlier in 1921 he had contacted Clarence Stein, chairman of the committee on community planning of the American Institute of Architects. That he communicated with an architectural association rather than the park service or some recreational administration may seem surprising. It was, though, a choice of avenue one might have expected of MacKaye—he viewed his scheme as one of regional planning, not one of recreation or conservation. He was setting out to improve people's lives, not help them pass the time, and he knew exactly what he was about.

In the words of Clarence Stein in his introduction to MacKaye's article:

> We need the big sweep of hills or sea as a tonic for jaded nerves—And so Mr. Benton MacKaye offers us a new theme in regional planning. *It is not a plan for more efficient labor, but a plan of escape* [author's italics]. He

When these two men first met, the history of the nation was changed. Benton MacKaye (right) *reminisces with Clarence Stein, who arranged the publication of MacKaye's revolutionary article, "An Appalachian Trail, A Project in Regional Planning," in 1921.* (Photograph courtesy of the Appalachian Trail Conference)

would as far as practicable conserve the whole stretch of the Appalachian Mountains for recreation. Recreation in the biggest sense—the re-creation of the spirit that is being crushed by the machinery of the modern industrial city—the spirit of fellowship and cooperation. . . .

To all of those to whom community or regional planning means more than the opening up of new roads for the acquisition of wealth, this project of Mr. MacKaye's must appeal. It is a plan for the conservation not of things—machines and land—but of men and their love of freedom and fellowship.

In "An Appalachian Trail," MacKaye makes his case deliberately. After stating his overall point, that modern workers need escape from the workplace and the living situations that it forces on them, he proceeds to illustrate why he feels his plan will suit those needs.

Why the Appalachians, for example? Simple! "These mountains," he explained, "in several ways rivaling the western scenery, are within a day's ride from centers containing more than half the population of the United States."

MacKaye, by the way, recognized the, well, radical aspects of his proposals. He was by then somewhat known for his broadmindedness, having virtually proposed cooperative farms as a solution to labor and farm production problems in the late teens. He also, in "An Appalachian Trail," suggested that for the United States to take on a project like the AT would require a "new deal in our agricultural system," as well as a "new deal" in our forestry methods. (I wonder if Franklin Delano Roosevelt ever read this work.)

The original proposal went far beyond the simple blazing of a trail. In order for industry, as he said, to "come to be seen in its true perspective—as a means in life and not as an end in itself," he was planning a vast wilderness complex, complete with recreational "community camps" throughout the range; "shelter camps," not unlike many of the hut-to-hut systems in place today; and finally, "food and farm camps" in which workers, in a "back to the land" experience, would provide "the food and crops consumed in the outdoor living," as well as the chance for citified workers to get back to the country, either as the first stage of an escape from industrial life, or as a temporary respite.

The Trail itself was proposed to be much like the AT as it exists today. The actual route was to run from Mt. Washington in New Hampshire to Mt. Mitchell in North Carolina, with side trails suggested in a variety of places. Among these a contemporary Trail walker will recognize a side route west from the AT in southwest Virginia to the Allegheny range, then south to the Great Smokies, and on into Georgia. Another leads up from Mt. Washington to Katahdin in Maine. Both are actually part of the route today. Another side branch leads off the AT to the west in the area of Shenandoah National Park, and leads north through western Maryland and into Pennsylvania, just like the Big Blue/ Tuscarora (only in MacKaye's plan it doesn't rejoin the AT).

MacKaye also clearly marks the cities served by the Appalachian Trail concept as well as the railroad lines that link them with the route.

In his final plea, MacKaye shows some of the effects of the still-recent Great War: "Indeed the lure of the scouting life can be made the most formidable enemy of the lure of militarism (a thing with which this country is menaced along with all others). It comes the nearest perhaps, of things thus far projected, to supplying what Professor [William] James once called a 'moral equivalent of war.' It appeals to the primal instincts of a fighting heroism, of volunteer service and of work in a common cause."

It's not that the idea of a through-trail over long distances was a new one. Quite the contrary. The Long Trail was well along, being blazed by the Green Mountain Club the length of Vermont, from the Massachusetts line to Canada, across some of the finest terrain the Greens had to offer. The New England Trail Conference (NETC) had already debated the possibility of creating a trail that would run from New York City up the Hudson River Highlands and to Quebec over the mountains of western New England (probably very close to the route of the AT today). There were other plans to extend the proposed Long Trail down the western New England route across the Hudson River and down the west Hudson Highlands to connect with a series of trails already under development in New Jersey—again, very much like the current route of the Appalachian Trail. Allen Chamberlain of the NETC wrote in May of 1922: "Whoever was privileged to see that plan [MacKaye's] recognized it at once as a logical extension of the New England Trail System."

But it took MacKaye to set the actual 2000-mile Trail in motion. This has surprised some people. MacKaye was something of an outsider, not officially connected with any of the major trail clubs, and not party to the discussions and plans that were already in motion when he published his article. How could

James P. Taylor provided the impetus for the Long Trail in Vermont, a major forerunner of the AT. (Photograph courtesy of the Vermont Historical Society)

he, a dreamer and planner without practical drive, inspire such action?

The answer, of course, is simple. It lies in the reasons why people wanted trails in the first place. It goes back to what I discussed in the Introduction. America was in the throes of a love affair with the wilderness that it didn't quite understand, but which it was powerless to resist. Already feeling themselves shredded and exploited by the advance of the Industrial Age, people longed for a return to less-complicated times, to a way of finding again the simpler virtues of the pioneers, the virtues that made the United States the new superpower. Adventure had gone from their lives, and they wanted to find it again.

Possibly the greatest adventurer of all time, polar explorer and Nobel Peace Prize laureate Dr. Fridtjof Nansen of Norway, used to assert that the spirit of adventure was a human imperative equal to—and at times greater than—the drive for survival. It was, he said, like the blank page that needed to be written upon. MacKaye also seemed to understand that notion, that there was some inexplicable need within people that could be satisfied by time well-spent in the wilderness.

The difference between MacKaye and other trail advocates, then, was this: Everyone else was being driven by this modern need to re-create themselves in the wilderness; MacKaye, while feeling that drive most powerfully, also understood it. When he proposed a linear park to run the length of the entire Appalachian range he wasn't merely responding to an urge that he felt but couldn't pin down. He knew why the urge was there, and what would satisfy it. And he had a plan.

When MacKaye published his plan in October 1921, people recognized the rightness of it (although agreement wasn't always unanimous, causing NETC Chairman Albert M. Turner to lament, "There are some people so hard-headed that the sudden impact of a vivid and iridescent idea makes no particular impact on 'em."). It was as though trail builders breathed a collective sigh of relief, as if to say, "Of course! That's it." Someone had finally explained why they felt the way they did, and given them a plan and a goal. And they went to work.

The beauty of the MacKaye plan was that it operated on several levels. Its purpose wasn't really to see a trail established, nor was it to provide simple recreation. In MacKaye's own words, it was a case of priorities: He wanted a way, through careful regional planning, to reduce the industrialized city to "a means in life and not an end in itself." Working at the factory was to be a way to an end, which in MacKaye's mind was nothing less than a better life for the worker. You worked because you needed money to survive. The rest of your time you spent enhancing your life. The Trail and the parks and camps that were to accompany it were also means of improving life. MacKaye saw them as no less important than a person's job. One offered money with which to buy food and shelter; the other provided sustenance of another sort—nourishment for the spirit.

Work progressed quickly in the early years, causing Albert Turner to declare, "Maybe this Maine to Georgia stuff is all a dream; I don't know; but the part east of the New York line is all in a day's work—we're at it." Within eighteen months the proposed route was on paper in more than just pencil. By the spring of 1922 newspaper articles had appeared in New York and Boston, written by early Trail luminaries Raymond H. Torrey, a founder that year of the New York-New Jersey Trail Conference (NY-NJTC) from its beginning in the old Palisades Park Trail Conference, and Allen Chamberlain, who was among the participants in the New England Trail Conference's earlier plans.

Soon, things were also underway on the ground level, so to speak. By the fall of 1923 the first trail miles had been blazed in Bear Mountain State Park, 40 miles north of New York City. Further plans had been laid, based on the obvious recognition that all that had to be done in some parts of New England was to link up the lower sections of the Long Trail in Vermont with some of the Dartmouth Outing Club's trails. From there, lead into the Appalachian Mountain Club's White Mountains system and you would have the better part of 300 miles of trail on-line.

Common wisdom has it that the early years of the Trail were high on enthusiasm and low on production, and that it took the appearance a few years later of people like Judge Arthur Perkins and Myron Avery to get things really off the ground. These two were among the heroes of the Appalachian Trail, second only to MacKaye himself. They were the men who took over the leadership of the Appalachian Trail Conference in the late 1920s when momentum began to flag, and it is often said these days that the effort to create the AT didn't really get going until they arrived. This is true and untrue.

It is untrue in the sense that, in point of fact, many things actually did happen. A core of the route was put together in the upper Mid-Atlantic states and New England, and the notion of the Trail was promulgated strongly in some quarters. The overall route was also largely mapped out during this period (although in places the precise route—and how it was to be put in—remained a mystery). And most important of all, the Appalachian Trail Conference (ATC) was founded with Major William A. Welch, the guiding light of the Palisades Interstate Park Commission and the newly formed NY-NJTC, as its first chairman. All this tends to be forgotten in later years, after Avery's formation of the Potomac Appalachian Trail Club (PATC) and later ascendance to the chairmanship of the ATC, when the histories were written by the Myron Averies themselves. One gets the impression that not much happened until they got there.

But it *is* true that on another level, certain things had not been done. In the early years the Appalachian Trail Conference did succeed in putting in hundreds of miles of trail, but these constituted the "easy miles." Fortunately, these were the parts of the AT route near the very urban areas where the need for the Trail was keenly felt even before MacKaye's proposal.

But in other areas, like Maine and the whole southern end of the proposed route, "tramping" hadn't caught on as a pleasurable pastime. Support of the Trail idea couldn't simply be evoked by a few newspaper articles, with the result of volunteers appearing and the Trail progressing. At times, the organization could be downright discouraging. Charlie Elliott, a founder of the Georgia Appalachian Trail Club (GATC), recalls that his boss at the Forest Service, Everett "Eddie" Stone, "said to me, 'I want you to organize the Georgia Appalachian Trail Club.' Just like that. Just like I could go out into the street and round up fifty people who would walk with me up the summit of a mountain. Most of the folks I knew had never seen a mountain."

Elliott did have his troubles. At the first meeting he called he was "the only living individual who stepped across the threshold . . ." The second time things were little better: "I was not alone. That night the janitor kept me company." Support for the Appalachian Trail in such places had to be earned and nurtured. And that took organization.

That arrived in the person of Judge Arthur Perkins of Connecticut. Filling a vacancy on the executive committee in 1926, he brought the organizational and leadership ability the ATC desperately needed. When, early the following year, Major Welch regretfully stepped down from the chairmanship of the ATC, Perkins was the obvious choice for his replacement. The time for the thinkers was past; people of action were needed now.

With Perkins came Myron Avery from Lubec, Maine, by birth, but then living in Connecticut and just beginning his law career with Perkins's firm. Soon, he would move to Washington, D.C., and a whole new chapter of the Appalachian Trail would begin.

The transfer of leadership that heralded the exciting but all-too-brief Perkins era occurred at the annual meeting of the NETC, and MacKaye was the invited speaker. He took the opportunity to give one of his finest speeches. Called "Outdoor Culture: The Philosophy of Through Trails," it might better have been called the "Barbarian Utopia Speech." It was one of the finest expressions ever made of the belief in wilderness as a cure for the ills of civilization.

MacKaye had come, he said, "to organize a barbarian invasion. . . . This crest line should be captured—and no time lost about it. . . . The Appalachian Range should be placed in public hands and become the site of a Barbarian Utopia."

The reasoning was disarmingly simple. Civilization was as "unthinking, ruthless," as a glacier. Citing Ancient Rome as an example, MacKaye theorized that overcivilization was the cause of its own downfall, that the barbarian invasions lent a cleansing influence (residents of the fallen city might have disagreed). By embracing the barbarian ethic, the free human spirit, common people could become heroes in their own lives, not needing fake heroes like cinema stars (MacKaye mentioned Douglas Fairbanks).

Later at that meeting, after the famous speech, Major Welch, all but overwhelmed by his responsibilities at the Palisades Interstate Park Commission, resigned as ATC chairman and Perkins assumed the job.

What followed was a whirlwind of activity. In 1927, Avery—by then an attorney with the U.S. Maritime Commission—formed the Potomac Appalachian Trail Club along with H. C. Anderson, P. L. Ricker, the Joseph W. Coxes (Sr. and Jr.), and Frank Schairer (who would go on to be the PATC's trail supervisor for many years). These are names that will be encountered again and again in Trail history.

They began blazing south of Harpers Ferry soon after (putting in a whopping half-mile their first trip, due, they said, to dull axes). That same year, Perkins and Raymond Torrey spoke at a meeting of the Blue Mountain Eagles Climbing Club—the organization that would be so important to the Trail in Pennsylvania. The next year Torrey would meet with the new Pennsylvania Trail Conference (PTC) (Torrey would die in 1938, a serious loss to the young movement). With the Northeast (with the exception of Maine) in good hands, Avery and the PATC turned their attention to the South, becoming, in MacKaye's words, a "maker of clubs."

With Perkins at the helm, things began to happen again. Contacts were made, little by little, in critical areas like Georgia (where the GATC was finally founded in 1930 by Everett Stone of the Forest Service, Roy Ozmer of the ATC, and Everett's not easily frustrated assistant, Charlie Elliott). The route was formalized through protected public land wherever possible.

With organization came a subtle change in emphasis. MacKaye, as active as always, nevertheless became more than ever the spiritual leader. In Perkins and his protégé, Avery, the ATC had found men concerned enough with the human condition, yet whose main interest was simply to see the Trail through.

One of the first problems was choosing a southern terminus. Several options were discussed. MacKaye's proposed ending spot, Mt. Mitchell, had its charm—it was the highest mountain in the South, just as northern-terminus-designate, Mt. Washington, was the highest in the North. But the two peaks were very quickly bypassed in favor of Katahdin in Maine, and "someplace in northern Georgia" in the South.

Just where was a mystery. At first, MacKaye's side trail past Mitchell to Georgia was considered, but at the insistence of the only existing hiking club in that part of the country, the Smoky Mountains Hiking Club centered around Knoxville, Tennessee, a more westerly route through the Great Smokies gained support. From there, several other options were available: Cohutta Mountain in northwest Georgia and Mt. Oglethorpe farther east. The Smoky Mountain club favored Cohutta, since that destination would allow the Trail to go all the way through Great Smoky Mountains National Park. Ozmer of the GATC preferred Oglethorpe as a better final destination than Cohutta, and as closer to the actual southernmost point of the Blue Ridge, on Springer Mountain. It was only after a compromise, allowing greater routing through the national park and then a kind of backtrack through the Nantahalas to Oglethorpe, that everyone was satisfied.

Things putted right along, and by 1932 1700 miles of Trail were complete. There were small gaps here and there: 6 miles in eastern Pennsylvania, 20 in North Carolina, 10 in Connecticut. And then there was Maine—all of it!

There was also a sadness in the ATC. Arthur Perkins, the dedicated, practical, and, not least, diplomatic man who had in a few short years given the ATC the organization it would need to extend the Trail into the remoter reaches of its route, died after an illness that had forced his resignation in 1930. Myron Avery had taken over the chairmanship upon Perkins's leaving and the ATC continued without breaking stride. Avery would put his stamp on the organization in the nearly twenty years he was chairman. Perkins's contribution in the critical two years of his chairmanship tends to go by the boards, relegated to a footnote begun with the words, "and efforts lagged until 1928, when Arthur Perkins, a retired judge from Hartford, Connecticut . . ."

During his tenure as chairman, Perkins succeeded in overseeing the organization of many local clubs who would do the actual work of the Trail, he saw the route of the AT become fixed, he inspired the blazing of hundreds of miles of trail. And he recruited Myron Avery.

Avery could best be described as the Irresistible Force. He hopscotched across the country, meeting with prospective club organizers, inspecting potential routes, and reinspecting trail already blazed. When the rest of the ATC cried out for the problematic Maine route—of which practically nothing had been blazed—to be abandoned, he went personally to the area (his home state, it must be remembered) and organized the Maine Appalachian Trail Club (MATC) in 1935. He would wear the additional hats of trail supervisor of the MATC until 1949 and president until his death in 1952.

Under Avery's leadership—described by the not-uncommon people who were less than fond of him as a kind of bullying—the Trail was essentially completed by 1936, except for a mile in Tennessee and 2 miles in Maine. A saying in the ATC has it that, in his single-mindedness, Avery had actually left two trails: one on the ground, blazed with metal markers and rectangles of white paint; the other a trail of bruised egos and hurt feelings. The niceties of tact were not said to be his long suit.

One of his real strengths, though, was his simple attention to detail. He was like the ball player who could do everything, including taking tickets at the gate. One example was something as simple as the Appalachian Trail blaze.

The Appalachian Trail Marker

From Maine to Georgia, the Appalachian Trail is marked by white painted blazes, 2 inches wide by 6 inches high. This method of marking came into style back in the 1930s. The design was evaluated and approved personally by Avery. "These dimensions," he later wrote, "are not the result of an accident. They were very definitely determined. A blaze of this size is in keeping with the shape of the tree, and hence creates an impression of proportion which is lacking in a blaze of other dimensions."

Also famous as trail markers were the metal AT signs that were nailed up at key sections of the Trail. These were the descendants of the first copper squares that Major Welch developed for the first sections in Harriman State Park in the mid-1920s. The next designs went to the diamond shape, but there were problems.

The first replacement for the copper square was a galvanized diamond with AT printed on it. This had a tendency to fade. It was for a time in 1933 replaced by a galvanized diamond with a Bakelite varnish. This peeled.

Finally, the ATC settled on a metal diamond that was anodized—the part surrounding the insignia was immersed in a chemical vat, which permanently altered the surface to a whitish cast, and the insignia itself was protected from contact with the chemical and thus didn't become discolored. This marker lasted longer. The main trouble with the metal markers was twofold: they were expensive to make and they were frequently stolen. Thus the popularity of the painted markers. But things may have come full circle. In southwest Virginia the Kanawha Club is experimenting with stick-on reflector patches in the same size as the painted blazes.

As hikers walk down the Trail in any section, the sight of the blazes acts as yet another reminder of the size of the idea in which they are participating. Not only is this selfsame blaze adorning everything from scruffy ridge-top balsam fir in Maine all the way down to giant yellow poplar in the Great Smoky Mountains, but the very shape of the blaze is significant. It is placed on the footpath at prescribed distances, sometimes in pairs to denote a major change in Trail direction. Blazes are not placed at random, but as part of a plan that was so well thought out that even the size of the blaze required a conscious decision at the highest organizational levels. It's a small part of what made the Trail work. And it's typical of the way Myron Avery operated. No task was too large—or too small—to warrant his attention.

By the way, if you run across one of the metal blazes and you're tempted to take it as a souvenir, please desist. You can buy one from the ATC in Harpers Ferry for practically nothing.

A logical question might be whether Avery, who was so task-oriented, had any real feel for the spirit of what the ATC was attempting to do beyond the mechanics of the day-to-day problems. The answer is simple: Yes, he understood what had been accomplished—who better? Not only had he pushed the effort with almost superhuman vision and endurance, but he also walked every inch of the Trail, becoming in 1936 the first person to walk the entire route (some of which was not yet blazed). In his victory statement, delivered a couple of months before an MATC trail crew completed the final 2 miles on Spaulding Mountain in Maine on August 14, 1937, he said: "To say that the Trail is completed would be a complete misnomer. Those of us, who have physically worked on the Trail, know that the Trail, as such, will never be completed." It was the simple statement not of a man whose single-mindedness was simply aimed at drawing a line on a map; it was said by someone who actually knew in spiritual terms what a trail of this kind meant, that it was a living, changing thing.

Since that day in 1937, the story of the Appalachian Trail has been one of preserving what has been gained. At the time, less than half of the AT route crossed publicly owned land. The rest passed over private land where the simplest dispute between a landowner and a hiker could break the 2000-mile chain. Much of the rest—875 miles—was in national forest, and the Forest Service isn't in the Agriculture Department for nothing: its priorities have always been more on the side of timber cutting than of preservation.

But if the bureaucratic purpose of the Forest Service was not concerned with conservation of the wilderness, the hearts and minds of many of its staff were. The first victory in the effort to preserve the route of the Trail came quickly, on October 15, 1938, to be exact. The Forest Service agreed to protect a zone on either side of the Trail for a mile. Timber cutting would be prohibited within 200 feet of the Trail. It was a significant act, though not as far-reaching as the ATC would later deem necessary to secure the route.

The Forest Service, in spite of its mission to promote timber harvesting, seemed to take on the AT as a project near to its heart. Perhaps it was that MacKaye had been one of them: To this day in United States Forest Service literature he is referred to as "Forester Benton MacKaye." But for whatever reason, wherever I have traveled on the AT, local-club members seem quite fond of their local Forest Service and proud of their working relationship. For their part, Forest Service staff seem exceptionally proud of their sections of the Appalachian Trail. The route is always included prominently on Forest Service maps (which are frequently among the best available for hikers).

With the Forest Service holding the line over a third of the route came the campaign to give the Trail itself legal status. It began in 1945 with congressional efforts to establish a national system of footpaths, and wouldn't end until the late 1960s and mid-1970s with the passage and subsequent funding of the National Trails System Act of 1968. Introduced by the great environmentalist Senator Gaylord Nelson of Wisconsin, the Act established the status of National Scenic Trail as a legal one, carrying certain protections, and designated two trails in that category: the Pacific Crest Trail and the Appalachian Trail.

The Act mandated the Park Service to take certain measures to protect the route and to acquire up to 25 acres per mile to maintain the wilderness feel of the Trail. The Forest Service responded by setting aside land along the Trail as it passed through national forest land.

But on the Park Service side, things lagged. The trouble was that Congress had mandated the protection of the Trail and acquisition of land for that purpose, but had not yet appropriated any funds for the Park Service to do it *with*. That would come with the "Appalachian Trail Act" of 1978. It appropriated $90 million to be doled out over a period of time, and upped the mandate for the trailway to up to 125 acres per mile to maintain the Trail's wilderness character. Within a year the Park Service had successfully negotiated its first land purchase, at Nuclear Lake in eastern New York state.

One more victory remained, and it came in 1984. On January 26 of that year the National Park Service signed over management of the lands acquired for the Appalachian Trail and responsibility for maintaining the Trail itself to the Appalachian Trail Conference. It was the first time in American history that responsibility for public lands of such magnitude had been placed in private hands. After the enormous hue and cry on the part of many for the "privatization" of federal lands, it is interesting that this is the only major example of it actually happening. But considering the high caliber of the ATC staff and volunteers, this is certainly not a situation over which we need to lose any sleep.

Benton MacKaye lived until 1975 and died peacefully just before he would have turned ninety-seven. He had been estranged from the ATC and the Trail he inspired and worked so hard to see blazed since 1935, over a dispute with Myron Avery (described in more detail in Chapter 11), but had in the early 1960s been reconciled with the Conference and had spent part of his last years meeting with members and corresponding with the leadership. In the interim, he had been involved in the formation of The Wilderness Society, working with environmental giants like Bob Marshall and Aldo Leopold (who considered him their peer), and becoming one of its presidents.

Still active in his later years, MacKaye would write and speak about the early days of Trail efforts. It's appropriate that his should be the final word on what it was all about, since it was his vision that set the whole thing in motion, more than sixty-five years ago: "The ultimate purpose? There are three things: 1) to walk; 2) to see; 3) to *see* what you see."

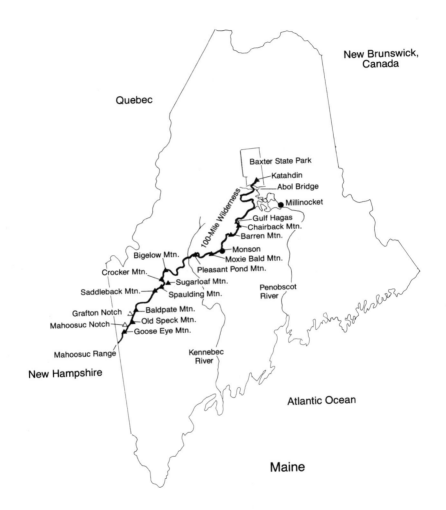

New Brunswick, Canada

Quebec

Baxter State Park

Katahdin

Abol Bridge

Millinocket

100-Mile Wilderness

Gulf Hagas
Chairback Mtn.
Barren Mtn.

Monson
Moxie Bald Mtn.
Pleasant Pond Mtn.

Bigelow Mtn.

Crocker Mtn.

Penobscot
River

Sugarloaf Mtn.

Saddleback Mtn.

Spaulding Mtn.

Grafton Notch — Baldpate Mtn.
Mahoosuc Notch — Old Speck Mtn.
— Goose Eye Mtn.

Mahoosuc Range

Kennebec
River

New Hampshire

Atlantic Ocean

Maine

4

The Maine Section

Trail Distance:

Katahdin to the Maine/New Hampshire
state line . . . . 278.3 miles

Maintaining Club:

The Maine Appalachian Trail Club: Katahdin
to Grafton Notch

INTRODUCTION

THE CHOICE of Katahdin as the northern terminus of the Appalachian Trail is appropriate for reasons other than including the greatest wilderness in the Northeast. It allows this singular Trail to begin on a singular mountain. Katahdin, or "The Greatest Mountain," stands alone in Maine, surrounded by lowland bogs and lesser peaks and ridges. In the process of creating the Trail, a long, thin oasis was established along the crest of the Appalachian range. Katahdin qualifies as a fitting northern terminus to that refuge, both physically and symbolically.

It was once so remote that for the first three hundred years of European settlement in North America, it was climbed only by a handful of people. In the minds of the local people, the

61

Penobscots, it was more remote still: It was believed to be the home of the evil deity *Bumole* (or *Pamola* in the English rendition), who would destroy anyone daring to approach. The Penobscots, in their oral history, had enough stories of hunters disappearing in the rugged region to keep the curious away. *Pamola,* for whom a peak in the Katahdin group was named, was said to kidnap hunters and warriors who ventured too close and hold them captive beneath the mountain. During their captivity he would often marry them to one of his sisters or daughters. The warrior would then be sent back to his people with the stern admonition never to marry or have relations with another woman. Those who forgot the warning (And who are we kidding? Most would and did, according to legend.) would disappear beneath the mountain forever.

The mountain's ruggedness could at times seem to be taking the form of some malevolent presence. Even Henry David Thoreau, the great American transcendentalist, on failing to climb Katahdin in 1846 had to alter a bit his romantic outlook of nature in favor of a more realistic, less benign view.

Of all the sections of the Appalachian Trail, Maine stands as the most remote in fact. Where the Trail farther to the south will cross roads and run within a few hundred yards of tract housing, in Maine it will plunge through woods that are still so deep that the imaginations of city dwellers will be tested there. To those wishing to make the trip, it should not be undertaken lightly; those with the necessary skills should try it if they possibly can.

Special note must be taken of the Maine Appalachian Trail Club (MATC). Its far-flung membership has the awe-inspiring task of maintaining the longest segment of Trail of any of the member organizations of the Appalachian Trail Conference (ATC), through the ruggedest, remotest country on the entire route. What's more, there is less of the Trail protected from development in Maine than anywhere else, which means more rerouting as land is purchased or as landowners change their minds and demand the removal of the AT from their domains. Though they won't brag about the job they do (or about anything else, for that matter), the Maine Club members deserve our admiration—and our thanks.

GEOLOGY ALONG THE TRAIL

The mountains of Maine from Katahdin through the Mahoosucs belong geologically to the White-Mountain province in many ways. Formed east of the suture line between the North American continental plate and the Eurafrican, they are variously composed of deep sea sediments and granitic plutons and batholiths.

Maine was formed in the middle phases of the Appalachian Revolution (around 350 million years ago) as the European and African continents crashed into North America to form the huge supercontinent of *Pangaea*. As the continents approached, they ploughed up sediments and rock from the deep ocean floor and pushed them up and onto the continental shelf, crushing the band of offshore volcanic islands against the North American coastline.

Eastern Maine may actually have been originally formed on one of the other continents—probably Europe—and left on North America after *Pangaea* began to break up, some 200 million years ago.

Katahdin itself was formed in much the same way that the Presidentials were in New Hampshire. It is a granite monadnock, a solitary peak thrust up among dissimilar structures, usually standing higher than the surrounding countryside. Mt. Greylock in Massachusetts is another monadnock that the Trail will cross on its way south.

Katahdin was originally molten rock that welled up through the deep bedrock, melting its way through as it rose. As it approached the surface it began to cool slowly, forming a giant mass of granite that was eventually exposed by millions of years of erosion. No one knows for sure what the mountains above looked like when the granite finally cooled. Katahdin as it appears today is the product of erosion. Its boulder-covered appearance prompted one geologist to say that it has been "buried under its own ruins."

The other ridges and ranges follow for the most part the northeast/southwest tendency of the whole Appalachian province. The rocks they contain vary, depending on how far inland they are and how much of the original mountain has been weathered away. Many are, like Katahdin, granite mounds that bubbled up some 200 million years ago as the Eurafrican continental plates began to drift away. A lot has been removed because the ice ages scoured these mountaintops completely. Many of the rocks exposed these days, however, are deep ocean sediments that have been metamorphosed, such as the slates that one finds in many parts of Maine. Many of the deep notches, such as Gulf Hagas, in Maine have been made more spectacular by the vertical layers of slate jutting toward the sky. These have in places been dotted and crisscrossed by many intrusions, such as basalt dikes and granite plutons. The roughness of the Maine Coast bears witness to the variable geology of the Maine bedrock, as well as to the sculpting of the glaciers.

Another legacy of the glaciers is the countless ponds, lakes, and bogs; the ice sheet left these in a couple of different ways. Many of the ponds are "kettle" lakes. These were formed by huge chunks of ice left buried as the glacier retreated. When the ice melted, a pond, often without an outlet, was left. Moraines, the huge piles of boulders and gravel left by a glacier at its terminus, could alter and impede the flow of water, forming huge lakes and wetlands. Many of the swampy lowlands in Maine were formed in glacially scooped basins kept wet by moraines.

NATURAL HISTORY ALONG THE TRAIL

Maine is the land of the sphagnum bog and the moose. Its glacially carved lowlands are dotted with ponds and lakes surrounded by the boreal and transitional deciduous forests of the North. At Maine's higher latitudes you don't have to go as far up on the mountain to reach tree line, and spruce-fir forests appear even in some lowlands.

Ponds and lakes are frequently surrounded by bogs. The city dweller might think of this as a drawback—city swamps tend to be the home of rats and junked cars. But in reality, a good bog is one of the most beautiful, fascinating ecosystems imaginable. Wetlands are among the most fertile life zones on earth, and the Maine bogs are home to countless waterfowl, fish, moose, deer, bear, raccoon, weasel, mink, otter, fisher, marten— you name it. You can find growing on the interlaced plant life that flourish out over the water on the edge of a pond or lake a variety of carnivorous plants: the pitcher plant (*Sarracenia purpurea*) and the sundew (*Drosophyllum rotundifolia*) are common. One of my favorite activities is pond-hopping in a small, light canoe.

Cold streams are home to brook trout (*Salvelinus fontinalis*, a variety of char) and Atlantic salmon (*Salmo salar*, only present if the stream has access to the ocean). Deep lakes contain hidden, hard-to-reach populations of a fish for which Maine is famous among anglers: the togue, which the rest of us call the lake trout (*Salvelinus namaycush*, another char), as well as populations of Atlantic salmon that were landlocked by the retreating glaciers. Moosehead Lake, along the route, is famous for both.

Another kind of Maine wildlife is also notable: insects. Be aware of the worst seasons for mosquitoes and black flies, and always carry strong insect repellent.

HISTORY ALONG THE TRAIL

When the colonists arrived from Europe the entire region that is now Maine was the domain of the various Abnaki tribes. These Algonkian peoples had organized into a loose confederacy in response to the threat presented from the west by the Iroquois Confederacy—and especially the Mohawks of eastern New York.

The two tribes that populated Maine were the Passamaquoddies and the Penobscots. They were the archetypal eastern woodlands people, traveling along their rivers in skillfully crafted birchbark canoes, hunting for most of their diet, and growing the rest through primitive agriculture. Unlike their more southern counterparts in lower New England, they were relatively unharmed by the European settlement in the seventeenth century, but in the early eighteenth they became embroiled in the ongoing conflicts between the English and the French (with whom they sided, as did most Algonkian peoples). By the 1730s they had suffered several brutal defeats at the hands of the British and had begun to retreat up into Canada, where many of them are today. The rest live largely on state reservations in Maine. Old Town, Maine, where the canoes are made, has long been a Penobscot community and source of

Abnaki hunting guides. In lawsuits brought by the Penobscots against the state in the 1970s, however, they have won back large tracts of their old domain.

The settlement patterns of Maine can still be seen in today's population centers along the coastlines and up the river valleys. The coastline was the first to be populated by European immigrants, starting early in the sixteenth century (Scandinavian claims that the Vikings first landed in the tenth century notwithstanding). Things were a bit difficult for settlement for quite some time. The French and the British were engaged in skirmishes in the area until around 1675, and in all-out war until much later in the eighteenth century.

When settlers finally did begin to arrive, they pushed up the river valleys in search of farmland and timber. These have remained two of the mainstays of the state's economy ever since.

So remote was the Maine interior that Katahdin wasn't climbed for certain until 1804, by Charles Turner, Jr. By 1846, when Henry David Thoreau made his attempt, only a handful of others had done the climb, mostly surveyors trying to map the features of the state. When Thoreau traveled to Katahdin it was through totally uninhabited country. To this day there are whole sections of the Appalachian Trail in central Maine where the only access—and that only occasionally—is by barely passable logging roads.

HISTORY OF THE APPALACHIAN TRAIL IN MAINE

"Nail it up," Myron Avery said.

It was "probably the shortest dedicatory speech on record," someone who was there at the time recalled. The date was August 19, 1933, and the place was the summit of Katahdin. The occasion was the symbolic claiming of the spot by the Appalachian Trail Conference as the northern terminus of the Appalachian Trail. Avery had just ordered one of his companions to nail the sign marking the terminus onto a white spruce post they had hauled to the summit and embedded in a rock cairn.

It was a far more important occasion than the speech might indicate. Katahdin almost lost its chance to be on the Trail at all. When Benton MacKaye first proposed the Appalachian

Trail, his choice for the northern terminus was Mt. Washington in New Hampshire. Once the idea took off, though, it was very quickly changed to Katahdin. It was, however, a switch that the ATC would very nearly come to regret.

In 1932, after Myron Avery had become the guiding spirit and goad of the Appalachian Trail Conference, things started moving all along the route. By that October the *Appalachian Trailway News* could report that 1700 miles of the proposed 2056 miles of Trail had been completed. It then listed the gaps: Smith Gap to Little Gap in eastern Pennsylvania (6 miles); Nolichucky River to Devil's Fork Gap (20 miles) . . . and the entire state of Maine: all 250-plus miles of it!

The trouble was that unlike the other regions through which the AT was to travel, there were few existing trails in Maine and no hiking clubs to take up the blazing and maintenance effort. Combine that with the fact that the area was remote and almost diabolically rugged and you can see the problem.

The *Trailway News* article also reported optimistically that

Staking their claim to the northern terminus, Myron Avery (center), *with Albert Jackman* (left), *and Frank Schairer* (right), *start from Katahdin on August 19, 1933, to blaze the trail in Maine. Their companion, Shailer S. Philbrick, took the photo.* (Photograph courtesy of the Appalachian Trail Conference Archives)

Perhaps the most famous wheel since Ezekiel's, in the hands of the man who rolled it the entire length of the AT—Myron Avery—who leads the way, as usual. (Photograph courtesy of the Appalachian Trail Conference)

"Eight months ago, the seeming hopelessness of the Maine situation led to suggestions of its abandonment and a substitute of some White Mountain Peak for Katahdin as the northern terminus of the Trail." That "some White Mountain Peak" was, of course, the majestic Mt. Washington as seen through the eyes of Maine-born Myron Avery, who was damned if his Maine terminus was going to be taken away by New Hampshire or anybody else.

The article went on to say that the chairman of the Trail Conference (Avery) had developed "exhaustive data" on the 175-mile region between Dead River and Katahdin, to go along with the exploration of Arthur C. Comey from Grafton Notch in the Mahoosucs to Dead River. In other words, they had looked over the region and had an idea of how the Trail might be routed using existing trails, roads, and mountain routes.

But it was a combination of Avery and "a Broadway actor and Maine Guide" who finally gave successful impetus to the efforts in Maine. The latter, Walter D. Greene, who actually *was* a Broadway actor with a summer home in Maine, had for years roamed out from his cabin on Sebec Lake to blaze trails in the remote areas—especially the terrifically rugged section in the

Barren-Chairback range, which he blazed in the sprin

The ATC expedition in the summer of 1933, whi
Avery to the summit of Katahdin, was more than just sym
They (Avery and companions Shailer S. Philbrick, Albert
"Jack" Jackman, and the redoubtable J. Frank Schairer, trail
supervisor of the Potomac Appalachian Trail Club) intended to
blaze the Trail off of Katahdin to Monson. And that's what they
did.

Coming down off Katahdin, painting the now-familiar
white blazes all the way, they followed logging roads, old trails,
and the Barren-Chairback route already blazed by Greene and
Philbrick, all the way to Monson—a distance that measured
118.7 miles on Avery's measuring wheel. The wheel itself is now
famous for having been in so many pictures with its owner.

Philbrick then went right back at it, blazing another 54.8
miles from Blanchard, near Monson, to Mt. Bigelow, bringing
the total for the summer to 173.5 miles. With less than 100
miles to go, there could be no further question that the AT would
indeed go all the way to Katahdin.

The ATC scored two major coups in 1935: the founding of
the Maine Appalachian Trail Club, with Greene as its first president and Avery (who was already chairman of the ATC and president of the Potomac ATC) as its first supervisor of trails; and the
agreement of the Civilian Conservation Corps (CCC) to take on
the blazing of the rest of the Trail as one of their projects. These
accomplishments virtually assured that the project would succeed, which it did when a CCC crew blazed the last 2 miles on
August 14, 1937, on the slopes of Spaulding Mountain. It was
the last link in the 2000-plus-mile Appalachian Trail route. Like
Avery's "dedication" on Katahdin, it was done without fanfare,
and the crew simply finished the job and moved on down the
Trail to another assignment.

Hikers on the AT will run across frequent reminders of the
contribution of the CCC, especially in national parks and national forests. These take the form of anything from cabins and
bridges to graded trail beds. In the South, where the AT was
displaced in the 1930s by the Skyline Drive and the Blue Ridge
Highway, the relocations were made by the CCC.

In the years following the completion of the Trail, the
Maine section has had a history similar to many other sections:

d World War and efforts by the main-
on with the ATC to protect the route
ifference in Maine is that the vast ma-
oss private land. The MATC never had
er mile of national forest land that the

test Maine Appalachian Trail guide, the
r 170 of its 277 miles since the early
erhuman effort to secure the route on
protected ıaııu. ....h that effort is now nearing completion,
it is further from the finish in Maine than it is anywhere else.
Hikers should remember as they cross any private land in Maine
that the MATC doesn't need irate landowners to make that job
any harder.

But in typical Maine fashion, the job will be finished, and
it will be finished without a lot of fuss; the way it has always been
done.

THE TRAIL IN MAINE

Katahdin

Katahdin isn't so much a mountain summit as it is an assembly
of summits. The highest point, also the highest in the state of
Maine, is Baxter Peak.

Henry David Thoreau's attempt to climb Katahdin (or
Ktaadn, as he spelled it) has given us perhaps our best view of
what the countryside was once like. Hiring Penobscot guides at
Old Town, Thoreau approached Katahdin by bateau up the West
Branch of the Penobscot. He is said to have camped on a point
of land within sight of Abol Bridge. He wrote that he and his
companions caught many fine brook trout on the spot. From
there, he and his party headed north, crossing Abol Stream and
continuing up a tributary toward Katahdin.

There were, of course, no trails in those days, and the
going was exceedingly rough. The forests were thick, and no
routes had yet been discovered around the many boulders and
blow-down thickets. For the most part, ascents of remote mountains were made up streambeds or slides.

Thoreau and company set up a base camp at the base of
Rum Mountain (another peak in the Katahdin group), and Henry

climbed it. From their base, the group continued up the stream until it petered out at its source. Thoreau, mistaking South Peak for the highest point, had intended to continue from there on a compass bearing (all other parties had taken the easier climb up the 1816 slide, which is the route of the Abol Trail). He reached his high point perhaps somewhere below the Table Land, or maybe farther east near the base of South Peak. Due to clouds, he wasn't sure exactly where they were and gave up the climb 1200 feet below the summit. He makes no mention of, and did not see, the spring that lies below the summit and bears his name. He didn't make it that far.

Hikers today need not worry about losing their way: The various trails to the summit are mostly very well marked. Myron Avery would later write: "If, on a clear day, the Trail across the Table Land seems overmarked, we would ask our critics to defer judgment until they attempt to cross the Table Land in a dense fog. Then, undoubtedly, they will find the paint blazes too far apart. For, in the fog, the real source of danger on Katahdin is the numerous misleading lines of cairns."

The Trail leads steeply off the summit of Baxter Peak to the southwest, soon reaching the comparatively level terrain at Table Land. Crossing that, at the distance of nearly a mile, it reaches The Gateway, at which point it begins to descend stiffly once again, down a heavily bouldered route toward tree line, 1750 feet below the summit. Once at tree line it passes by The Cave, a space beneath a large boulder that can be used as a refuge in an emergency.

Reaching Katahdin Stream, down which it will run to the bottom, the Trail passes by some beautiful 50-foot waterfalls and finally reaches Katahdin Stream Campground just over 5 miles from the summit. It has completed perhaps the ruggedest descent on its entire length, having dropped over 4000 feet in those 5 miles.

This is one of the most popular accesses to Katahdin. Run by Baxter State Park, the Katahdin Stream, Daicey Pond, and Abol Campgrounds offer a place to set up a base camp and leave your car. However, you need reservations in advance to do either. You can also make them at Abol Bridge Campground, which is privately operated. None of these sites has a phone.

Now in the lowlands, the Trail has reached the wet regions

of Maine. Thoreau wrote later in his story of his Katahdin hike (in *The Maine Woods*) that "The primitive wood is always and everywhere damp and mossy, so that I travelled constantly with the impression that I was in a swamp. . . ." The Trail will weave its way among the thousands of lakes and ponds that the ATC trail guide describes as looking from the summit of Katahdin "as if a mirror had been broken and scattered over the mantle of dark green spruce and fir forest cover, with the myriad lakes reflecting the sun's light to the observer." Passing by two impressive waterfalls (accessible by short side trails), the AT descends into the valley of the West Branch of the Penobscot.

The West Branch, which the AT crosses on the Abol Bridge, is a wild river that features some of the best whitewater in the Northeast. There are a number of rafting and guiding operations in Millinocket that can take you down.

The One-Hundred-Mile Wilderness

After descending into the valley, the Trail crosses the Abol Bridge (Abol is short for *Aboljackamegassic,* which is recorded as meaning "bare ground" in Abnaki, or, in the case of Abol Falls, just below the Trail, *Aboljacarmegus,* or "smooth ledge falls"). It then approaches the entrance to the "100-mile Wilderness." Actually, it's about 98 miles, and it's nothing to be taken lightly. This most remote of all AT sections is crossed by primitive timber roads in only a few locations, and it's no easy walk out on any of them.

If you're an easterner who has been frustrated by an inability really to get out on your own, far from civilization, this is your chance. If you want to attempt the crossing, allow eight to ten days and be sure to make arrangements with the Great Northern Paper Company's gatekeeper to leave your car at the control gate at the site. Or, better yet, get somebody to drop you off and leave your car in Monson. That's where you're going to end up.

As it enters the 100-mile Wilderness, the Trail heads first for Rainbow Ledges and Rainbow Lake. It was there in 1954 that "Grandma" Emma Gatewood's first attempt to thru-hike the AT failed. She got lost, and after spending the night out in the bush made her way back to Rainbow Lake to find her rescuers pitching horseshoes. They had given up on her.

They might have saved themselves the trouble entirely,

because Grandma could take care of herself. The following year, 1955, she set out from Mt. Oglethorpe in Georgia, and by September had become, at sixty-five, the first woman to thru-hike the AT. She then did it two more times, and hiked the Long Trail, the Oregon Trail, and a number of others in the bargain. She was only the sixteenth person to hike the AT in sections and the eighth to thru-hike the entire route, but she stands as perhaps the best-known and best-loved of them all. She died in 1977 at age eighty-five after a short illness. To this day, along the route people will tell you "Grandma Gatewood slept here."

On the route she *did* complete on her first attempt, though, she would have walked generally uphill toward Rainbow Ledges from the West Branch. These are part of a relatively steep unwooded knob overlooking Rainbow Lake from the east. They are bare because of a forest fire in 1903 that was evidently hot enough to kill the trees and burn the ground cover away completely.

The Rainbow Lake area is uninhabited except for some private camps. Hikers should stay away from them except in emergencies. The Trail follows the south shore of the lake to near its outlet, and then follows Rainbow Stream down toward Nesuntabunt ("Three Heads") Mountain and Nahmakanta Lake. On the way it crosses a logging road that leads out toward Millinocket. The Trail climbs Nesuntabunt (a short, steep pitch with good views toward Katahdin from a ledge down a side trail) and then goes down steeply to Nahmakanta Lake. This lake, with its sandy beach and fabulous views, is worth a long weekend all by itself—it's almost 23 miles from Abol Bridge, making it a destination in itself—especially if its name, "Plenty of Fish," still means anything.

The Trail then takes off to the southeast, passing by several other beautiful lakes (Pemadumcook and Jo-Mary, the latter named for a Penobscot guide) and some low-lying boggy country, on its way to the White Cap Mountains and nearby Gulf Hagas, the "Grand Canyon of the East."

The White Cap Range

White Cap and its neighbors run in the 2750- to 3500-foot range. White Cap, the first the Trail reaches, is 3644 feet high and has an open summit noted for its spectacular view. Nearby

Hay Mountain (3244 feet) and Gulf Hagas Mountain (2683 feet) offer less in the way of view. The range is accessible on either end by very rough logging roads, described on the MATC's trail guide map. They involve passing by control gates operated by the paper companies, so check in advance for any arrangements you may need to make. The Maine ATC trail guide lists which logging companies control the various logging road accesses.

Gulf Hagas and The Hermitage

At the southern end of the White Cap range the Trail passes near Gulf Hagas. Access is from The Hermitage, a stand of 130-foot-tall white pine owned by The Nature Conservancy (no camping and no fires!). The trails into the Gulf area were blazed by Walter Greene in 1934.

The Gulf itself is a 2.5-mile-long gorge cut down into tilted layers of slate—the remnant of deep-ocean sediment pushed inland by the Acadian Orogeny 350 million years ago. The West Branch of the Pleasant River cascades down over a series of falls until it reaches still or "dead" water near The Hermitage. Gulf Hagas Brook also enters here, with the spectacular Screw Auger Falls just above the confluence.

Access to this section is through the Katahdin Iron Works, an old smelting operation that is now a museum. It is off of Route 11 near Brownville Junction, and it's a 7.4-mile walk from the Ironworks to The Hermitage but you can drive in as long as you park out of the way of the logging trucks.

The Barren-Chairback Range

Next, as the 100-mile Wilderness winds its last miles into Monson, it enters one of its true gems: the Barren-Chairback range, blazed by Walter Greene in the spring of 1933 in anticipation of Myron Avery's arrival and to prove that the Trail could be blazed in Maine.

The AT enters the range from the Chairback side, climbing up the "Chairback Cliffs," from which it got its name. It seems they reminded somebody of a ladderback chair.

The range is noted for its steep ups and downs. Even though the mountains are only in the 2200- to 2600-foot range, they are exceedingly rugged, and there are open summits on a couple—Chairback and Barren (with its abandoned fire tower) being notable.

The range is a favorite for overnights, suitable for a long weekend. There are two shelters high in the range that can afford a lot of privacy if you're not there in the height of the season.

The Trail comes down off Barren Mountain steeply, and heads once again into a low knob-and-valley region, climbing over a series of parallel ridges as it heads southwest into Monson. Some of the streams don't have easy crossings—if you hadn't heard, there aren't always bridges over bodies of water in Maine the way there are farther south. If you don't believe it, wait until you get to the Kennebec River.

Moxie Bald and Pleasant Pond Mountains

Through this section, a lightweight fly rod and a Maine fishing license are required equipment. I, at least, can't bear to pass by clear streams like this without at least dropping a line once or twice.

The Trail, by the way, doesn't actually go *into* Monson—it hits the shore of Lake Hebron a couple of miles up the road and moves away to the west.

Passing by the lake to the west, the AT enters another lowland wilderness. It enters almost immediately the slate canyon of the West Branch of the Piscataquis River. The route will be through the canyon for 5.3 miles. There is good swimming in the pools if you don't bother the fishermen.

Once through the canyon the Trail fords the Piscataquis and follows the Bald Mountain Stream up toward the boggy northern end of Bald Mountain Pond. Then it's a steep climb up Moxie Bald Mountain, a 2630-foot peak with, as you'd expect from the name, a bald summit. Then, it's quickly down and up again to the top of 2477-foot Pleasant Pond Mountain, with views to be had from ledges around the summit.

Can Pleasant Pond be far away? No. A fast descent off of Pleasant Pond Mountain brings you to this moderately developed lake with road access to the small village of Caratunk on the Kennebec River.

Crossing the Kennebec

The Kennebec is big trouble for thru-hikers. Day hikers don't worry so much because they can simply start or finish their hikes on either side, using their cars to get around the ford. But on occasion even short-term users come face to face with the problems of crossing this wilderness stream.

With no bridge across it and 150 feet wide, the Kennebec's fording situation is complicated by a power station upstream that regularly releases large amounts of water. If you're on the water when the wave comes you stand to be in deep trouble—what was knee-deep when you started crossing can quickly go over your head and wash you away. The MATC and the ATC have jointly been providing ferry service to avoid accidents. Get hold of one or the other to find out if the service is still running and, if so, what the ferry schedule is.

If you really can't arrange to use the ferry, it's important first to accept that you're going to get your feet wet. Second, it's important to get an early start—the power station doesn't release water until after 8:00 A.M. Use a walking stick for stability, cross quickly, try to stay on the sand bars, and make some provision for keeping your pack dry. The ATC discourages fording the Kennebec. Use the ferry if you possibly can.

Carry Pond Country

Once across the Kennebec, the AT heads immediately into the low-lying terrain around the three Carry Ponds: East, Middle, and West. It was through this wet, marshy section that Benedict Arnold—a Patriot at the time—passed in November of 1775 on his way to an unsuccessful surprise assault on Quebec. The Arnold Trail was reopened in the 1930s and the AT follows the route for a couple miles between Middle Carry and West Carry ponds. The Arnold Trail then heads to Flagstaff Lake, which is actually the dammed-up Dead River, up which Arnold traveled toward the St. Lawrence.

The hardships endured by Arnold and his seven hundred men would seem to give little advance warning of his later betrayal of his country. How could a man willing to undertake such an expedition turn coat? But there is perhaps the grain of a hint: After putting forth so much effort, Arnold would later feel unappreciated when he was passed over for promotion. Perhaps if the expedition had succeeded . . . But it didn't, and the result will be described in Chapter 7.

After leaving the Carry Pond region and the Arnold Trail, the AT heads for the Bigelow range. The Trail rounds the south end of Flagstaff Lake and starts climbing.

The Bigelow Range

This high range is known for its spectacular views and its brutal ups and downs. From Flagstaff Lake the AT will climb nearly 3000 feet and drop and rise sharply several times on its traverse through the range.

Bigelow Mountain is the third highest peak on the AT in Maine, after Katahdin and Crocker mountains. It consists of West Peak at 4150 feet, Myron Avery Peak (a well-deserved honor, I think) at 4088 feet, and several other smaller summits in the 3000- to 3500-foot range.

Both Avery and West peaks feature open alpine summits that contain fragile ecosystems with rare plant and animal life. An abandoned fire tower on Avery Peak helps the Bigelows lay claim to some of the finest views in the entire state, rivaling even Katahdin. The entire range is a popular short, strenuous backpacking trip of 17.8 miles, especially when you consider that some of the campsites—such as Myron Avery Memorial Lean-to in the shallow notch between Avery and West peaks—offer such memorable accommodations, being among the highest in the North. Also, don't forget Horns Pond, with a couple of lean-tos on a classic tarn lake. It's perched at 3100 feet at the base of South Horn, a 3831-foot beauty with an open summit.

The Bigelow Range Trail continues west toward Stratton, Maine, while the AT cuts sharply south a couple miles down the trail from Horns Pond.

Crocker, Spaulding, and Saddleback Mountains

The 30-mile section from Stratton Brook at the base of the Bigelow range to the Sandy River at the southwest end of the

Saddlebacks is among the ruggedest sections of the entire AT. The net up and down in either direction is around 10,000 feet.

In the first 5.5 miles the route climbs nearly 3000 feet to its second highest point in Maine, the North Peak of Crocker Mountain at 4168 feet. It has that honor because nearby Sugarloaf Mountain, at 4237 feet the second highest in Maine, had to be taken off the route in the early 1970s due to widespread ski-area development on the mountain. Continued building threatens to force more relocation even now.

Once past the two main peaks of Crocker Mountain (North and South), the AT descends sharply into the valley of the South Branch of the Carrabasset River, through which a dirt logging road passes that may usually be used as an access for day hikers. It then climbs up the flank of Sugarloaf Mountain to a point on the ridge about three-quarters of a mile and 700 vertical feet below the summit (which is accessible via a side trail). Hikers passing by this point toward neighboring Spaulding Mountain should keep in mind that it was this section, blazed on August 14, 1937, that formed the final link in the 2000-mile route of the Appalachian Trail.

Once past Spaulding Mountain (3988 feet), the AT takes a sawtooth descent into the steep valley of Orbeton Stream and then immediately ascends sharply into the Saddlebacks. These are characterized by open summits and a traverse of over 3 miles from the east side of The Horn to just west of the summit of Saddleback Mountain over bare granite, alpine ridges, and peaks. The weather can brew quickly, so be prepared in case you get caught out on this section.

From the 4116-foot summit of Saddleback, the fourth highest on the AT in Maine, the Trail drops drastically again, bottoming out in the Sandy River valley at around 1500 feet, 5 miles later.

The Saddlebacks are among the best short-hike and day-hike destinations in Maine. Ambitious climbers can do a day hike of Saddleback, hiking out to the Saddleback ski area to the north if desired. Relatively frequent road access at various points adds numerous dimensions to hiking in these wild 4000-foot hills.

Sandy River to Bemis Valley

For those with a naturalist's bent, the next section won't seem like a letdown. Mountaineers might give it a pass, unless they're on their way to the Bemis range and don't mind a few miles in which to stretch their legs.

Anybody interested in the ponds and bogs of Maine's lowlands will adore this section. It passes by a half-dozen wilderness ponds, each more pristine than the last, and crosses a number of wild streams and sphagnum bogs.

The MATC recommends hiking this section from north to south to take advantage of the sandy beach and swimming on Long Pond, near the southern end.

I'd avoid this section in June, though. We New Yorkers are fond of touting our Adirondack black flies as the most ferocious on earth, but I wouldn't want to argue the point in these bogs at the height of the black fly season.

The Bemis Range

Crossing the Bemis Stream, the AT begins a fairly gradual ascent toward 3592-foot Bemis Mountain. This is an area of open summits and a series of rocky knobs that don't require a whole lot of descent in between. The entire range covers around a dozen miles and has four main peaks, including 3762-foot Elephant Mountain, just off the Trail, and Old Blue Mountain, 3600 feet, which is on it. The MATC advises hikers to carry water.

Dunn Notch and the Baldpates

After passing by Wyman Mountain and several lower ridges and intervening notches, the AT reaches Dunn Notch, a deep cleft in the ridge line cut by the West Branch of the Ellis River. There are a number of cascades and waterfalls there. From there, the Trail ascends steeply into the Baldpates, West and East Peaks. Both are open summits and afford fine views of the Mahoosucs to the south. If you can spot your car at either end, this makes a fine 10.1-mile day hike.

Dropping down off of West Peak, the Trail heads into Grafton Notch. This spectacular 1000-foot-deep valley marks the end of the Maine Appalachian Trail Club's responsibilities. From the Notch, day hikers can range out over quite a variety of trails, most up into the Mahoosucs to the south. The Baldpates make a good up-and-back ascent.

The Mahoosuc Range

Maine was just bound to go out with a bang. The wild Mahoosuc range is many a thru-hiker's choice as the roughest, toughest section along the entire AT. The only rival is said to be the Nantahalas, the last range on the route before it heads into Georgia and the finish at Springer Mountain. There are those who say that trail builders and maintainers in North Carolina have done such a good job on the Nantahalas that it has lost some of its flash and dash. Decide for yourself, if you get the chance. My choice is the Mahoosucs, though there are parts of the Nantahalas that I've missed. You can't go wrong in either range.

The Mahoosucs, though, are truly something special. Uncrossed by roads for its entire thirty-mile length, the Trail here features open peaks and boulder-scrambled glacial valleys that require the skills of a human fly to cross.

The Trail first climbs up the flank of Old Speck Mountain, at 4180 feet the third highest in Maine. The hiker is presented with a choice: taking the southern route around the Eyebrow Cliffs, or taking the Eyebrow Trail to the north and traversing the top of the escarpment.

The AT then heads up a ridge leading south to the West Ridge of Old Speck, approaching to within 0.3 mile. A side trail completes the ascent. The East Spur Trail off the other side leads to an alternate return route to Grafton Notch.

After descending the southern slopes of Old Speck, the AT passes by Speck Pond and its shelter and climbs over the open summit of Mahoosuc Arm, a 3777-foot knob. It's then a steep descent into Mahoosuc Notch.

This is reputed to be the ruggedest mile on the entire AT. The notch itself is a glacially carved valley with exceptionally steep walls and strewn with huge boulders. The Trail clambers up and over, down and under, and—when possible—between. Allow lots of extra time for the passage. Mahoosuc Notch is listed on the National Register of Natural Landmarks.

The last 6 miles of the AT in Maine climb up into the Filling Mill Mountain-Goose Eye Mountain section of the Mahoosucs. These are largely open summited peaks interspersed by high-elevation bogs that feature interesting—and rare—plant life. Goose Eye is perhaps the most impressive peak in the Mahoosucs, even though it's only 3794 feet high. Altitude isn't everything.

From near the summit of Goose Eye the Goose Eye Trail leads 3 miles down to the Success Pond Road, meeting it at the same point at which the Carlo Col Trail sets off on a 2.6-mile ascent of neighboring Carlo Mountain. The two trails can be linked up with the AT for a fine day hike that takes in both mountains.

The last peak the AT crosses in Maine is 3562-foot Mt. Carlo, with an open summit that offers fine views of what's ahead and behind. The Mahoosuc range continues into New Hampshire, with the border 0.9 mile southwest of Mt. Carlo. You'll know it when you get there by the yellow blazes.

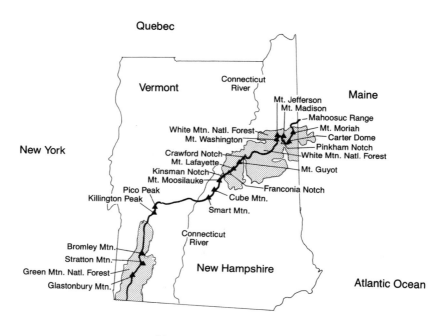

Quebec

Vermont

Connecticut
River

Maine

Mt. Jefferson
Mt. Madison

Mahoosuc Range

White Mtn. Natl. Forest
Mt. Washington

Mt. Moriah
Carter Dome
Pinkham Notch
White Mtn. Natl. Forest

New York

Crawford Notch
Mt. Lafayette
Kinsman Notch
Mt. Moosilauke

Mt. Guyot

Pico Peak
Killington Peak

Cube Mtn.

Franconia Notch

Smart Mtn.

Connecticut
River

Bromley Mtn.

Stratton Mtn.

New Hampshire

Green Mtn. Natl. Forest

Glastonbury Mtn.

Atlantic Ocean

Massachusetts

New Hampshire and Vermont

5

The New Hampshire / Vermont Section

Trail Distances:

> *Maine/New Hampshire state line to New Hampshire/Vermont state line* . . . . *157.9 miles*
>
> *New Hampshire/Vermont state line to Vermont/Massachusetts state line* . . . . *137 miles*

Maintaining Clubs:

> *Appalachian Mountain Club: Grafton Notch, Maine, to Kinsman Notch, New Hampshire* . . . . *128.8 miles*
> (Maine miles: *14.4*)
>
> *Dartmouth Outing Club: Kinsman Notch, New Hampshire, to Vermont Route 12* . . . . *75.5 miles*
>
> *Green Mountain Club: Vermont Route 12 to Vermont/Massachusetts state line* . . . . *115 miles*

INTRODUCTION

WHEN BENTON MacKaye first envisioned the Appalachian Trail, the immediate choice for the northern terminus was Mt. Washington. At 6288 feet, it is easily the most impressive mountain in the entire Northeast. Called *Agiocochook,* or "Home of the Great Spirit," by the local tribes, it is, even in the defaced commercialization of late years, a mountain to be reckoned with. The highest wind speed ever recorded was clocked on its summit: 231 miles per hour. Its soaring peak perches a full 1000 feet above tree line, making its slopes the longest open running on the entire Appalachian Trail.

But the roads and railways and souvenir stands on Mt. Washington aren't the whole story of this state or this region. Though it's a shame that it had to be the Home of the Great Spirit that drew the attention of the developers, even Mt. Washington itself is mostly wild. It's the great secret that hikers know, the inspiration for Benton MacKaye's whole concept: All you need to do to get away from the plastic and the glitter is to put your boots on and walk for about half an hour. Soon the gum wrappers and soda cans that bloom in the shadow of the snack bar are replaced by sedge and rare cinquefoil; the croaking of ravens and song of winter wrens take the place of screaming kids and the inane conversation of people who didn't earn their way to the summit.

Besides, once the developers had built their road and their cog railway up Mt. Washington, they left most of the other peaks alone. The New Hampshire/Vermont region is a wild, wonderful area all the way from the Mahoosucs to the Berkshires.

GEOLOGY ALONG THE TRAIL

The geological history of New Hampshire and Vermont is about as complicated as you'd expect of two areas that were formed on separate continents. As the Trail continues in a southeasterly direction it nears the old continental boundary, which it will cross near Norwich, Vermont, in the Connecticut River valley.

Before that, though, it crosses a complex series of formations, ranging from plutons to dike structures to metamorphosed volcanics. Huge basaltic dikes pushed through the rock strata, later to be eroded out by rivers into spectacular flumes through which icy streams cascade. Glacial melt-off, milky with powdered rock, scoured out immense potholes and channels through the bedrock. A lot happened in this narrow strip of land.

In the beginning, 600 million years ago, the eastern areas of New Hampshire, like those in Maine, lay either on the western edge of the Eurafrican plate, or on the bottom of the ocean. As the European plate neared the North American across *Iapetus* and the uplifts began on the continental shelf and on into Vermont and down the eastern coast, volcanic islands formed out in the ocean. As the onrushing continents (speeding in at literally inches per year!) closed in, the band of volcanic islands, the sea floor and continental shelf, and all, were squished up onto the Taconic and Berkshire mountains that awaited them. When the impact occurred 350 million years ago the result was a huge continent, *Pangaea*, joined at the present Connecticut River valley with the volcanic band squashed in at the suture line.

The great crunch in New Hampshire and Vermont did much the same kind of thing it did elsewhere: rocks that were once deep under the ocean were ploughed up onto the land, folded, compressed, and bulldozed over the often younger bedrock farther west. Sediments were so crushed and heated that they either turned into advanced metamorphic structures or re-melted entirely into granite. Vast plutons welled up and widespread volcanic activity sprang up everywhere.

The structure of New Hampshire bears certain similarities to Yosemite National Park in California. Many of the mountains there are the remains of ancient granite plutons that welled up through the rock and hardened as they reached the surface. It's the basic geological story of New Hampshire—reason enough to call it the Granite State.

One characteristic of New Hampshire is the *ring dike.* These were formed when overlying bedrock sank into a magma chamber beneath, opening cracks around the edges for magma to squeeze up through toward the surface.

After passing over the volcanic band left by the precollision islands that were welded into the fabric of the North American continent, the Trail passes into Vermont and an entirely different situation. The Vermont structures bear more resemblance to the ridges that will be encountered in Virginia and

North Carolina. Mostly the remnants of the sea floor and continental shelf that were thrust over the edge of the ancient Grenville continent, these folded and faulted ridges are in places eroded all the way down to the core Grenville rock. You find absolutely no Grenville rock anywhere in Maine or New Hampshire because these areas were formed elsewhere.

To the north of where the Trail crosses into Vermont, the plutons that formed the commercially important Barre granite pushed their way up through thick layers of rock strata. The sheath rocks surrounding the plutons themselves are composed of metamorphic rocks that some geologists theorize must have been formed by pressure that would be present only beneath 12,000 to 15,000 *meters* of overlying rock. This would mean that the mountains formed along the northern end of the Vermont/New Hampshire border could have been 50,000 feet high, half again as high as Mt. Everest! How would you like to try the first ascent of one of those?

NATURAL HISTORY ALONG THE TRAIL

Alpine Summits

When Henry David Thoreau first climbed Mt. Washington in 1839 he spent much of his time observing the plant life, trying to determine its relation to his increased elevation, and from there, to the equivalent increase in latitude. He figured at the time that every 400 feet of ascent was equivalent to traveling 70 miles farther north.

The many alpine summits in New Hampshire are the ecological counterpart of the tundra of northern Canada. The scruffy balsams and firs of the high-elevation boreal forests give way completely to a kind of high-altitude desert; trees are replaced by grasses and sedges, each clinging desperately among the boulders. The true monarchs of the alpine summit are probably the lichens. This is a desert governed by cold and a short growing season, not by lack of moisture.

The upper limits of the White Mountains are home to quite a variety of species not found below. The White Mountain butterfly (*Oeneis melissa*), found nowhere else, is a famous example; the dwarf cinquefoil grows only on the Madison Flats of Mt. Washington. These are species left over from the last Ice

Age. As the glaciers retreated, the higher elevations became refuge to species that could not survive in the oncoming warmth.

What resulted was a unique role for the alpine summit: that of island amid a sea of more temperate environments. Species that fell back to the mountaintops became effectively isolated by the warm, hostile conditions surrounding them below. Examples abound. The Canaan valley of West Virginia is a sequestered boreal environment more typical of something on the Canadian shield. Several northern species find their southernmost ranges there. The subalpine peaks of the Blue Ridge and the Smokies also form islands—in their case islands of boreal fir-spruce forest.

But the few truly alpine summits of the east—Katahdin, the White Mountains, a handful of peaks in the Adirondacks—form the most complete islands of all. Their plant varieties are literally hundreds of miles from where they can survive anywhere near sea level. So they remain up there, perched on their ridges.

HISTORY ALONG THE TRAIL

The hills of New Hampshire were the haunts of a number of Algonkian peoples. The largest group, the Pennacooks, lived in central and southern New Hampshire. To the north lived bands of Abnakis, the people who controlled the lion's share of Maine. They extended all the way down into northeastern Vermont.

Pennacook apparently meant "At the Bottom of the Hill/ Highland." This might suggest that they made their homes for the most part outside the mountains, though they may on occasion have hunted there. The White Mountains may, then, have been mostly the domain of the Abnakis.

Vermont was apparently divided among the Abnakis to the north, the Pennacooks in the east, the Mahicans in the west, and the Pocumtucs of Massachusetts in the south. The action of *Northwest Passage,* Kenneth Roberts's famous novel/biography of Major Robert Rogers, is concerned with a 1760 British raid through Vermont into southern Quebec against the Algonkian St. Francis tribe, allies of the French, who were probably Abnakis.

The Europeans Arrive

In 1630 the first Chases arrived in Massachusetts Bay Colony. They were William, a ne'er-do-well carpenter (my great-some-odd grandfather), and his two pious cousins Thomas and Aquila. William, never one to take a stand on matters of faith, remained in his obscurity on Cape Cod, surviving fairly regular scrapes with his neighbors and the authorities and parenting another equally undistinguished member of my family tree.

Thomas and Aquila, on the other hand, stayed only a few years. In the early 1630s they ran afoul of the Colony's rulers on a theological matter. Rather than bend their principles, they decided to leave. They went to New Hampshire.

The same hardheaded independence that sent the brothers even farther into the terrifying wilderness on an issue of principle is evident in everything from the state's license plates ("Live Free or Die") to the annual town meetings that still control the course of most New Hampshire townships and constitute one of the last vestiges of pure democracy anywhere in the world.

Although the southern reaches of Vermont and New Hampshire were settled as early as the 1630s, the north remained rather inhospitable until shortly before the American Revolution, especially in Vermont. The mountainous areas became warpaths for marauding French and their Algonkian allies coming down from Quebec. It wasn't until the 1760s that the northern invaders were finally defeated and settlement could proceed north of the lowlands.

One favorite route for the northern raiders went through what was described as "The Notch"—a narrow defile said to be only 22 feet across. After the raids ceased, the route was lost until the 1770s, when it was rediscovered by hunters. It probably refers to Crawford Notch. English chronicler John Josselyn in the 1700s described the country north of the Notch as "daunting, terrible; being full of rocky hills as thick as mole hills in a meadow, and clothed with infinite thick woods." He dubbed the "rocky hills" with a name: The White Mountains.

Once the French were defeated and settlement began in earnest, Vermont became a bone of contention. Claimed by both New Hampshire and New York, the territory was subject to land grants for the same land being issued from two separate authorities. Ethan Allen and his Green Mountain Boys, famous for their action against the British during the Revolution, were originally organized to block New York settlers—Yorkers—coming into Vermont from the west. The vigorous Yankees of this region, their minds irrevocably made up on many things, were strong Patriots during the Revolution, enthusiastic abolitionists before and during the Civil War, and a bastion of Republican conservatism ever since.

HISTORY OF THE APPALACHIAN TRAIL IN NEW HAMPSHIRE AND VERMONT

Unlike Maine, New Hampshire and Vermont were relatively easy to include in the Appalachian Trail route. Much of the Trail already existed in the form of the Appalachian Mountain Club's (AMC) White Mountains system, the Dartmouth Outing Club's trails, and the Green Mountain Club's (GMC) Long Trail and its side routes.

It was, in fact, already under discussion to link up these trails into a longer route. The various organizations were meeting together under the banner of the New England Trail Conference (NETC) before Benton MacKaye proposed the AT.

Trail historians Guy and Laura Waterman point out that although there were many trails blazed over the years in recreational hotspots like the Presidentials and the Franconia Notch area, it wasn't until the widespread appearance of the automobile that it became practical—or even desirable—for them to be linked up into longer routes. Once the Tin Lizzy made trailheads more accessible, though, things moved quickly. It's not coincidence, they suggest, that efforts to blaze the Long Trail in Vermont began in 1910, the year Henry Ford took the first step toward putting a car in every garage. It's also not surprising that, in 1933, the Green Mountain Club, like the Appalachian Trail Conference at about the same time in Virginia and North Carolina, faced efforts by well-intended commerce-boosters to pave a ridge-top road the length of the Green Mountains. (The Watermans's writings on the subject have mostly been confined to magazine articles; they are said to be working on a comprehensive history of the AT, which we all hope they publish soon.)

In the year of 1916 to 1917 there was a great deal of debate among the principals of the NETC regarding longer routes. Allen Chamberlain, a columnist with the *Boston Evening Transcript,* proposed extending the Long Trail down the Taconics to New York City. Another plan suggested linking the Long Trail with Green-Mountain-Club-member Professor Will S. Monroe's existing trails in New Jersey.

It's unclear whether these plans were or were not on Mac-Kaye's mind in 1921 when he proposed his Appalachian Trail. He was, however, well acquainted with Allen Chamberlain, and had been since the early teens.

Of all the trails then in existence, the Long Trail must stand as notable. Begun in 1910, it was the brainchild of school-master James P. Taylor. The whole idea came to him on Vermont's Stratton Mountain as he waited for the weather to clear. Perhaps coincidentally, Benton MacKaye would later claim that the inspiration for the AT came to him on Stratton Mountain. There must be something about the place. Thank goodness that, after an absence of several years, it's back on the route.

By the time MacKaye published his proposal for the Appalachian Trail, large chunks of the still-incomplete Long Trail were already in existence. When the Long Trail was finished in September of 1931, flares were lit simultaneously on fourteen mountaintops along its crest. In its southern sections it had already been incorporated into the route of the AT. Today the two routes run concurrently for nearly 100 miles.

THE TRAIL IN NEW HAMPSHIRE

It's appropriate that the Trail should cross from Maine to New Hampshire in perhaps the wildest, ruggedest range on its entire length. The Mahoosucs are always near the top of any thru-hiker's list when it's time to tell stories about hardships on the Trail.

Because the 31-mile section through the Mahoosucs is unbroken by roads, they are usually hiked through in their entirety. For that reason, both the Maine and the New Hampshire/Vermont trail guides include the section in Maine from Grafton Notch to the Maine/New Hampshire state line.

The Appalachian Trail crosses the state line in a shallow notch between Mt. Carlo in Maine and Mt. Success in New Hampshire. The spot is marked by yellow blazes. The Trail then climbs up the meadowed summit of 3565-foot Mt. Success, 1.8 miles to the southwest.

Through the rest of the way to the Androscoggin River the AT sticks to the ridge line, descending into valleys at Gentian Pond, Moss Pond, Dream Lake, and Page Pond. The country is characterized by high-elevation meadows and ledges, many of which give superb views of the other peaks in the Mahoosucs or even the Whites to the southwest.

The New Hampshire section of the Mahoosuc Range is accessible by side trails that intersect the AT at regular intervals. These generally offer approaches of somewhere in the neighborhood of 3 miles. A particularly nice hike ascends from North Road near Shelburne, New Hampshire, to Gentian Pond Campsite, and the Dryad Falls Trail is available for a pleasant loop past some nice waterfalls. Be prepared, though, because the last quarter mile of ascent to Gentian Pond is exceptionally steep.

The Appalachian Mountain Club system trailhead is on Success Pond Road, near Berlin, New Hampshire.

The Trail used to continue straight down the ridge from the summit of Mt. Hayes into Gorham's Upper Village. In 1976 it was rerouted from Mt. Hayes south, to cross the Androscoggin nearer to Shelburne. The new section, built on the centennial of the Appalachian Mountain Club, is called the Centennial Trail. The old section is still open as a side trail.

The Androscoggin, by the way, is known as a fine trout stream, especially along its upper reaches, and as an exciting river to paddle.

From its crossing of the Androscoggin, the Trail quickly heads back up into the mountains. In the next 5 miles it will ascend nearly 3000 feet, which foreshadows the radical up-and-down that will characterize it through most of New Hampshire. It soon tops 4000 feet in Mt. Moriah as it enters the Carter-Moriah range on its way to the Presidentials.

Most of the Carter-Moriah range is in the White Mountains National Forest. Fires are prohibited above tree line (defined as areas where trees are less than 8 feet high), and near trailheads and shelters. Check with the Forest Service for specifics: White

Mountains National Forest, P.O. Box 638, Laconia, New Hampshire 03247, (603) 524-6450.

Another access to the Carter-Moriah range is over the Carter Moriah Trail out of Gorham. It joins the AT on the summit of Mt. Moriah and continues concurrently with it to Carter Notch Hut. From there, the Trail follows the Wildcat Ridge Trail to Pinkham Notch.

Throughout the Carter-Moriah range the AT remains above 4000 feet except in the steep-sided notches. Once across Wildcat Mountain it descends a knee-popping 2000 feet in under 2 miles on its way to Pinkham Notch.

The Presidential Range

Located at Pinkham Notch is the Appalachian Mountain Club's mountain facility, Pinkham Notch Camp. It is the gateway to the Presidential range, the highest, most spectacular mountains in the Northeast.

Most guide books to the White Mountains begin with long strings of warnings in bold-faced print, capital letters, italicized, quoted, in parentheses, in the middle of the page. Writers are afraid that readers will underestimate these mountains, go off and do something stupid, get themselves killed, and blame it on them.

The Whites *are* deceptively dangerous. Situated in stormy New England smack dab in the crossroads to several major weather paths, they are also high enough to create their own bad weather. Storms can blow up quickly and they can be among the most violent on earth. So here goes—the obligatory (and necessary) warning: When in the Presidentials, *ALWAYS PREPARE FOR COLD AND STORM, EVEN IN SUMMER.* You'd follow that dictum in any mountain range, but in the Whites, it should be a religion. Just don't be *too* afraid of them. They *can* be safely visited without an undue fear of death if you take the proper precautions.

The White Mountains, and especially the Presidentials, have been a recreational attraction for over one hundred years. The road to the summit was begun as early as the 1850s, with a number of mountain lodges built in the area to house tourists and hikers. The famous cog railway, the first of its kind in the world, began operation in 1869.

Human visitation began long before that. The first ascent of Mt. Washington evidently belongs to one Darby Field, who explored the "tops of the white hills" in 1632, possibly looking for gold or gems. He returned to civilization to report seeing some kind of "shining stone," and then retreated into obscurity. Others followed the same year, apparently looking for the shining stones. One was the deputy governor of Maine, Thomas Gorges, who reported traveling "about 7 or 8 miles upon shattered rocks, without tree or grass, very steep all the way. At the top is a plain [sic] about three or four miles over, all shattered stones, and upon that is another rock or spire [Sugar Loaf], about a mile in height, and about an acre of ground at the top." In the 1700s Major Robert Rogers, of *Northwest Passage* fame, evidently failed in his summit attempt. He reported 4 or 5 miles of thick beech, hemlock, and white pine, followed by 6 or 7 miles of black spruce covered with "white moss," and beyond that "scarce any thing growing." His particular route is not known.

Henry David Thoreau's 1839 route *is* known, as is his path in 1858. In the first instance, in August and September of 1839, he and his brother John began their mountain adventure at Franconia Notch, approaching Mt. Washington from the west. Once on the summit they went back the way they had come to Crawford House in Crawford Notch, and then back south to Conway.

In 1858 they ascended to the base through Pinkham Notch. Hiring a local packer, they took the Tuckerman's Ravine route to the summit. Thoreau himself, not as strong as he had been nineteen years before (he would die four years later), took a couple of bad falls on the way up. The packer let the camp fire burn out of control, incinerating a couple of acres. To this day, many local people attribute the fire to Thoreau himself. He *had* been responsible for a bad one in his hometown of Concord, Massachusetts, several years before.

Once the Trail leaves Pinkham Notch it takes a long counterclockwise arc north, crossing the lowland for about 4 miles, passing the Mt. Washington auto road and several trail junctions. Once it passes the point where the Madison Gulf Trail branches off, however, it begins a relentless uphill climb for the next 2.4 miles, during which it will ascend nearly 2800 feet to the summit of Mt. Madison. This part of the route climbs up the Osgood Trail, named for B. F. Osgood, who blazed it in 1878. It is the oldest route to the summit of Mt. Madison still in use.

When the AT passes above the tree line on the southeastern slopes of 5363-foot Mt. Madison, it won't go below it for another 12.7 miles. It won't dip below 5000 feet for 10 miles, until it descends from Mt. Franklin. This is the longest high-elevation distance through unwooded territory on the entire AT. You're totally exposed out there, and you should not attempt this section without taking proper foul-weather precautions.

The alpine ridges and peaks constitute an exceedingly delicate ecosystem. Tiny plants cling to crevices between the rocks, accomplishing an entire year's growth in a matter of weeks. In several places the AT has been rerouted to avoid particularly fragile areas. Don't leave the Trail if you can avoid it: Even walking over the boulders can damage the lichens on their surfaces; the rocking of the boulder your footsteps cause can crush or uproot small plants.

Once above the tree line, the AT heads once again in a more southwesterly direction, inscribing a huge counterclockwise arc along the ridge line. Crossing Mts. Adams (5798 feet), Jefferson (5715 feet), and Clay (5532 feet), it makes its way toward the giant, Mt. Washington. The other summits mentioned are to the side of the AT route, but can easily be reached by side trails.

Mt. Washington's summit has been easily accessible since the 1850s. There is a concession building there, with souvenirs and a snack bar, as well as toilets, a post office, and public phones. A short way off is a weather observatory and radio towers. There is even a horse corral. As on Whiteface Mountain in the Adirondacks, hikers work very hard to climb Mt. Washington, only to be confronted by red-faced tourists with their ankles nearly crippled from pressing the accelerator all the way up the mountain.

Frankly, though I do wish all that stuff wasn't on top, it doesn't spoil my climb. The view is much the same, once you turn your back on the development, and for the most part the tourists don't talk to you (beyond the inevitable few who ask if you *really* walked all the way up—a dumb but easily answered question). I make a quick trip to the summit, maybe buy a candy bar or something, and then retreat down to a more remote knob along the trail. Some of the tourists probably watch me going down the meadows and wonder where I'm headed. What they don't know doesn't hurt a thing.

Once off Mt. Washington, the AT descends sharply to Lakes of the Clouds, where there is an Appalachian Mountain Club hut. A short loop to 5385-foot Mt. Madison branches off the AT nearby. From there, descending gradually, the Trail passes nearby 5004-foot Mt. Franklin (not a president, but some think he should have been); 4761-foot Mt. Eisenhower; 4310-foot Mt. Pierce (president, but some think he shouldn't have been—he *was* a New Hampshire man); 4052-foot Mt. Jackson; and finally 3910-foot Mt. Webster (formerly Notch Mountain, evidently considered low enough to be named for Daniel, a mere congressman).

The Presidentials are crisscrossed by too many trails to enumerate here. Far better to get hold of the Appalachian Mountain Club's excellent *White Mountain Guide,* which does for the Whites what the ATC guides do for the Appalachian Trail.

The AT comes to earth in Crawford Notch. Named for the family that lived there, it is the site of one of the first traveler's hostels, the Willey House, founded by the Willey family in 1825. Their tenure there ended tragically the following year when a freak rock slide wiped out the hostel and the Willeys with it (though rock slides occur regularly in the mountains, it is freakish for them to hit anyone). The site can be seen today, about a mile to the north of where the AT crosses the Saco River valley.

North of the Notch is the site of the Crawford House, where Thoreau stayed in 1839. Though the last incarnation of the original house burned in 1976, the AMC has purchased the land and runs a hostel and information center on the site. There's a shortcut to the hostel from near the summit of Mt. Pierce, where the Crawford Path (the route to the summit of Mt. Washington along which the AT travels, cut in 1819 by Abel Crawford and his son, Ethan Allen Crawford) diverges from the AT. It was Thoreau's route in 1839.

Crawford Notch to Franconia Notch

Traveling west out of Crawford Notch the Appalachian Trail heads into the longest uninterrupted wild section in New

Hampshire or Vermont. It is a rugged, precipitous range, and the Trail will go steeply up and down a great deal.

Climbing over a low shoulder of the 4300-foot mountain named for the unfortunate Willeys, the Trail goes several miles at about the 1500-foot level until it reaches Thoreau Falls (there is no evidence that Thoreau ever passed by here).

Following Whitewall Brook the AT passes up the steep-sided Zealand Notch on the old roadbed of the Zealand Valley Railroad. It was put in there to haul logs out from the timbering operations in the late 1800s.

The path then climbs up 4560-foot Mt. Guyot—the first of two mountains on the 2100-mile route of the Appalachian Trail (the other is in the Great Smoky Mountains)—named for Arnold Guyot, the famous Swiss geographer of the mid-nineteenth century. It continues to near the summit of 4902-foot South Twin Mountain (a side trail goes the 1.3 miles to North Twin), and then descends steeply to Galenhead Hut. Then, it's up to a mislaid president, 4488-foot Mt. Garfield, down again, up to 5249-foot Mt. Lafayette, over to 5089-foot Mt. Lincoln, and then to Mt. Liberty (4459 feet). One section between Mt. Lincoln and neighboring Little Haystack is a precipitous knife edge—be careful in windy or slippery weather. Viewed from Franconia Notch, Mt. Liberty resembles a reclining profile, giving rise to one of its traditional names, Washington Lying in State.

You'll be lying in state soon yourself, because your knees won't support you: Over the next 2.5 miles, the Trail is going to drop nearly 3000 feet!

What you're dropping into is famous Franconia Notch. Thoreau *did* pass by here in 1839, and he marveled at the sights. Most famous is the Old Man of the Mountains, a rock formation on the side of Profile Mountain. It's on the west side of the Notch a couple miles north of where the Trail crosses.

Closer is The Flume, a chasm cut by Flume Brook (which has its source on Flume Mountain, if you're interested). It's a vertical-sided canyon (a basalt dike, with the basalt eroded out by stream action), 60 to 70 feet high, 800 feet long, and in places, only 12 to 20 feet wide. Admission is charged.

Closer still to the Trail crossing is The Basin, a 20-foot-diameter stream pothole cut 25,000 years ago by the melt-water of the retreating glacier. Thoreau called it "the most remarkable instance of [its] kind . . . the well known Basin on the head waters of this stream—where a mere brook, which may be passed at a stride, falling upon a rock has worn a basin from 30 to 40 feet in diameter. . . ." There is another pothole, 100 feet in diameter and 40 feet deep, off a side path near the Flume. Admission is charged.

Franconia Notch to Kinsman Notch

The Trail follows Kinsman Ridge most of the way to Kinsman Notch. Ascending gradually (it regains the 3000 feet, only this time it spreads them over 7 miles), it crosses the North and South peaks of Kinsman Mountain (4293 and 4358 feet, respectively), just southwest of the backside of Profile Mountain.

After passing by the AMC's Lonesome Lake Hut ("dormitory-style lodging"), it joins up with the Fishin' Jimmy Trail, which it follows all the way to Kinsman Pond, 1.8 miles to the west. Fishin' Jimmy (blazed in 1930) and the Kinsman Ridge Trail (1917) were among the original AMC trails that were tied together into the AT in the White Mountains. After hopping over Wolf Mountains and several other knobs, it makes its fairly gradual descent into Kinsman Notch.

The Notch is site of the Lost River—a formation one would be more likely to find in the limestone-underlain Great Valley areas of Virginia and Tennessee. It's an underground river. The cause, however, is not water action dissolving soft limestone. What has happened here is that the Lost River first gouged out a course deep into the bedrock, perhaps along a fracture line, perhaps scouring out a narrow dike of softer volcanic rock. Later, large boulders dropped down over the top of the narrow gorge, effectively burying the river. It gurgles along for about half a mile underground. You can get down to it via special trails, boardwalks, and ladders.

Kinsman Notch to Glencliffe, New Hampshire

After leaving Kinsman Notch, the AT enters the region maintained by the Dartmouth Outing Club. The first section begins with another 3000-foot grunt, up Mt. Moosilauke. This 4802-foot alpine-summited peak can be done as a day hike from either direction, but shouldn't be attempted by the weak of leg (or lung).

The summit of Moosilauke was once topped by the Prospect House, which was served by a 5-mile carriage road from the south. Prospect House burned in 1942, and its foundation is still visible on the summit. The carriage road is now a hiking trail.

The Trail on the western side of Moosilauke is another case of aggravated assault on your knees: It descends around 3700 feet in about 4 miles.

Glencliffe to the Connecticut River

This last section in New Hampshire demonstrates vividly how lucky Trail hikers are that the Dartmouth Outing Club already had trails in place when the AT was proposed. Surrounded on all sides by roads, farms, and houses (it does traverse a number of cleared fields), the Trail nevertheless passes through pleasant wilderness, and is an especially good place for backcountry skiing for adventurous souls.

There are two major grunts in this section: Mt. Cube (2911 feet) and Smarts Mountain (3240 feet). They are the tallest of some half-dozen sawtooth ridges the AT crosses on its way to Vermont. There are a number of side or alternate trails in the area, making it a grade-A destination for day hikers. The area just east of the Dartmouth Skiway toward Smart Mountain is especially well served by side trails.

As it approaches the Connecticut River, the Trail enters the zone of the Ammonoosuc volcanics. These are the remains of the volcanic islands that formed out in the proto-Atlantic Ocean, before Eurafrica hit North America. These rock formations are the last stop before leaving what was probably once part of Europe and crossing the ancient coastline of North America.

After passing through the college town of Hanover, New Hampshire (home of Dartmouth College and the Dartmouth Outing Club), the AT crosses a small bridge over the Connecticut River near the Dartmouth College boating houses and into Vermont.

THE TRAIL IN VERMONT

The first 40 miles inside Vermont are the same sort of broken-field running that the AT did in the last sections of New Hampshire. These are former farm fields in the process of reverting to woodlands. They're not the most adventuresome miles on the route, but they make splendid short walks and picnic trails. What the heck: This is Vermont, after all!

After entering Vermont, the Trail heads up into the low hills east of the main Green Mountain chain. The first elevation it attains is on Griggs Mountain, at about 1570 feet. It then follows Podunk Brook (yes, Virginia, there is a Podunk!) across Interstate 89 to the White River. Crossing the river, it goes into the hills near West Hartford, Vermont. Then it's through more varied country until it reaches Vermont Route 12 north of Woodstock. Here, the responsibilities of the Dartmouth Outing Club end and the Green Mountain Club takes over.

The next 18 miles are over still more open and closed territory, running between the official boundary between the White Mountains and the Green Mountains. As the Trail passes over the Ottauquechee River near Sherburne Center, it is within a mile of the Green Mountain Club's Long Trail, which it joins at Gifford Woods State Park. From there, it enters the Green Mountains in earnest, passing by several ski areas on its way to Massachusetts.

The first of these is reached very quickly after the AT joins the Long Trail. It climbs over a shoulder of 3957-foot Pico Peak. It and nearby Killington Peak (at 4235 feet the second highest mountain in Vermont after Mansfield, which is not on the route) host major ski resorts, both of which are threatening to encroach upon the Trail wilderness.

As it passes through the Coolidge range (named for dour New Englander and local boy Silent Cal, whom Theodore Roosevelt's acerbic daughter Alice Longworth once described as looking like he'd been "weaned on a pickle"; informed of his death, she quipped, "How can you tell?") it's again time for a lot of up-and-down. Killington is the last time the Trail will pass above 4000 feet until Virginia.

Pico and Killington are two of the last contested areas on the entire AT, which is now nearly completely protected. The ski industry in the Northeast has been unable in recent years to keep up with the demand placed on its slopes and facilities. Pico, the first major ski area to appear on the AT, and (especially) Killington are among the most vigorous developers in the area, and they are trying to meet the demand of ever more skiers by expanding still more their slopes and lifts. The Appalachian Trail Conference is currently negotiating with the areas, while at the same time trying to prevent development from infringing on the Trail route. We all hope that some compromise can be reached.

As long as the facilities are there, though, some people may as well derive benefit from them. One possibility is to engage in "downhill mountain climbing"—taking the lift to the summit of one of these peaks and then walking down, nice and slow. It could be a real welcome alternative for people with physical problems that prevent them from activities that are too strenuous—like climbing a 4000-foot mountain. A lift ride usually costs only a few bucks and you're soon out of sight of the top station and rotating lift bullwheel. Cross-country skiers do it all the time, riding up and then touring for miles and miles, all downhill.

Besides the chair lifts and gondola, though, Killington is also reached by several trails. There is a shelter, Cooper Lodge, near the summit, and the views of Vermont, New York, and New Hampshire are spectacular. Basing out of a camp somewhere along the route, hikers can spend several days exploring the area.

The general sequence that the Trail follows in this part of Vermont takes it from trailheads in the valleys through the lower hardwood forests (dominated by the sugar maple that forms such an important part of the Vermont economy) up to the spruce groves on the ridge crests. Once out of the Coolidge State Forest, the Trail descends into the Mill River valley near Cuttingsville and Clarendon. The valley, like most in New England, is characterized by fields and young woods. The Trail then climbs up into the Wallingford hills, hopping up and down between around 1500 to 2000 feet. There are a few crossroads in the middle of the section but some nice walking over rocky knobs in hardwood forest with spruce groves along the ridge lines. At Greenwall Shelter the Trail enters the Green Mountain National Forest, through which it will pass for the next 73 miles. The 5.1-mile Green Mountain Trail runs a nice side loop over the rocky ridge of Green Mountain, which parallels the AT just to the west.

The Minerva Hinchey and Lula Tye shelters draw some comments for their names. They were christened for two former secretaries of the Green Mountain Club who, between them, served from the 1920s to the late 1970s.

After it crosses the Danby-Landgrove Road, near Danby, the Trail moves up to the main crest of the Green Mountains, crossing west of the summits of Buckball and South Buckball peaks on its way to Baker (2850 feet) and Peru (3429 feet) peaks. It crosses 3394-foot Styles Peak and 3260-foot Bromley Mountain before descending once again into the valley at Route 11.

This section has a number of good side trails, including the 5.3-mile Old Job Trail (the former AT) which diverges from the AT near the Danby-Landgrove Road and rejoins it 5.1 miles down the Trail. From the road, the two offer a loop of over 11 miles, which cuts a circuit around the Buckball mountains.

At Route 11 the Trail once again passes by ski areas—Big Bromley and Snow Valley. The Trail actually descends Bromley Mountain on a wide ski trail. Manchester, Vermont, is just a few miles to the west.

The AT leaves Route 11 and climbs gradually up onto the ridge again, reaching Stratton Pond after 10.4 miles. The guidebook warns that Stratton Pond is the most popular area on the entire Long Trail (as well as the largest body of water), and that the Green Mountain Club has taken precautions to minimize impact to the environment. They ask that hikers obey the caretakers.

In recent years the AT has veered away from Stratton Mountain at Stratton Pond. The 8.6-mile Stratton Mountain Trail (blue-blazed) diverged from the main AT at Stratton Pond and came back in again at Black Brook, 3.9 miles down the Trail. As this is written, though, a rerouting is being completed on Stratton, to take the Appalachian Trail once again to the summit of the mountain on which its birth was first contemplated by Benton MacKaye. The International Paper Company finally agreed to sell the land to the Forest Service, but there was a hitch. As a condition of the deal, IP insisted that the sale (for a reported $3.2 million) appear on their books during the first quarter of 1986. The Forest Service, unable to come up with the cash in time, had to rely on a friend, The Nature Conservancy, which purchased the land and held it in trust for the Forest Service until they could acquire it. Dedicated conservationists usually find a way.

South of the Arlington-West Wardsboro Road, where the new Stratton Mountain section joins the old route, the Trail climbs up to around the 3000-foot level, crossing over several smaller peaks on its way to 3748-foot Glastonbury Mountain. There are a number of beaver dams in a couple of the notches near Story Spring Shelter, near the beginning of this section. They may make the Trail somewhat mucky.

On Glastonbury Mountain the summit, like most in this region, is wooded, but there is an abandoned rickety fire tower there, which might still be climbed with extreme caution. I don't know what shape it's in these days, so you're on your own if you decide to go up. If it can still be climbed, there are impressive views, especially of the famed "ski valley" of Vermont, home to Haystack Mountain, Mt. Snow, and other ski areas.

Just south of Glastonbury Mountain the West Ridge Trail diverges to traverse the conspicuous ridge visible to the west of the AT, also crossing the summit of 2857-foot Bald Mountain at the southern end of the ridge. It travels 7.8 miles to the steep-sided Wallomsac Brook gorge. Hikers can complete a loop of around 20 miles by heading out of Woodford Hollow at the end of the gorge and back up the City Stream valley on Route 9 (about a mile) until it crosses the AT.

The AT itself takes a more easterly route to this point, climbing over several knobs, including Little Pond Mountain and Maple Hill, on the way. After Route 9 it again ascends into the woods for the last stretch before the Massachusetts border. This part of the route continues to go over small knobs and down into valleys, many damp from beaver activity. Just to the north of Seth Warner Shelter it crosses its last high point for many miles—a nameless peak of 3025 feet.

The AT crosses into Massachusetts on a short knob in the woods above Williamstown, Massachusetts.

Vermont   New Hampshire

Mt. Greylock State Reservation ─┤
North Adams
─Mt. Greylock
Cheshire
Dalton

October Mtn. State Forest ─┤ ── October Mtn.   Massachusetts

Beartown State Forest ─┤
East Mtn. State Forest ─┤
Torrington
Mt. Everett Reservation ─┤ ── Mt. Everett
─Race Mtn.

Housatonic State Forest ─┤
Macedonia Brook State Park ─┤

Cornwall Bridge

New York   ● Kent   Rhode Island

Housatonic
River

Massachusetts and Connecticut

6

The Massachusetts/ Connecticut Section

Trail Distances:

> *Vermont/Massachusetts state line to*
> *Massachusetts/Connecticut state line* . . . . . . *87.7 miles*

> *Massachusetts/Connecticut state line to*
> *Connecticut/New York state line* . . . . *48.9 miles*

> *Section total* . . . . *136.6 miles*

Maintaining Clubs:

> *Berkshire chapter, Appalachian Mountain Club:*
> *Vermont/Massachusetts state line to*
> *Massachusetts/Connecticut state line*

> *Connecticut chapter, Appalachian Mountain Club:*
> *Massachusetts/Connecticut state line to*
> *Connecticut/New York state line*

INTRODUCTION

AS THE Appalachian Trail leaves Vermont near Pownal and Stamford, it heads into what has long been called the "Lake Region of America." It was called thus both because of its many lakes and scenic streams and because of a similarity with the Lake District of northern England, a favorite haunt of British ramblers, as hikers there call themselves.

It is also the Trail's first foray into the Industrial Belt. Of course, the gentle rolling Berkshires and Litchfield Hills over which the AT courses for the next 136 miles could hardly be termed urban blight. In fact they are, in their way, among the most scenic miles of all. But roads crisscross frequently; the land around the Trail, if not right underneath it, is largely privately owned; and some valley crossings are hard for the Appalachian Trail Conference to maintain without running sections over roads.

As the southbound hiker sniffs the air atop 3491-foot Mt. Greylock—one of the most frequently climbed peaks in the world, as it happens—some thought should be given to what lies to the south. Within 100 miles of the Trail for the next 850 miles sits the greatest, dirtiest, not to mention most heavily populated, problem-plagued, sprawling, and (to me at least) ugly band of industrial wasteland in North America, if not the world. For here, plastered to the East Coast like a fungus, lies a megalopolis—the hectic New Hampshire-to-Virginia inhuman beehive of human activity that Benton MacKaye had in mind when he created his idea for an Appalachian Trail. Here is where the people live who are in such desperate need of Clarence Stein's beguiling vision of re-creation, for an escape from the noise and dirt and tension of their everyday lives.

The Appalachian Trail is about to enter the area for which it was created. Standing on Greylock, the hiker should feel a powerful sense of awe—and not just for the spectacular scenery of the place. A greater awe should be reserved for the mere thought that in this blighted region such a place as the Trail could exist at all.

And thanks to the volunteers, past and present, the Appalachian Trail, green, rocky, sweet-smelling, harmonious to the ear and eye, will pass by those cities, within easy striking distance of every last citizen in megalopolis. Paradise really is just a couple of hours away for anyone with a car, bus fare, or a thumb they're not too proud to stick out on the highway.

GEOLOGY ALONG THE TRAIL

The north/south line of the Green Mountains of Vermont, the Berkshires and Taconics of Massachusetts and eastern New York, and the Litchfield Hills of Connecticut, represent the very first uplift of the Appalachian Revolution. As such, they are composed of extremely old crystalline rocks that have been metamorphosed many times.

Much of this cordillera was once part of the sea floor off the continental shelf of eroding Grenville-era North America. The last mountain-building was at least half an eon past. *Iapetus* was at its widest point.

As the continental plates began to shift again, though, and Europe (with Africa to follow) first headed for its rendezvous with the North American coast, things began to happen. This was to be the Taconic Orogeny, the first round of mountain-building.

The sea floor at first began crashing together at a rift in the relatively thin ocean-floor plate off the North American continental shelf. The European side rode up and over the North American side, shoving the sea floor up and toward the North American plate. This was out in the ocean, beyond the limits of the rather wide continental shelf. As the sea floor was pushed toward North America it was raised up, lifting sea-floor material up out of the water, the volcanism released by the subduction creating a series of volcanic islands just to the east.

Once the onrushing landmass had managed to push the whole structure—gathered up like a deck of cards off a table-top—right up against the solid Grenville core of the continent itself (which was at the time the shallow continental shelf on the edges of the continental plate), the relatively thin ocean-floor plate began instead to subduct beneath Europe on the other side of *Iapetus*. This took the pressure off the North American side of the ocean and mountain-building stopped for the time being. What was created was a band of land off the North American shore, with a shallow inland sea over the continental shelf that had not yet been uplifted. The main mountain range that was formed was the Green Mountain/Berkshire cordillera. Where slabs of broken, overthrust strata were pushed over the western edge of the Berkshires and into the inland sea, the Taconics were formed.

In the 100 million years before the next impact, erosion, which is always with us, worked its will on the Taconic and Berkshire ranges that were created. Eroded rock material was washed into the ocean as well as the shallow inland sea, forming new continental shelves and deltas. These would be uplifted themselves in later rounds of the building of the Appalachian ranges. The coast of the shrinking *Iapetus* was approximately at the current site of the Connecticut River valley.

As the Taconics eroded, layer upon layer of the original Cambrian and Ordovician ocean-floor material wore away. Where the Grenville rocks have been thrust up and over the more recent Paleozoic (Cambrian and Ordovician) layers, they can be seen along the western New England cordillera of the Greens, Berkshires, Taconics, and Litchfield Hills. Much of the more recent rock remained, though, the limestones and silt-stones of the Precambrian ocean floor that would later, when Europe finally arrived, be metamorphosed into the famous Vermont marble.

The cordillera wore away further during the two major ice ages of the Cenozoic Era, finally emerging as the low, rounded, rolling hills we recognize today. As the glaciers retreated, leaving in their wake the lakes and the huge, erratic boulders seen in every farmer's field in New England, mastodons and other bizarre animals moved in—along with human beings. The stage was set for the coming of History.

HISTORY ALONG THE TRAIL

At the time of the first European settlement of North America, the region through which the AT travels in northern Massachusetts was the territory of the then-powerful Mahican tribes. The name means "Wolves," and the French referred to them by that name—*loups* in their own language.

And powerful they must have been, too, for in the early 1600s, when the first Europeans (the Dutch) met them, they were at war with the mighty Mohawk Nation.

They weren't tough enough, it seems. In 1664 the Mohawks, members of the then newly formed Iroquois Confederacy, had gained enough power of their own to force the Mahicans to leave a part of their territory near Albany, New York, and settle in the area of Stockbridge, Massachusetts (yes, the same Stockbridge where Alice had a restaurant). As outlying clans migrated away from the increasing European settlement, selling their lands and disappearing, the core group—by then known as the Stockbridge Indians—stayed around Stockbridge, gradually decreasing in numbers and selling off their land to survive. Eventually, most of them packed up and moved to Wisconsin.

In the Northeast it is sometimes difficult to determine exactly where certain tribes actually lived. Always in motion through wars and migrations, things deteriorated quickly for the Native American nations once the white settlers arrived. All we have in most places is a snapshot of their lives at the time the first Europeans met them. It is pretty certain, though, that this was Mahican turf, though nobody knows for certain how long this had been the case. To the east was the territory of the Pocumtucs, the Mahicans' cousins. Prior to 1664, when the Iroquois forced the Mahicans eastward, the Pocumtucs may have hunted in the Berkshires as well.

The Mahicans extended down into Connecticut. A band called the Wawyachtonocs were known to live in the northwest corner of the state, where the Trail crosses the state line. Then it runs into the territory of the wampum-makers, the Wappingers. These Algonkian cousins of the Mahicans lived on the east bank of the Hudson from the Bronx to Poughkeepsie, New York, and all the way east to the Connecticut River valley. Their name means "Easterners," and they were among the most prolific makers of wampum belts in the country.

During the Revolution, perhaps anxious to reverse the British tendency to push them off their lands, the Wappingers sided with the Continentals. Their chief, Daniel Nimham, was killed fighting a rearguard action to enable Washington to escape from his defeat at White Plains. Encouraged by Washington to escape too, Nimham is said to have responded, "I am an old tree. Let me die here."

Like most eastern tribes, the Wappingers were eventually forced off their traditional lands. Today I "own" about a half acre of their patrimony—by whose original title I have no idea. It's a past crime we all live with.

For their part, the Wappingers threw their lot in with their Mahican cousins, various groups migrating off in different directions. Many found their way to Stockbridge and shared the journey of the unfortunates to Wisconsin, where they remain today. They have passed out of the story of the Appalachian Trail.

Considering their place in "Historic New England," it's somewhat surprising that history doesn't play a greater part in the area crossed by the Appalachian Trail in Massachusetts and Connecticut. But by quirks of geography and history, though, the western portions of the two states remained relatively free from the conflict that usually spells "historical interest."

During the early colonial days these areas lay outside both major areas of colonization. They were too far to the south for much beyond an occasional raid arising out of the conflict between England and France over control of Vermont and New Hampshire. They were separated from their parent colonies at Massachusetts Bay by the Connecticut River. Though it doesn't appear to be too much of a geographic hurdle, the river evidently did present a cultural barrier between east and west. Evidence for this division can be found to this day in language patterns: The Connecticut is the division between the Boston-based "Pahk the cah in Hahvahd Yahd" dialect, and the more Mid-Atlantic pronunciations to the west.

Originally an agricultural area, western New England gradually went fallow as the farming might of the country was dominated by the huge farms to the west. Its recent history has been one of increasing development as bedroom communities for nearby urban areas. This is especially true of Connecticut.

HISTORY OF THE APPALACHIAN TRAIL IN MASSACHUSETTS AND CONNECTICUT

There is probably less to tell about the blazing of the Trail in western New England than there is about keeping those blazes put. When the first electricity sparked across New England in 1921 and 1922 about the new Trail that was to link the entire Eastern Seaboard, action in this part of the country was swift. Albert Turner of the New England Trail Conference (NETC) was right: Other parts of the country might have trouble getting their sections of the Trail together, but east of the Hudson they were already "at it."

When the AT was first proposed the New England Trail Conference was already in existence and had, in fact, been discussing just this kind of thing since the mid-teens. The plan—and that's all it was at the time, just a plan—was to link up the Green Mountain Club's Long Trail with existing trails in New York and New Jersey via other trails down the Berkshires and Taconics. Many of these already existed, too.

Western New England was the bailiwick of the Appalachian Mountain Club, one of the oldest hiking clubs in America. A major player in the NETC, it was already nearing its half-century mark when the linking up of the AT was begun in the mid-1920s. They had many trails through New England, including along the ridges of the Taconics and Berkshires.

However, keeping the Trail was another matter. When it was first blazed, the AT in Massachusetts and Connecticut crossed over much farmland and—better yet—unused farmland. But as the Industrial Revolution expanded outward from New York, Albany, Providence, New Haven, and Boston, more and more people came to live in these hills.

Most problematic were the valley crossings. There, residential areas would pop up, while the ridge lines remained relatively wild. The Nature Conservancy had holdings in these areas, which helped, but in many areas road walking became more and more the norm.

The solution wasn't anything earth shattering. Trail supervisors and workers from the AMC simply met each challenge, made each rerouting, plotted and planned until the route in New England is now mostly secure. The state of Connecticut and commonwealth of Massachusetts have been useful in establishing several state parks and forests along the ridges, and the Scenic Trails Act gave a boost to the final efforts, but on the main it has been a simple case of hard work that has preserved the Trail's unbroken route. That's the New England way.

THE TRAIL IN MASSACHUSETTS

The Trail enters Massachusetts in the shadow of The Dome and Pine Cobble, two knobs in the southern Green Mountain chain, each in the neighborhood of 2000 feet. It enters near Williamstown, Massachusetts, a small, scenic town, home of Williams College (it only *seems* that every small town in Massachusetts is home to some institution of higher learning or other). After descending about 1500 feet into the Hoosic River valley (a major tributary to what will become the Housatonic), it immediately ascends sharply onto the flanks of the Mt. Greylock massif.

Greylock itself, at 3491 feet the highest peak in Massachusetts, is one of a number of monadnocks scattered around New England. It amounts to a core of harder igneous rock that remained long after the surrounding strata had eroded away. Greylock's name comes from an eighteenth-century chief of the Waranoke tribe. It was another of the many peaks climbed by Henry David Thoreau in his various ramblings.

The Mt. Greylock State Reservation, though very popular, nevertheless makes a fine destination. The 11,500-acre reserve hosts over 10 miles of the AT and more than 50 miles of trail total. The stated emphasis of the reservation management is "hiking." There are thirty-five campsites and a visitor's center. The Mt. Greylock Reservation contains, besides Greylock itself, several others of the highest mountains in Massachusetts. There are many ski trails, and it makes a great getaway for cross-country skiing enthusiasts.

Also in the area is the Taconic Crest Trail and the Taconic Skyline Trail. These don't hook up with the AT, but run for 26.4 and 20 miles respectively along the ridge of the heavily eroded Taconics just to the west of the Berkshires. They make nice parallel routes.

After crossing the summit of Mt. Williams and a side spur of Greylock, Mt. Fitch, the Trail crosses the summit of Greylock itself only 6 miles from the trailhead on Route 2 in North Adams, Massachusetts. From there, it weaves down through the woods of the reservation, passing some of the last boreal bogs on the AT and meeting the junctions of some of the many side trails maintained by the Reservation staff. It finally bottoms out at about 1000 feet above sea level at Cheshire, Massachusetts.

The AT then heads up on some residential roads and toward North Mountain, a southern extension of the Hoosac range, a north/south escarpment of the Berkshires. First going by The Cobble just uphill from Cheshire (from which there are some good views), it passes through some wooded, ponded country before hitting the road again near Dalton, Massachusetts (this is real broken-field running).

After the trail leaves Dalton it crosses the Housatonic River immediately, and after less than 2 miles on roads, heads into the woods again. From here it will be in wilder land—mostly state forest—all the way to the Connecticut state line.

First comes the entry into October Mountain State Park, 8 trail miles south of Dalton. At 14,189 acres it's the biggest state park in Massachusetts. The AT keeps to the ridge line most of the way, across the peaks of several of the mountains on the way—all in the neighborhood of 2000 feet.

After crossing the Massachusetts Turnpike near Stockbridge (where the Mahicans found their refuge from the Mohawks), it heads into a Natural Area protected by the National Park Service. A nice place to hike, but no fires or camping. After several miles of road walking (not highway walking, and all things considered, not that bad), it once again enters the woods.

This section runs through Beartown State Forest and crosses over Mt. Wilcox, which features a fire tower. An old charcoal pit is there, remnant of the industry that is primarily responsible for deforesting the Northeast. This is a presaging of the many charcoal pits the Trail will pass in northern New Jersey and farther south.

After crossing Route 23 the Trail ascends East Mountain, a precipitous escarpment with fine views to the west and rocky scrambles to get up and down the ledges. This section runs through East Mountain State Forest.

After once again crossing the Housatonic River (renowned for its trout fishing), the Trail enters the popular Bash Bish Falls State Forest. The falls for which it is named, while not on the Trail, are well worth the extra time to visit and afford superb swimming. Right on the New York state border, Bash Bish Falls is complemented by another park at Copake Falls on the New York side. From here, the Trail will head up into the Taconic range.

The section the AT enters here is one of the best day-hiking destinations along the whole route in Massachusetts. The Trail runs though some of the best wild areas (still in Bash Bish Falls State Forest) and is accessible by side trails on either side of Mt. Everett and near Race Mountain. The latter, which runs up from the east from Jug End Road (local Route 41) to near the summit of Race Mountain, passes several waterfalls and makes a fine outing.

The AT here is following the eastern escarpment of the Taconics. Another trail, the South Taconic Trail, follows the western flank from Mt. Whitbeck in Bash Bish Falls State Forest and ducks back and forth across the state line for over 15 miles.

As it travels from Jug End (a 1700-foot summit just to the south of South Egremont, Massachusetts) and heads for the Connecticut state line, the AT crosses several more peaks: Mt. Bushnell (1834 feet), Mt. Everett (2602 feet), and Race Mountain (2365 feet). The open summit of Mt. Everett affords superb views—on a clear day you can see the Catskills spread out over the western horizon. The Trail leaves Massachusetts at Sages Brook—the border is in the woods.

THE TRAIL IN CONNECTICUT

Connecticut is generally lower in elevation than is Massachusetts. In fact, the highest point in Connecticut is actually *in* Massachusetts—it's on the flank of Mt. Frissell, the summit of which is north of the border in the Bay State.

The highest mountain that lies entirely within Connecticut's borders is Bear Mountain, which the Trail crosses within 2 miles of entering the Nutmeg State. The approach is made through some especially scenic woodlands, past waterfalls and streams (once it approaches the top of Bear Mountain, over some treacherous, and therefore exciting, rock slabs), until the summit (2316 feet) is reached. From there, it leaves the Taconics and descends into the Housatonic River valley, passing by Lions Head, the southernmost peak of the Taconics. The Appalachian Trail will not reach the 2000-foot level again until Quirauk Mountain in northern Maryland.

The Trail route in Connecticut is short (49.9 miles) and runs in and out of civilization. Some of the valley crossings have proven exceptionally difficult for the ATC to protect.

However, the woodland areas of the AT in Connecticut offer some of the finest easy walking in the Northeast and have the advantage of being among the most accessible of the Trail miles. One of my favorite walks anywhere is the section around Kent Falls and Macedonia Brook, where the Trail runs for 5 miles along the banks of the beautiful Housatonic River. Friends of mine have caught brown trout in there that looked like nuclear submarines. The Trail passes sheltered hollows filled with hemlock groves and pine woods planted years ago and grown large.

In the Housatonic valley the AT passes through several state parks on its way to the New York state line. South of Falls Village, the sections formerly east of the Housatonic (the "Seymour Smith" section, after the Watertown man who maintained these miles for thirty years in the 1950s, 1960s, and 1970s) are now blue-blazed and known as the Mohawk Trail and managed by the Connecticut Forest and Parks Association. In 1988 the Trail was relocated to the Sharon Mountain area in the Housatonic State Forest, on the west bank of the river. Once the relocation was completed, the old route became part of the extensive blue-marked Connecticut side-trail system. By hooking the AT up with the Mohawk Trail a fine backpacking loop of about 35 miles can be made.

As it nears the New York state line, the AT continues in a generally southwesterly direction. It actually crosses into New York once, but has to cut back into Connecticut to Bulls Bridge before making its final approach, as it were. Just before crossing the line it also fords the Ten Mile River on a fine bridge put in just for the Trail a few years back. The Ten Mile, by the way, is one of my favorite trout-fishing haunts. One piece of advice: From sad experience over the years I can warn you to watch out for hornets' nests on Schaghticoke Mountain.

Thanks to efforts on the part of many environmental groups and trail clubs, the wilderness feel and the wild avenue for the Appalachian Trail that remain in Connecticut have largely been protected. Don't be surprised if a wild turkey buzzes you as you walk down one of the damp hemlock-wooded sections of trail in this otherwise developed state. When you consider what trail crews and ATC member organizations are up against, the Connecticut section of the AT stands as a solid tribute to their efforts.

Massachusetts

New York

Hudson
River

Schaghticoke Mtn.

Delaware
River

Canada
Hill

Pawling Nature Conservancy

Pawling

Shenandoah Mtn.

Clarence Fahnestock State Park

Greymoor Monastery

High Point

West Point

Bear Mtn.

Anthony's Nose

High Point State Park

Harriman/Bear Mtn. State Park

Connecticut

Greenwood Lake

Kittatinny Mtn.

Wawayanda State Park

Delaware Water Gap

Worthington State Forest

New York City

Pennsylvania

New Jersey

Delaware
River

Trenton

New York and New Jersey

7

The New York / New Jersey Section

Trail Distance:

> *Connecticut state line to New Jersey*
> *state line* . . . . *89.7 miles*

> *New York state line to Delaware Water*
> *Gap* . . . . *73.4 miles*

Maintaining Club:

> *New York-New Jersey Trail Conference and its*
> *participating organizations and individuals*

INTRODUCTION

AS APPALACHIAN Trail states go, New York and New Jersey are perhaps less impressive in sheer Trail miles, wildness of country, and shelter availability than are the more out of the way places such as Maine and North Carolina. That's to be expected: Even in the early 1920s, nearby New York City was extending its sphere of influence northward and westward. Westchester County, which comes as far north as the Trail's Hudson River crossing at the Bear Mountain Bridge, was fast becoming the bedroom of Manhattan's white collar workers; the state of New York was eyeing sites, including one at Bear Mountain, for a large prison to shut away human products of urban blight (Sing

117

Sing Prison was finally built in Ossining, 30 miles north of the city and 20 miles south of the Trail, and the phrase "sent up the river" was born).

The Trail in this megalopolis, however, is amazing in its way. First, considering the seemingly invincible juggernaut of development in the area, it's literally astonishing that any land has been preserved for the Trail to cross at all. And second, the trail system created and maintained by the New York-New Jersey Trail Conference (NY-NJTC), of which the AT is a part, offers weary urbanites copious opportunities to "re-create" themselves in precisely the sense in which Benton MacKaye intended when he first conceived the idea of the Trail.

Traffic permitting (which it does on rare occasion), you can be from Times Square to the Trail in about an hour and a half or less. The area in which you find yourself, the Hudson Highlands, the Reading Prong, and the Kittatinny Ridge, form one of the most spectacular, historically rich, geologically interesting, and scenically beautiful areas in the East.

GEOLOGY ALONG THE TRAIL

New York

The Hudson Highlands are actually an extension of the Reading Prong. It was all uplifted as part of the Taconic Orogeny 450 million years ago, give or take (what's a few million among friends?).

So much erosion has gone on since the uplift (including at least two major ice ages) that all that is left of what was probably a substantial mountain cordillera is the bones—literally. The rocks of the highlands are Grenville rocks—many over a billion years old. They are the remnants of the original Appalachians from the dim past, laid down in an episode of mountain-building before life began and uplifted anew during the formation of the current ranges.

The Grenville Event may well have been a similar occurrence to the Taconic and Acadian Orogenies that formed the highlands you see today. Radioactive dating fixes the Event in New York at 1145 million years ago, plus or minus 50 million years, with another uplift sometime later. The rocks you see in the highlands are crystalline in nature, running from gneisses and schists in the general structure to granites in the many plutons in the area (which formed in the neighborhood of 950 million years ago as the Grenville uplift came to an end). The Canada Hill Pluton (the Trail goes right over it, just north of Anthony's Nose) is one of them. Any pieces of grayish white equigranular granite you see probably came from there. Anthony's Nose itself is made mostly of a *paragneiss,* a gray to bluish gray equigranular rock.

One of the things for which the Reading Prong has been famous (or infamous) recently has been radon. The ancient rocks of the Prong contain significant deposits of radioactive elements that emit the dangerous gas as they break down. Radon gas collects in basements of houses and poses a health threat unless the homeowner takes steps to keep it out or vent it away. Anthony's Nose (owned by the military, which takes a dim view of prospectors poking around) has long been rumored in the valley to contain uranium deposits.

In the New York area the various ridges of the Appalachians do continue but get compressed quite a bit. A few dozen miles to the northwest the next ridge of the great range, formed during the later Alleghany Orogeny and consisting of the westernmost ridges of the Appalachians (Kittatinny Mountain in New Jersey, the Blue Mountain complex in Pennsylvania), continues as the Schunemunks and the Shawangunks. Just above that is the Catskill Plateau. The Catskills, you understand, are not really mountains at all, but rather a huge plateau dissected by streams. The plateau was formed by an enormous river delta deposited into the great inland sea off of the eroding Taconic Mountains and uplifted in later rounds of mountain-building.

New Jersey

It is in New Jersey that the Trail finally reaches the long ridge that it will follow with only occasional interruptions all the way to Harrisburg, Pennsylvania. After crossing the New Jersey state line at Bearfort Mountain (part of the comparatively recent, 400-million-year-old Devonian rocks of the Schunemunks) near Greenwood Lake, it travels west over the broken country of the New Jersey Highlands. These consist mostly of Precambrian valleys and small ridges and knobs until the Trail reaches Kittatinny Mountain near High Point, not coincidentally the highest point in New Jersey. From there, it heads in a generally southwesterly direction to the Delaware Water Gap. It continues through Pennsylvania, where it is now known as Blue Mountain.

Geologically, Kittatinny is of an entirely different province from the New York highlands. Unlike the older Precambrian rock found in the highlands, Kittatinny is made of the same Shawangunk quartzite found in Pennsylvania's Blue Mountain complex. In origin, it is Silurian, deposited as sand on the shores of the great inland sea that formed west of the uplift of the Taconic Orogeny. It was then metamorphosed into quartzite in the various orogenies that uplifted these hills.

HISTORY ALONG THE TRAIL

The river over which the Trail passes was perhaps the most important waterway in colonial America. It was first discovered in 1524 by Florentine navigator Giovanni da Verrazano, but nobody bothered to explore it until nearly a century later, in 1609. Henry Hudson, an English navigator, sailing at the time for the Dutch, arrived in search of a passage to Asia (to this day he is on occasion remembered in the valley as "Hendrick" Hudson). He became the first to enter the river, sailing upstream about 150 miles to a point near Albany. His little ship, the *Half Moon,* thus became the first European vessel to pass through the river at Bear Mountain, where the Trail crosses it. Once at Albany, Hudson determined rightly that the river did not, after all, go all the way through to the Pacific (New York City ignorance of upstate geography is such that to this day many urbanites seem not to realize this). Forbidden by the English to sail again for other nations, Hudson nevertheless sent his logs to his sponsors in the Netherlands. Based on his information, Dutch settlement of the valley began in 1629. The Dutch owned the valley until 1664, when they were forced out by the British.

When Hudson arrived in the valley he found that, like most other places in the New World, it was already inhabited. The people on the east bank north of Manhattan Island were the Wappingers, whom we have already met in Connecticut.

On the west bank were the Lenni Lenape people who would later be named for the Delaware River that ran through their territory, which was in turn named for a family of English nobles. It is not recorded if they were consulted in this renaming. The Lenni Lenape subdivision, which inhabited the southern New York and northern New Jersey woodlands through which the Trail passes, were known as the Munsees.

One bequest of Dutch rule was the land-ownership system of manor owners ("patroons" under the Dutch) supported by the labor of tenant farmers. Huge estates owned by the few were worked by the many, who existed in conditions resembling serfdom. The unrest this created (there were occasional uprisings— a major one happening in 1754 around Quaker Hill in Wingdale, where the Trail crosses into Connecticut) was eventually to be a factor in the Hudson Valley's role as one of the powderkegs of the Revolution. This instability could not have happened at a worse place, from the British point of view.

After Lexington, the hotbeds of the Patriot cause were obviously centered in Boston and Virginia. The British moved quickly to isolate the two factions, invading and taking New York City very early on. From there they attempted a two-prong attack on the valley, trying to divide the rebellious colonies in half. It was a game effort, but failed.

The two key reasons are well known. First, the Battle of Saratoga in October of 1777, far to the north, is considered by many to be the turning point of the Revolution. An invading army, coming down from Canada under the command of General Burgoyne, was defeated and captured by superior forces under General Horatio Gates.

The second, more infamous, episode occurred mere miles north of Bear Mountain Bridge, within sight of the Trail. One-half of the British pincer was the continuing effort to push forces north up the river. The British found the way by land barricaded by colonial forces and their artillery batteries, and by rugged country in which their movements were severely limited. The rocky hills of Putnam and Dutchess counties, through which the Trail winds, are dotted by overgrown redoubts thrown up by Patriots worried about a British advance. The rolling hills of northern New Jersey are dotted with the sites of battles and skirmishes marking where the British tried to cut Patriot lines from the west.

By river the British were blocked by everything the Patri-

ots could muster, from iron-tipped booms set at angles just below the water's surface and ready to gut any ship that struck
them, to enormous iron chains (including one at the site of the
Bear Mountain Bridge) strung all the way across to a string of
forts and batteries that controlled key passages. Much of this
effort was centered around the more easily defended highland
narrows from Stony Point, past Bear Mountain and West Point,
up to Newburgh. If you stood on the banks of the Hudson in
1778 where the Trail crosses today and looked up and down,
you'd be gazing over an armed battle zone.

After failing to take the river by force, the British tried
subterfuge. (Their seizure in 1779 of the fort at Stony Point just
south of Bear Mountain is an exception, though it was quickly
recaptured by forces under the command of "Mad Anthony"
Wayne, an event commemorated by a historical side trail on the
route to battle.) Opportunity knocked when the British command was approached secretly by the hero of Saratoga, colonial
general Benedict Arnold. Passed over for promotion (his occasional rashness tended to alienate his peers), severely wounded
and partially disabled at Saratoga, veteran of the grueling and
unsuccessful march through Maine to Quebec, and now married
to a wealthy Tory from Philadelphia, Arnold offered in 1780 to
turn over his new post, the critical fortifications at West Point, to
the British. Had he succeeded, this would have effectively eliminated the most powerful batteries overlooking the river, as well
as the base for much of the Patriot resistance.

He never got the opportunity. His contact, British Major
John André, was captured by chance by a group of local ruffians
loosely organized into a band of Patriots. They turned the major
over to the colonial army where his papers gave away the
planned betrayal. Arnold quickly crossed the river to the east
bank and, after staying a night at the Robinson House (the site is
on Route 9D a few miles north of the bridge), he made his way to
Canada, leaving André to hang.

As the focus of the war moved to other areas, the tense
standoff continued. However, the actual number of engagements
trailed off until the war ended at Yorktown. To this day, though,
those of us who grew up in the valley feel that, although the
Revolution may have started in Massachusetts and may have

ended in Virginia, it was largely fought by New Yorkers in New York.

The end of the Revolution brought change to the Hudson River valley. With few exceptions, the manor owners were Tories. As a result, after the war their seignorial titles (i.e. granted by the Crown) were void, their estates were taken from them (most of the dispossessed emigrated) and were for the most part distributed among their former tenants. (Lord Fairfax's ingenious method of getting around similar seizure will be described later.) It was one of the first (and most effective) incidents of land reform in history.

The subsequent history of the Hudson Valley is largely concerned with commerce. River towns served as whaling ports during the War of 1812 as a way of protecting the fleets from British aggression. In 1825 the Erie Canal was completed, making the Hudson the most important waterway to the West. Railroads followed, and with them, names like Vanderbilt and Harriman entered the scene.

Development continued with gusto until late in the nineteenth century, when it turned out that even industrial New York was not immune to nostalgia for the American wilderness. As Benton MacKaye said, industrial lords and workers alike began to wilt under the pressure of life in the industrial age. Robber barons like J. P. Morgan built "Great Camps" in the Adirondacks, palatial "cabins" where they would hold court in the wilderness (Morgan named his camp "Uncas" after the renegade leader of the Mohegans). Lesser lords and workers blazed trails and hiked. This wilderness sentiment combined with fortuitous circumstance to ensure a place for the Trail to pass over.

The state of New York began building a prison in the area of the circle just west of Bear Mountain Bridge. That didn't line up very well with the plans of Mary Williams Harriman, widow of railroad tycoon Edward Harriman. It seems she was in the process of building a park at Bear Mountain (valley legend says that the Harrimans, snubbed by a downstate country club, decided to build their own). As so often happens in New York, when the rich dip their oar into the water, the boat snaps to. The plans for a prison magically relocated to Ossining (at about the same time a large tract at Bear Mountain was donated to the state as a park). To secure her plans for her own park, Mrs. Harriman and her family built—at their own expense, $5 million—Bear Mountain Bridge in 1923 to 1924. That fact, combined with generous grants of land to the Palisades Interstate Park, made Bear Mountain the logical place for the Trail to cross the Hudson when planning for the route had begun in earnest after 1921. It was on Harriman-granted land that the first section of the AT was blazed in 1923.

The prominent peak called "Anthony's Nose" or "Antony's Nose," which rises above the eastern end of the Bear Mountain Bridge, provokes some historical disagreement. The Anthony is said (probably inaccurately) to have been affixed in honor of General "Mad Anthony" Wayne, a local hero of the Revolution; some hold (probably with more justification) that it was named for the patron of nearby St. Anthonysville (now called Manitou). However, some old maps tend to favor Antony, and a vocal minority of native valley people attribute the name to Mark Antony and the hill's resemblance to a good Roman nose. Mad Anthony, though, probably deserves the nod. A tannery owner from Pennsylvania, he served with distinction in many widely separated fronts during the Revolution.

It was during the action on the night of July 15, 1779, to recapture the fort at Stony Point that Wayne earned his celebrated nickname. On a mission that was generally considered foolhardy, he added a twist of his own. Attacking by night, he had his men stick slips of white paper into their hats so that they could recognize one another. The first wave stormed the fort with muskets *unloaded.* It was their job to shout loudly, "The fort is ours! The fort is ours!" It went according to plan: By the time the second wave arrived with muskets loaded, the wakening British, convinced by the theatrics of the first that they had been defeated, surrendered.

HISTORY OF THE APPALACHIAN TRAIL IN NEW YORK

That the first tailor-made section of the Trail was blazed in New York should surprise nobody. Nowhere was the urge for recreation felt more strongly than in that metropolis. In fact, the creation of the New York section, along with those in certain parts of New England, were perhaps so easy that the infant Appalachian Trail Conference was, in the end, unprepared for the task of pushing the Trail through in areas where support was not as easy to find.

But in New York in 1923 it would have been harder to *prevent* the blazing of the Trail than it turned out to be to arrange it. Major William Welch and his Palisades Interstate Park had been a force since 1900; hiking clubs had been flourishing in the area for years and then the Harrimans announced the construction of the Bear Mountain Bridge. It was perfect.

Then, too, there was Raymond Torrey. A journalist in New York, he had already done much to begin the trail system on the west bank, between Bear Mountain and the Delaware River. Benton MacKaye credits Torrey with the first major public relations coup for the infant Appalachian Trail idea: Torrey had, on April 7, 1922, published a glowing exposition and endorsement of the whole concept on the "Outdoor Page" of the *New York Evening Post*. Two weeks later the New York-New Jersey Trail Conference was officially formed, with Benton MacKaye in attendance at the first meeting.

As with most other sections that came later, the blazing of the New York section followed a soon-to-be-familiar pattern. The NY-NJTC leadership (formed from the original group that included Welch, Torrey, and Clarence Stein) spent the first year gathering members and mapping out the potential route. As in most areas where the Trail got a quick start (and unlike the wilder areas like North Carolina and Maine, where the Trail idea was slower to take hold), New York had a lot to work with. There were already routes crisscrossing the Hudson Highlands on both sides of the river. The route was designed to take advantage of both the best topography and existing trails.

So it wasn't until more than a year later that the NY-NJTC actually had to blaze a new section. Work parties met on October 7, 1923, at the site of the bridge (under construction at the time) on the west bank and began blazing a 16-mile section from the bridge to the Ramapo River near Arden, New York. It was the first section of Trail blazed especially to create the Maine-to-Georgia link.

The new section received an official dedication of sorts on October 26 to 28, as the new New York-New Jersey Trail Conference met at the Bear Mountain Inn, virtually at the side of the Trail. There, a group of conference members and interested parties, including MacKaye, Welch, Torrey, and Stein, as well as Alan Chamberlain of the New England Trail Conference, met to continue plans for the Trail. It was on the third day that Welch officially introduced his proposal for a Trail logo—the familiar AT, with the two letters sharing the same crossbar. It was adopted and immediately put to use on the original square copper marker, again designed by Welch.

Over the years, the New York section, like most sections, has had to be rerouted any number of times. One of the most successful was in 1981, when the Trail was moved off local roads and onto a beautiful new area just off the ridge line of Hosner Mountain, onto land obtained by the U.S. Park Service. The first such purchase under the funding of the Scenic Trails Act was at Nuclear Lake near Pawling, on the Connecticut border.

THE TRAIL IN NEW YORK

Contrary to popular belief, there is a wide range of hiking to be had in New York. True, throughout most of it it's hard to find any place you can pitch a tent with a reasonable expectation of solitude—not in the same sense as, say, up in the White Mountains in New Hampshire.

But that's okay. With so many people living nearby, the proper role of the Appalachian Trail isn't as a wilderness adventure anyway. What people need this close to home is the day-to-day renewal that a pleasant walk in the woods can give. And that's what you get on the AT in New York and New Jersey.

Starting at the Connecticut border (which is somewhat confused, with the Trail ducking into New York only to duck right back out again), the Trail route offers splendid day hiking. Coming out of the scenic gorge of the Housatonic River, it enters the eastern hills of the Reading Prong—Schaghticoke Mountain (pronounced *skatticoke*), Gardner Hill, Ten Mile Hill. It loops around the Ten Mile River—a fine trout stream—and up onto the ridges of Leather Hill and Hammersly Ridge.

This is unexpectedly wild country. The valleys are abrupt here and much of it is protected, either by the state, various scout camps, or local preservation groups. The Pawling Nature

Preserve, a large tract up on Hammersly Ridge, is a simply superior place for a nature walk—it's the only place in the state of New York where I've seen some of the flora one finds there. It's part of The Nature Conservancy, and information and permits can be obtained by contacting them at: Chestnut Ridge Road, Mt. Kisco, New York 10549.

Once the Trail leaves Hammersly Ridge, it heads down the ridges of the Hudson Highlands along their generally southwest/ northeast axis. If you enter the Trail at Route 55, heading southwest onto Depot Hill, you'll find several rock ledges cresting the ridge that offer wonderful vistas of the rolling hills of the area. Since the lowlands are largely covered by maple-beech deciduous forest, it's a sight to be remembered in the fall.

Crossing the Taconic State Parkway, you reach one of the best opportunities for extended wilderness trekking (in the New York sense) on the New York section—Clarence Fahnestock State Park. It's an enormous tract of land and the Trail has for years traveled the length of it.

Ascending from the Taconic Parkway, the Trail reaches the summit of the long ridge of Shenandoah Mountain (why this name persists so far north is a mystery to me). At 1282 feet it is, according to the guidebook, the highest point in this section. Though it has a rocky summit like its higher northern New England counterparts, I have yet to contract a nosebleed from climbing it.

From there, the route heads generally south through some wonderful oak-hickory forest. Keep an eye out for the scrubby shoots of American chestnut sprouting along the route. You'll also see huge logs on the forest floor—the remains of chestnuts that died in the 1920s and 1930s.

Fahnestock Park is a good base. You can day-hike out onto the AT in either direction or stay around the park and take advantage of the fishing, boating, and camping, which can be had for a reasonable rate (thru-hikers stay free). Of particular interest are the old iron mines that operated here during the Revolution and after. Part of the Trail south of Fahnestock goes along the route of a railroad built to take the ore to the foundry at Cold Spring. Pieces of iron ore can still be found. Just be careful of the mines.

The woodlands in and around Fahnestock Park are riddled with trails, both marked and unmarked. Unmarked trails in the Highlands tend to run along old abandoned carriage roads and railroads, and can make for pleasant walks. One interesting side hike in the park goes to Sunk Mine Lake. It's exactly what it says it is—the main iron mine at Fahnestock, filled with water. It was near there that the Wappingers tribes had one of their main villages.

Southwest of Fahnestock Park the Trail goes through the heart of the contested area of the east bank during the Revolution. Names like Fort Hill and Fort Defiance Hill commemorate the crude, largely earthwork redoubts that defended the passes through the Highlands against a British advance. U.S. 9 travels up one pass that was a major worry to Patriot commanders.

At Route 9, the Trail skirts by the monastery of the Friars of the Atonement at Graymoor. A favorite stopping place for thru-hikers, the monastery is also popular with local Catholics looking for an alternative to Sunday services in their home parishes. Graymoor friars are well known in the area also because they frequently help out in local churches.

As the Trail continues southwest over Canada Hill, it reaches South Mountain Pass at Manitou. From there, it starts to ascend the northern flank of Anthony's Nose. This section was closed during the Second World War because of its proximity to the military facility at Camp Smith. There were once copper mines in this section, but the Trail has been rerouted away from them. Besides being dangerous—they're ugly shafts straight down, filled with dangerous gasses—they're not really much to see.

After a fairly steep descent down the western side of Anthony's Nose, the Trail finally reaches the river at Bear Mountain Bridge. Crossing on foot costs a dime.

With the exception of the Fahnestock Park trail system, and an unmarked loop to the summit of Sugarloaf Hill (splendid view of the Hudson Valley and West Point, site, at its base on the west, of a Continental Army encampment and the Robinson House, Benedict Arnold's refuge his first night on the lam), there are relatively few side trails on the east bank of the Hudson. This is certainly not the case on the west bank.

As soon as the Trail crosses the Hudson, it enters Harriman and Bear Mountain State Parks. These are the gifts of the Harriman family, and site of the first sections of the AT to be blazed. With just a few minor relocations, the route is the same one that was blazed back in October of 1923 by Raymond Torrey, Frank Place, and other early Trail luminaries, along with the usual assembly of anonymous workers who have shown up at convenient moments.

From a hiker's point of view, the parks are a gift of true magnificence. More than 20 miles of Trail pass through some of the last wild land in southern New York. As the Trail winds through, seeming by its circumspect routing to be reluctant to leave the relative solitude, it skirts ridges, knobs, lakes, and marshes left by the glacier that stopped not far south, the only civilization nearby being the few roads that pass through the parks. It passes by Hessian Lake, said to be site of a Continental victory, after which the bodies of Hessian mercenaries were dumped into the lake, giving it its name. An act of true patriotism, no doubt. There are two conveniently located shelters—among the few in the entire New York section.

Besides the AT, though, the entire Bear Mountain State Park is crisscrossed by trails. Most hikers like to climb Bear Mountain itself (the AT goes up there), but that's not all that's available. If you have a historical bent, there's the 1777 and 1779 trails. The first follows the route of the British in their expedition in 1777 to capture Forts Clinton and Montgomery, which dominated the Hudson from the west bank on either side of the Bear Mountain Bridge site. The second follows the route of Continental general "Mad Anthony" Wayne and his 1300 patriotic semiregulars to recapture the fort at Stony Point 12 miles to the south.

Once out of the Harriman State Park, the Trail crosses the New York State Thruway—a harsh shock back into reality. From there, it knob-hops over Precambrian uplands until it reaches the Schunemunk ridge at Bellvale Mountain. It ascends from a low point of around 700 feet at Fitzgerald Falls at the base of Bellvale to over 1200 feet at its summit. The route then resumes its southwesterly direction down the ridge into New Jersey at Greenwood Lake.

THE TRAIL IN NEW JERSEY

If the existence of a wilderness trail in New York is surprising, in New Jersey it astonishes most people.

But there it is. Though there are no impressive mountains

in the Garden State, the Trail nevertheless passes through some pleasant woods and along a wonderful ridge well worth a Saturday stroll or a weekend in a tent.

About halfway down the lake the Trail takes a sharp right, heading in a generally westerly direction. For about 21 miles it hops cross lots off the Schunemunks and over the Vernon valley (home of New Jersey's only major ski areas), never more than a mile or so from the New York border. This section has recently undergone several reroutings, most of which have taken the Trail off secondary roads and into the woods.

Throughout the southwestern New York and northern New Jersey section, hikers are liable to run across circular depressions in the forest floor. These are the sites of charcoal pits where local hemlock was burned into the charcoal needed for iron smelting. The charcoal industry denuded the woods from Jersey to Connecticut. There are charcoal pits listed in the trail guide in the section of New York between Route 17 and Bellvale Mountain. They're not the only ones along the Trail route—not by a long shot—but they're especially thick here.

Charcoal burning wasn't an easy job. To keep the wood from igniting, an elaborate mound was built, with wood carefully stacked inside. Over the wood, the mound's tender put a layer of ferns or wet leaves, covered by a thick layer of sod. Once it was ignited, he had to watch carefully, daubing any hot spots with a wet charcoal paste to smother flames.

It was slow, demanding work. A small mound could take a week or two to finish smoldering; a large mound—one up to 30 feet or so in diameter—could take up to a month. The tender of the mound had to watch it like a hawk, sleeping in short naps to prevent flame from consuming his work. It was dangerous, too. Tenders often had to climb up onto the mound to smother trouble spots. Occasionally, one would fall through.

After the Trail gets up onto the long Kittatinny Ridge, hikers will find some of the best walking in New Jersey. Starting almost immediately with the short side hike to the top of High Point and continuing down the ridge toward the Delaware Water Gap, the Trail consists of easy ridge-line walking. Once again, there are shelters—lean-tos—at intervals along the Trail. Elevations, except in the gaps, are consistently in the 1100- to 1400-foot range, with occasional points up to 1600 feet or so.

Because of side parallel trails, day hikers can often set up loop hikes. An example is the series of round trips that can be arranged to the Normanook Lookout tower (Culver Fire Tower) overlooking Culvers Gap and Culvers Lake. By starting from the north side of Kittatinny Mountain, at one of a couple of trailheads near the State School of Conservation at Lake Wapalanne, hikers can take trips of 8, 10, or more miles. It can even be turned into an overnight, with Gren Anderson Shelter within easy walking distance. Perhaps the most popular area for day hiking is the series of looping trails on Mt. Tammany, which forms the New Jersey side of the Delaware Water Gap and affords superb views of the Gap. The entire ridge system has dozens of such trails.

An invaluable book for those wishing to hike the ridges of New York and New Jersey is the famous *New York Walk Book,* first published in 1923 by the New York-New Jersey Trail Conference. The first edition was written by AT founding fathers Raymond Torrey, Frank Place, Jr., and Robert L. Dickinson. The authors have changed, but the NY-NJTC still publishes it, and for any hiker living in the New York metropolitan area, it's a work beyond price.

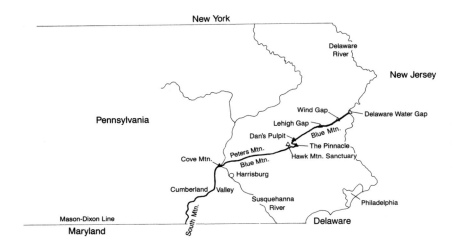

New York

Delaware River

New Jersey

Pennsylvania

Wind Gap

Delaware Water Gap

Lehigh Gap

Dan's Pulpit

Blue Mtn.

Peters Mtn.

The Pinnacle

Hawk Mtn. Sanctuary

Cove Mtn.

Blue Mtn.

Harrisburg

Cumberland   Valley

Susquehanna River

Philadelphia

Mason-Dixon Line

South Mtn.

Delaware

Maryland

Pennsylvania

8

The Pennsylvania Section

Trail Distance:

> Delaware Water Gap to Pennsylvania/Maryland
> state line . . . . 229.5 miles

Maintaining Clubs:

> The Keystone Trails Association and its affiliated
> organizations:

> > Springfield Trail Club: Delaware River
> > to Fox Gap . . . . 7.2 miles

> > Batona Hiking Club: Fox Gap to
> > Wind Gap . . . . 8.1 miles

> > Appalachian Mt. Club, Delaware Valley chapter:
> > Wind Gap to Little Gap . . . . 15.1 miles

> > Philadelphia Trail Club: Little Gap to Lehigh
> > Furnace Gap . . . . 10.2 miles

> > Blue Mountain Eagles Climbing Club: Lehigh
> > Furnace Gap to Bake Oven Knob; Tri-County
> > Corner to Rausch Creek . . . . 65.5 miles

*Allentown Hiking Club: Bake Oven Knob to
Tri-County Corner* . . . . *11.7 miles*

*Brandywine Valley Outing Club: Rausch Creek to
Pennsylvania 325* . . . . *11.2 miles*

*Susquehanna Appalachian Trail Club:
Pennsylvania 325 to Pennsylvania 225* . . *9.2 miles*

*York Hiking Club: Pennsylvania 225 to
Susquehanna River* . . . . *7.8 miles*

*Mountain Club of Maryland: Susquehanna River to
Pine Grove Furnace State Park* . . . . *46.5 miles*

*Potomac Appalachian Trail Club: Pine Grove
Furnace State Park to Pennsylvania/Maryland
state line* . . . . *36.6 miles*

INTRODUCTION

PENNSYLVANIANS ARE proud to call their home the Keystone State, testament to its position in the demographic (if not precisely the geographic) center of the Eastern Seaboard. It's a notion that holds some merit.

One example of why is Pennsylvania's border on Maryland, better known as the Mason-Dixon line (named for Charles Mason and Jeremiah Dixon, the two Englishmen who surveyed the line during 1765–68, in large part because the peaceful Quaker, William Penn, had a history of border disputes with his neighbors). Hovering as it does on the edge of two worlds, Pennsylvania has a character quite unlike that of its neighbors, be they northern or southern. It's a true link.

It's also a link between East and West. The Pennsylvania pioneer routes, hooking up as they do with the Ohio River and heading from there throughout most of North America, was one of the most popular in the seventeenth and eighteenth centuries.

If you've never been to Pennsylvania, you'll immediately

be impressed by its greenness (if you're not there in the winter, of course). It's a fertile place, notable for its farmland and wooded ridges. Myron Avery wrote in 1936 that there were more deer killed by hunters in Pennsylvania than in any other state; hunting figures may have changed, but the deer population is still there. Pennsylvania is a wide-open state.

GEOLOGY ALONG THE TRAIL

If the Appalachians are the most orderly fold mountains in the world, nowhere are they more perfect than in Pennsylvania. In scribing what Myron Avery called a perfect arc, with Washington, D.C., at the axis, the Blue Mountain/South Mountain system and the Alleghenies farther west, the Appalachian cordillera forms row after row of neat, sinuous ridges that cross the state. So neat are they that near Harrisburg, several ridges are known simply as First Mountain, Second Mountain, and Third Mountain. Put simply, they look like a slightly curved washboard.

Like nearly all Appalachian formations, the ridges of Pennsylvania are underlain by crystalline Grenville rocks. But here, the later structures haven't been removed yet, as they have been in the Hudson Highlands. Pennsylvania rocks are largely of the Paleozoic Era—between 240 and 570 million years old. They are likely to be of the Silurian, Devonian, Mississippian, and, yes, Pennsylvanian periods. In some of the earlier sediments hikers may find fossils of trilobites and eurypterids—strange beasties that once lurked in the shallow inland seas before Europe and Africa arrived to hurl the sea beds thousands of feet into the air.

The younger rocks have endured for a very simple reason: The glaciers of the ice ages came only as far down as northern Pennsylvania and no farther. Shortly after the Trail leaves the Delaware Water Gap it crosses the terminal moraines of the last ice age (the sand and gravel around Wolf Rocks are it). The ridges of the central and southern parts of the state have not been scoured clean by ice.

It was during the Acadian Orogeny, 350 million years ago, and especially during the later Alleghany Orogeny, that the Paleozoic rock strata of Pennsylvania were crushed together like an accordion. As the onrushing European and African plates hit the coast, the millions of years of sediment that had accumulated in the inland sea started bending. The most recent deposits—the layers rich in organic material that formed in the marshes that surrounded the suture area between the plates as the ocean disappeared—were uplifted, perhaps even as they were forming. These were crushed by the weight of sediment above and the forces that were uplifting them into some of the largest coal beds in the world. And as the continental game of bumper cars squished the rocks, it changed them, creating quartzite where there was once sandstone, and anthracite where there was once a thick layer of rotting vegetable matter.

The kind of sediment found in a given area depended on what was going on there at the time. If the deposits were at the edge of the sea, under mountains already uplifted, the layers would probably consist of sand. In the middle of a sea, mud might be deposited, forming shale. A shallow-water "carbonate bank" would form limestone or dolomite. "Dirty sand," or a mixture of sand and mud, might form siltstone or graywacke, common, albeit nondescript, kinds of sedimentary rocks. Add heat and pressure and the sediments would be welded into generally more durable metamorphic quartzites (from sandstone), slate (from shale), marble (from limestone), or gneiss or schist.

The Pennsylvanian ridges are excellent examples of how fold mountains erode into parallel ridge systems. The original mountains formed by the Acadian and Alleghany orogenies were much, much higher—possibly by tens of thousands of feet. As they eroded down over the 230 million years or so since the mountain-building stopped for good, softer layers wore away quickly, while hard rocks remained to form the new ridge lines. Once the top of a fold ridge was eroded away, the mountain might evolve into twin parallel ridges lower down, where a particularly hard layer wore down more slowly. Good examples abound in Pennsylvania.

For instance, from the Delaware Water Gap all the way to Indiantown Gap, the Trail follows a ridge made up mostly of Shawangunk Formation quartzite, deposited as sandstone during the Silurian period and since metamorphosed into the harder quartzite. It wore away much more slowly because the quartzite is a superhard, exceedingly durable rock. The softer siltstones, shales, and limestones of the bordering Martinsburg and Bloomsburg formations wore away, leaving the ridge where the Shawangunk Formation persisted.

Another, more dramatic, example is Cove Mountain, on the west side of the Susquehanna River where the Trail crosses. Cove Mountain scribes a neat parabola on the earth's surface (I flew over it once, and was astounded that such a pronounced and perfect formation could actually exist). It represents the edges of a syncline, or downward fold in the rock strata, which has eroded down to the more erosion-resistant Pocono Formation sandstone. This particular syncline is not parallel to the earth's surface; rather, it is tilted up toward the west-southwest, and Cove Mountain is where the Pocono sandstone from the ridge on either side of the syncline meets up. Farther down the syncline, toward the east-northeast, the center of the syncline is filled with Llewellyn Formation and Pottsville Group sediments—Pennsylvanian period rocks that contain the anthracite coal that hikers keep running into in the DeHart Reservoir and Yellow Springs areas.

One noted (though not universally beloved) characteristic of the Trail in Pennsylvania is the boulder fields. They, too, are peculiar to this area for a reason.

Since the glaciers came down only about as far as the very upper part of Pennsylvania, the rest of the state was in what is called a *periglacial* area. This meant that the ground and exposed bedrock were subjected to constant freezing and thawing, as well as substantial melt-off from the foot of the great glaciers. This tended to "seep-freeze" and pry out chunks of bedrock as the water would work its way down into seams in the rock, freeze, and loosen huge chunks.

Occurring over more than half of the Trail in Pennsylvania, the bedrock is that bombproof Shawangunk quartzite. The chunks of that hardy stuff, once broken off, tended to roll down the hill and then stay there. Since quartzite weathers slowly, the boulders didn't wear away. Frost heave and water action rounded them out a bit, but that's all. Hikers' feet probably erode them away as fast as anything else that's working on them these days.

The geology of Pennsylvania is as interesting as any area on the Trail. Just walking down the south slope of Cove Mountain takes you—in the space of 6 or 7 miles—through over 140 million years of geological history. Several places along the Trail are paleontologists' delights, offering fossils of plants and animals extinct for upward of 400 million years. Those Paleozoic seas were trilobite heaven. Perhaps the best place to look is where the Trail passes by Interstate 81 on Pennsylvania Route 72. The Martinsburg shale in the road cut is full of little critters.

HISTORY ALONG THE TRAIL

When the first Europeans arrived in Pennsylvania, the land along what would become the Trail route was inhabited by two basic groups of people: the Munsee clans of the Lenni Lenapes along the Delaware Valley to the east, and the Susquehannocks, an Iroquoian people, in the central part of the state.

The Munsees of Pennsylvania followed essentially the same road as did their New Jersey neighbors. For the most part peaceably, though inexorably, shoved off their land, they dispersed to the west with the many other groups who fled that way in the eighteenth and nineteenth centuries.

The Susquehannocks' fate was being sealed even as the settlers arrived. At that time they were at war with their cousins, the powerful Iroquois Confederacy to the north. In 1677 they were roundly defeated and forced to move—lock, stock, and hearth—to Oneida, in central New York. There they remained for decades.

When their captors finally relaxed their guard, sometime in the middle of the eighteenth century, the battered remnants of the once proud and numerous people gradually drifted back down toward their old haunts near Harrisburg. To their dismay, they found everything changed—the settlers in William Penn's vigorous colony were solidly in control.

It must have been truly pitiable. Over the ensuing years the Susquehannocks diminished to a ragged band of about twenty souls. These met their end in 1763, when they were massacred by whites in some Indian scare or other. A noble victory, beyond question.

Generally speaking, though, the history of Pennsylvania since the European settlement was relatively peaceful. This is due in part to a couple of factors.

First, it's undoubtedly true that having the major inhabitants of the territory you want to occupy vacate the premises just as you arrive is quite convenient. It surely enabled William Penn, who was granted his land in 1681, a good incentive to insist upon good relations with his Native American neighbors. Why not? Most of them were already out of the way.

Second, though, was Penn's undeniably good administration of his domain. Attempts were made from the outset to parcel the fertile land to settlers fairly, and the colony was governed for the most part in an enlightened manner. Settlers prospered, and more settlers arrived. The German and Scots-Irish who arrived in the 1720s and 1730s would a few decades later be the driving force for the settlement of western Virginia and Tennessee, down the long valleys of the Cumberland and the Shenandoah.

HISTORY OF THE APPALACHIAN TRAIL IN PENNSYLVANIA

The Trail in Pennsylvania was blazed by a number of local clubs, some of which were organized in the early days of the AT by the crew of Arthur Perkins, Raymond Torrey, and Myron Avery. It must have been a slick job, because these clubs work together within the Keystone Trails Association, and each keeps its section in top shape.

Although it's difficult to single out one club from the others, it seems that there were three prime movers early on: the Blue Mountain Club in the east, organized in Reading in 1926 by a Lafayette College professor, Eugene C. Bingham; the Blue Mountain Eagles Climbing Club in central Pennsylvania; and Myron Avery, Fred Schairer, and the rest of the Potomac Appalachian Trail Club (PATC) in the southwest. The Blue Mountain Eagles, organized in 1916, was already a vigorous organization when the AT idea arrived. They were recruited to the task in the fall of 1926 by Professor Bingham, and under the leadership of Dr. Harry F. Rentschler had completed their section from Schuylkill to Swatara gaps by 1930. They, like the PATC, also acted as a breeder club, enlisting various other groups to take over neighboring sections.

The Blue Mountain Eagles began as part of a completely

different, largely European, tradition. They arose out of an in-
formal group of Pennsylvania Dutch weekend walkers, the
Fussgaengers, who would get together each week to walk and
socialize, sing German songs, and tell stories at wine gardens in
the area. This is quite reminiscent of the northern European
tradition of taking walks with family or friends on weekend after-
noons and evenings, and it still can be seen in many German
and Dutch villages (Pennsylvania Dutch are actually of German
ancestry—the "Dutch" here is a corruption of *deutsch,* or
"German").

In 1916, the *Fussgaengers* went with Dr. Rentschler on a
hike to Eagle's Nest, hunting for an actual eagle's nest that Rentschler had seen in the area. The hike, which took place on
October 12, is remembered as the official founding of the Blue
Mountain Eagles Climbing Club. The Eagle's Nest hike became
an annual event and the Club always made one other climb each
year to a new peak. In the German tradition, each hike was
followed by a feast at a local inn.

Small wonder that it was such a strong and enthusiastic
group that the Blue Mountain Club's Dr. Bingham addressed on
October 30, 1926, to recruit for the effort to blaze "The Skyline
Trail" as part of Benton MacKaye's Maine-to-Georgia scheme. By
May of 1930, their whole 102-mile section, from the Lehigh
River to the Susquehanna, was complete.

The PATC, on the other hand, had a problem. The route
from Blue Mountain west of Harrisburg to South Mountain, leading into Maryland, had to cross the Cumberland Valley. In 1930–
31, Avery and Schairer finally settled on a route toward Michaux
State Forest, where it runs today. But they had to include a
traverse of the Cumberland Valley that remains controversial to
this day.

Since that time, several newer clubs have taken over responsibility for some of the sections that were originally blazed
by the founding organizations. Some of these groups live miles
from their sections.

The true history of the Trail in Pennsylvania, though, is
apparent to anybody who walks it. The trail workers don't erect
their monuments to organizations but, rather, to individuals.
You'll see a sign to the guy who built the bridge, a plaque to the
crew who reroofed the lean-to, a set of steps named for the lady

who sends out the newsletter. There's a woman along the Trail who likes to give ice cream cones to thru-hikers, and a couple who have hikers trained to walk out of the way to get fresh vegetables. It's characteristic Pennsylvania modesty and hospitality. And the recognition is a darned good way to keep volunteers happy and working hard.

THE TRAIL IN PENNSYLVANIA

As the Trail enters Pennsylvania it's more or less a matter of picking up where it has left off in New Jersey. It will roughly follow that same single-ridge system from the northeast corner at the Delaware Water Gap on the border with New Jersey to the southcentral border with Maryland, in a generally northeasterly-southwesterly direction.

In New Jersey, the Trail makes a switch from the Reading Prong (the ridge group that it has followed since it crossed into New York from Connecticut), to Kittatinny Mountain, which is the beginning of what will become Blue Mountain when the ridge gets a few miles into Pennsylvania. At the border, formed by the Delaware River, Kittatinny has been gashed deeply by the cutting action of the water. Crossing into Pennsylvania on the I-80 roadway, the Trail quickly ascends the ridge of Pennsylvania's Kittatinny and heads southwest. After the Trail crosses Wind Gap, the name of the ridge changes to Blue Mountain, a designation it will keep all the way to the Susquehanna and beyond. The AT stays on the ridge line, only descending to cross gaps or switch to neighboring ridges, all the way to the Cumberland Valley.

Just below the Cumberland Valley it picks up on South Mountain, which goes south into Maryland all the way to the Potomac River.

From the Delaware River it quickly climbs about 1100 feet to the top of Mt. Minsi, which forms the eastern knob of Kittatinny Mountain in Pennsylvania, or the western escarpment of the Delaware Water Gap.

Soon after leaving Mt. Minsi, the Trail reaches Wolf Rocks and the farthest southern point of the great ice sheet that retreated ten thousand to twelve thousand years ago. The boulders and gravel banks in the vicinity tell the tale: the glaciers stopped here, dumping their load of stone and sand as they melted.

As the Trail leaves Wolf Rocks, it meanders across the wide top of Kittatinny, sidling over to the south onto the beginnings of Blue Mountain. Here, it's just a spur of Kittatinny, going down to Wind Gap to the west.

Traversing Northern Pennsylvania on Blue Mountain

From this point onward, the Trail traverses the long ridge of Blue Mountain all the way to Swatara Gap, a distance of some 100 miles. It leaves it there only to avoid a military installation at Indiantown Gap (an area through which it traveled prior to WW II). Except for the periodic gaps in the ridge line, it stays about 1400 to 1500 feet above sea level and follows the outcropping of Shawangunk quartzite all the way.

The Blue Mountain ridge is a narrow, steep-sided finger of wooded and rocky hill that travels like an arrow nearly due east and west, the Lehigh River to the north and the rich farmlands and rolling hills of Lebanon and environs to the south. On the not-infrequent occasions when rocky knobs top the ridge, Blue Mountain affords splendid views of the surrounding countryside, often in all directions.

One of the most spectacular stretches of Blue Mountain is the exceptionally narrow steep-sided section west of Lehigh Gap. First reaching Devil's Pulpit overlooking the gap and the Lehigh Valley to the north, it offers several other lookouts just as good: at Bake Oven Knob, Baer's Rocks, and then a knife edge that the guidebook calls simply "The Cliffs."

West of this section, there is a crimp in the Blue Mountain ridge. Partly due to a complexity in the folding of the strata, and partly due to a series of faults in the rocks, the quartzite layer that the Trail has been following since way up in New Jersey takes a dogleg to the south and then continues westward again. The Trail stays right with it.

It is on this section, by the way, that the Blue Mountain Eagles Climbing Club first started work on the Trail, way back in 1926.

If you're a dedicated bird-watcher, you might someday want to keep on going west rather than take the jog to the south. The blue-blazed trail that keeps going straight ahead leads

2 miles into the Hawk Mountain Sanctuary, where you'll find a rocky lookout, the sanctuary headquarters, and a small museum. It's one of the finest places in the country to watch birds of prey on their annual migration, from mid-August to mid-December. In a given year, thirty thousand eagles and hawks of all kinds may pass through. There is a small fee for hiking in the Sanctuary. For more information, write to: Hawk Mountain Sanctuary, Route #2, Kempton, Pennsylvania 19529.

There are several impressive lookouts in the Hawk Mountain region: Tri-County Corner, where the first blaze in the new Trail went in back in 1926; Dan's Pulpit, named for Blue Mountain Eagle founding father Dan Hoch; and The Pinnacle and Pulpit Rock, where Blue Mountain zigzags around the Eckville Fault and gets back onto its westward axis. Hikers can also see the remains of more charcoal hearths much like the ones in New Jersey. This section ends in the steep-sided water gap of the Little Schuylkill at Port Clinton.

Like most narrow ridges, Blue Mountain has short spur trails leading up to the AT from below at frequent intervals. These can be used to gain access to the uplands for short hikes and to form interesting loops from the highway crossings in the gaps. Between Port Clinton and the point at which Pennsylvania Route 183 crosses the ridge, there are two such trails: Marshall's Path, which runs out of Bellmans Gap off Mountain Road; and the Tom Lowe Trail, which runs a nice loop out of a parking area where Northkill Creek leaves its narrow valley source.

Just west of the Lowe Trail the Eagles Nest Trail cuts off to the south. It was this knob that became the focal point for the Blue Mountain Eagles Climbing Club, founded in 1916 on a hike to the knob.

As the Trail draws closer to Swatara Gap, where it will finally leave Blue Mountain, it passes along a particularly steep section of the ridge. As it leaves the parking area at Route 183, it passes the marker for old Fort Dietrich Snyder, built under the direction of Benjamin Franklin in 1756 to protect the way from Indian attacks. The Trail then keeps close to the steep southern slope of the ridge.

One of the nicest things about hiking in Pennsylvania is that the blazers of the Trail have taken care to recognize their members who have played important roles in the building of the

AT. Typical is the side trail to the Shanaman Marker and the Showers steps. The former recognizes William F. Shanaman, once mayor of Reading and dedicated Trail worker; the latter consists of five hundred stone steps leading down to a spring, built by Lloyd Showers, another Trail worker, and named logically enough after him. Far better to remember a selfless builder than to suffer the usual inscriptions to armchair generals.

The Trail crosses Swatara Creek on history of another kind. The handsome iron bridge over which the route passes is the old Waterville Bridge, relocated to its present site in 1985 to preserve this fine example of a nineteenth-century lenticular structure. It takes this name from the shapes of its trusses, which, viewed from the side, bear some resemblance to a lentil. It was built in 1890 over Little Pine Creek, and was moved to Swatara Creek only because it was too narrow for modern automobile traffic. The loss to motorists is a gain for shanks' mare.

At Swatara Gap the Trail takes its leave of Blue Mountain. The ridge continues down toward Harrisburg, while the AT heads northwest over several ridges (Second Mountain, Sharp Mountain/Stony Mountain, and Peters Mountain). It passes several historic sites enroute, such as the old Cold Spring Railroad Station at Cold Spring Military Reservation on Dresden Lake (0.9 mile on the Horseshoe Trail, downhill from Sharp Mountain), and the ruins of Yellow Springs Village. It also heads right through St. Anthony's Wilderness, the largest roadless area in eastern Pennsylvania.

As the Trail passes through Rausch Gap, it enters the area of the famous Pennsylvania anthracite (hard) coal. It passes right near old coal beds, and hikers will run into many remnants of the old industry—building foundations, old earthworks for mining operations and the transportation systems that helped move the coal to market. There are also cemeteries, wells, and a thousand other pieces of debris from once-thriving communities in these valleys that are now ghost towns and ruins. Once the Trail has descended into Clarks Valley, good fossils of plants (*lipidondendron*) can be found in the old mine dumps near De Hart Reservoir, located about a mile and a half up the valley.

Clarks Valley is the bottom of a long syncline, of which Sharps and Peters mountains are the two sides, and Cove Mountain across the Susquehanna is the end. From the air the whole complex looks like a tube that has been buried on its side, slightly tilted up at one end and then cut off near the ground for its entire length. What's left is a huge parabola on the earth's surface.

At the crest of Sharps Mountain the rocks are Pocono Formation sandstone and siltstone. These are relatively new rocks from the Mississippian period (about 330 million years ago), and they're indication enough that these hills could only have formed in the later Alleghany Orogeny. Down in Clarks Valley the rocks are newer still—Pennsylvanian period siltstone, sandstone, and shale, and anthracite beds within (300 million years old). Then, when the Trail crests Peters Mountain, it will follow the relatively hard Pocono rocks all the way to the Susquehanna across to Cove Mountain and leave them only when it turns south toward the Cumberland Valley.

The route down Peters Mountain is much like the rest of eastern Pennsylvania: along the crest of an arrow-straight ridge, maintaining an elevation of around 1250 feet all the way. There are occasional side trails reaching up to the crest of the ridge from the valleys below, but the AT doesn't turn right or left until it reaches the impressive water gap where the Susquehanna carves its way through between Peters and Cove mountains— which are, with Sharps Mountain, actually part of the same long U-shaped ridge.

The AT crosses the Susquehanna on the Duncannon Bridge at the confluence of the Juniata, a major tributary. The two rivers are excellent for canoeing, offering easy Class 1 and Class 2 paddling, good fishing, and a fine array of water birds. Paddlers regularly run into huge herons, egrets, and the like— there is a major rookery of these birds on an island in the Susquehanna a few miles downstream, just before Harrisburg.

Within sight of the Juniata the Trail once again climbs steeply, this time up Cove Mountain, the first of several mountains of that name the Trail will pass on its way south. It offers splendid views of the water gap and the surrounding countryside before it makes its way two-thirds around the huge "U" of Cove Mountain and descends to the south. Once off Cove it isn't long before the AT runs into the northern end of the Tuscarora Trail, the Appalachian Trail's own child. It's appropriate that the meeting takes place back on Blue Mountain (yes, the name con-

tinued across the Susquehanna), the ridge that the AT has followed most of the way from New Jersey. The Tuscarora/Big Blue
Trail left the AT in Virginia, along the Blue Ridge.

The Tuscarora and its southern reaches, called "Big Blue"
in the Virginias, were blazed starting in the early 1960s, when
the ATC became convinced that they could no longer guarantee
the unbroken AT in northern Virginia. So, they mapped out and
blazed a western route along the last of the Appalachian ridges,
the Alleghenies to the west.

The Tuscarora/Big Blue system runs around 500 miles
until it regains the AT in the northern section of Shenandoah
National Park in northern Virginia. One Potomac Appalachian
Trail Club member that I met down that way told me that there
was some support for offering recognition for people who thru-
hiked from Maine to Georgia (or vice versa) using the Tuscarora/
Big Blue route instead of the traditional northern Virginia trail.

Once off Blue Mountain (for the last time), the Trail heads
into the famous road-walking section through the Cumberland
Valley. Thru-hikers seem to have a love/hate relationship with
the valley. Some love getting off the boulder-strewn trails and
onto a flat surface for a change. Those who get there in the heat
of the summer find it oppressive, since there's no place to hide
from the sun and heat. For the most part it doesn't get a lot of
day hikers—for obvious reasons. But it's actually a pleasant
area, for a residential community, even if it's not what you'd
consider a wilderness experience. The ATC has been trying for
years to relocate the Trail to a more remote ridge-top route.
Knowing them, they'll succeed eventually.

As the Trail reaches the southern edge of the Cumberland
Valley you can get glimpses to the southwest of your next big
ridge: South Mountain. At its northern terminus at Mount Holly
Springs it is quite a sight to behold, a narrow tongue of steep
highland reaching up to the edge of the Cumberland Valley.

It's in the shadow of South Mountain that the Trail gets
back into the woods. This is precipitous country, full of sharp
ridges and sheer cliffs. The Trail hasn't made it into large wilderness yet, so there's not much in the way of side trails, but there
are again a few access points on the ridge tops from the valleys
below. When Pine Grove State Park is reached, on the southeast
flank of South Mountain (which the AT hasn't climbed yet), the

Trail finally crosses over into territory maintained and watched over by the formidable Potomac Appalachian Trail Club. Some of the route ahead was blazed under the direct supervision of Myron Avery, Fred Schairer, and the rest of that whole gang who did so much to put the Trail through back when it was just Benton MacKaye's dream.

In 1936 in his short work *The Appalachian Trail on Pennsylvania's South Mountain,* Myron Avery wrote, "Not as high as the Blue Ridge, it nowhere exceeds 2,200 feet, yet for expansive outlooks, majesty of forest growth, the excellence of its trails, its peculiar topographic features and its economic and historical background, Pennsylvania's South Mountain Region is a worthy peer of its better-known rival."

The ridges in the southern section of Pennsylvania are littered with the remains of the old iron industry. From Pine Grove Furnace all the way to the Maryland border there are reminders of the industry that thrived from around the time of the Revolution to about the Civil War. Again, as it has all the way from northern New Jersey, the AT passes the circular clearings that indicate the old sites of *more* charcoal mounds. At Pine Grove Furnace the Trail passes old smelters and the ore hole (now Fuller Lake) before passing at last up the slope of South Mountain. Once again, the AT passes largely over the public lands of Michaux State Forest, and once more there are side trails and little-used or unused roads that can form day-hike loops and exploration routes.

The knobs and gullies in this section can be quite steep because the ridges form up around harder quartzite layers with softer strata in the valleys. In some places this will be the Antietam Formation quartzite, a dull gray variety that in places contains streaks that are actually the holes of *Skolithos* worms, a sand-dwelling tubeworm of 500-plus million years ago. Cliffs and lookouts are everywhere in these hills, so take advantage of the second and keep an eye out for the first.

As the Trail descends back down to Caledonia Gap at Caledonia State Park, it walks back into history. It was through this gap that Robert E. Lee and his Army of Northern Virginia passed on their way to Gettysburg. According to Myron Avery, the army rested at Travelers Spring, a local water hole in the area. Perhaps coincidentally, Lee's favorite horse's name was

Traveller. It was near here that Captain John Cook, one of John Brown's aides during his abortive raid on Harpers Ferry, was captured in 1859.

The Trail continues down along South Mountain, which in its northern section is a series of broken ridges and knobs, quite unlike the straight-run escarpment that it will become in Maryland. It makes for some of the most interesting—and pleasant—hiking in Pennsylvania. Lookouts like Chimney Rocks and Buzzard Peak offer fine views at frequent intervals. From there the Trail descends into Antietam Cove and the headwaters of Antietam Creek. It was across this small stream that Lee and McClellan fought the bloodiest battle of the Civil War in 1862, miles to the south near Sharpsburg, Maryland.

"Cove," by the way, is one of the first appearances of the term along the Trail (Cove Mountain is another). As the AT progresses farther south, it will appear regularly on all the maps, meaning simply a valley extending into the hills from the flatlands below.

Having just passed the halfway point of the AT, it's appropriate that another milestone should be counted. As the Trail pulls into Pen-Mar, it passes over the Mason-Dixon line: We have passed from the Keystone of the East into the True South.

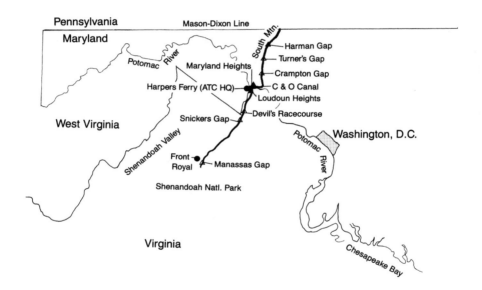

Maryland and Northern Virginia

9

The Maryland/ Northern Virginia Section

Trail Distances:

> *Pennsylvania-Maryland state line to the*
> *Potomac River* . . . . *40.5 miles*

> *Potomac River to Front Royal, Virginia* . . . . . *54.6 miles*

Maintaining Club:

> *The Potomac Appalachian Trail Club*

INTRODUCTION

THE WHOLE feel of the AT is about to change as it enters the South in earnest. History, geography, industry, culture—all will be quite different from what they were in the North.

This is a land of many ghosts. Great armies and other movements passed by here on the way to their destinies, and the story of these hills is written in their blood.

It is also a place where the mountains acted as a barrier. Settlement to the west could not take place until routes were traced through the seemingly endless line of the Blue Ridge and roads were built on them. It is for that reason that the same gaps, the same towns, appear in the history books in the French and Indian War all the way to the Civil War. Harpers Ferry is among the most contested spots in American history.

151

So walk, if you will, with John Brown and Stonewall Jackson. In these hills their memories are as alive today as they were a century ago.

GEOLOGY ALONG THE TRAIL

In the early Paleozoic era 600 million years ago, Maryland was in a vast sea over the continental shelf that formed so much of the rock strata later to be uplifted into the Appalachian Mountains. When the uplifts occurred during the great continental crashes of 450 and 350 million years ago this area was uplifted, forming the eastern border of the vast inland sea that extended to Minnesota. When the sea itself was uplifted 250 million years ago it was drained, with much of the flow exiting through the Potomac Gorge.

South Mountain, the ridge over which virtually the entire length of the Maryland section travels, is capped mainly by Paleozoic layers like the Weverton and Loudoun Formation metamorphics—sediments laid down in the early Paleozoic era, at the dawn of life, metamorphosed by the heat and pressure of their uplift into a mountain range. The Weverton Formation is characterized by gray quartzite, a hard, tough rock that would tend to prevent erosion of the ridge crest. Some later Paleozoic fossils can be found in younger layers at the very top of the summits, but in many places the rock has been eroded down to the 870-million-year-old metamorphosed lava flows that once lay under the sediment.

Like the rest of the Blue Ridge, South Mountain's rock strata is tilted upward toward the west. For that reason the western side will be somewhat steeper (although the difference won't be that great in a ridge this old and this weathered) and any cliffs or rock outcroppings will more likely be on the western side. It is divided by major water gaps in four places: Buzzard Knob, Turner's Gap, Crampton Gap, and finally at the Potomac River at the Virginia border.

HISTORY ALONG THE TRAIL

Maryland

The gorges on the Potomac or at Turner's Gap were among the most popular passages through the multilayered ridges of the

Appalachians. Coming up from the current site of Washington, D.C., a settler or explorer would be given a choice of continuing up the Potomac to the northwest, or branching off onto the Shenandoah to the southwest, toward the rich inland valleys of Virginia. It was through here that the settlers—largely German and Scots-Irish—passed on their way to settle their dream farms. It was also one of the most important trade routes, linking the Ohio valley with the East. The main road for a number of years in the early eighteenth century was the "Israel Friend's Mill Road," through Crampton Gap, which ran along the route of an old well-established Indian trail.

It was through Turner's Gap, though, that General Braddock, commander of British colonial forces during the French and Indian War, a young George Washington by his side, passed in 1755 on his way to defeat near what is now Pittsburgh. The retreating Washington, his general dead, may have paused there to refresh himself at the South Mountain Tavern, which still stands. What is probably the first monument to the first president has stood since 1827 on Monument Knob, just north of the gap.

On their way through, though, Braddock and Washington and their men created a wagon road that was later to become the famous National Road to the West. It was through here that most of the early traffic passed from Washington, D.C., to the Ohio valley and beyond. Abraham Lincoln stayed at the South Mountain Tavern on his way to Congress.

Western Maryland was crossroads for more than pioneers and traveling politicians, though. Located as it is, right on the Mason-Dixon line, ideas, runaway slaves, and, finally, armies passed this way as well.

South Mountain was an avenue for slaves escaping captivity. As they traveled along the present route of the Trail they lived in constant fear of the slave hunters, who kept careful watch in the mountains farther north, living on the bounties they received for captured escapees.

But the spirit of abolition made its presence felt in earnest in 1859 as zealot John Brown and a small army of sixteen white and five black followers arrived to strike a blow for Brown's dream of making part of Maryland a haven to escaping slaves. Over the summer they set up a headquarters in a farmhouse in the Maryland hills and waited. Then, on October 16, Brown and his band crossed the Potomac to Harpers Ferry and into history. Cornered by federal troops (under Robert E. Lee, as it turned out), he surrendered and was taken to nearby Charles Town, where he was tried, convicted of treason, and hanged. Several of his followers are said to have escaped north over South Mountain.

When the Civil War finally broke out, Maryland found itself in a precarious position. With sympathies that generally ran in favor of the South, the state had the ill fortune to be host to the Northern capital. Tensions around South Mountain quickly came to a head. Situated as it was at the mouth of the Shenandoah, the region was viewed anxiously by Confederate leaders. It was, after all, the gateway to the rich Shenandoah Valley, the "breadbasket of the South."

In 1862, Stonewall Jackson and Robert E. Lee took the offensive. The Southern army crossed the Potomac at South Mountain and proceeded north along its eastern flanks. After crossing to the west at Crampton Gap, Lee sent Jackson south again to capture Harpers Ferry and himself began maneuvering north toward Hagerstown for a run at Washington, D.C., from the northwest.

General George McClellan, the Union's boy wonder, marched with the Army of the Potomac to meet the threat. He had an incredible advantage beyond the fact that he vastly outnumbered his foe: One of his soldiers had found Lee's marching orders wrapped around three cigars, and had actually recognized their importance. They were delivered to McClellan forthwith. McClellan, on the other hand, spoke of his find openly, finally alerting Lee that he had the secret orders and also diddling away his advantage by endless rehashings of his line of attack.

The first skirmishes occurred at Turner's Gap and Crampton Gap as the Confederates under A. P. Hill fought to buy Lee time to reassemble his divided army. They bought several hours (McClellan's indecision gave them another whole day)—just long enough for Jackson to capture Harpers Ferry and return. The Washington Monument above Turner's Gap served for a time as a Union lookout (it is said to be haunted by the ghosts of a Union deserter and his lady fair, who shriek each year on September 17, anniversary of the battle of Antietam).

The two armies finally met at Sharpsburg, facing off

across Antietam Creek a few miles west of Crampton Gap, and they got down to cases. Lee had gone there to gather his scattered army and waited with eighteen thousand men on a bluff overlooking Antietam Creek for McClellan to arrive with his eighty-one-thousand-man hoard.

Arrive he did. And then he waited. For a whole day he pondered his battle plans, until Jackson arrived from Harpers Ferry and doubled the size of Lee's force. Then, cautiously, he engaged the Confederates. He succeeded in pushing them back and was actually on the verge of routing them when his many delays played their final trick: Another large unit (A. P. Hill's) arrived to Lee's aid. McClellan, tired of the fight, let the Confederates get away. But twenty thousand men died on the field at Antietam in what was to be the bloodiest battle in a bloody war. It was the costliest single engagement in American history.

Later in the war the huge armies swung to and fro on their way to their last confrontation in the North, at Gettysburg, just 20 miles or so from where South Mountain crosses the Pennsylvania line. The route of the Appalachian Trail stays fairly far from the site. It is true that Harpers Ferry changed hands from time to time during those days in 1862 to 1863. But in general the northward progress of the great armies occurred mostly to the east or west.

After the war, Maryland, spared the rigors of Reconstruction, settled back to business as usual. The moonshiners returned to South Mountain, where they had pursued a prosperous antebellum cottage industry, and other commerce such as textiles and the enterprise on the Chesapeake and Ohio Canal began to fade away. Floods on the Potomac occasionally washed out the bridges down in Harpers Ferry, and the countryside waited.

South Mountain waited until Myron Avery got his cohorts in the Potomac Appalachian Trail Club (PATC) moving. It was they, in the winter of 1931 and spring of 1932, who blazed the Trail along essentially the route it follows today. The greater part of the trailway is now protected.

Virginia

If you looked at the Shenandoah Valley from space you'd see a vast system of valleys running from Vermont and central

New York all the way to North Carolina and into Tennessee. This wide, fertile region formed one of the early breadbaskets of the United States.

The river and its valley have born the name Shenandoah for so long that the origins of the word have been lost and can only be guessed at. One tradition has it as a local Indian name meaning "Beautiful Daughter of the Stars." It could also have come from an Iroquois chief named "Sherando" who was at war with some of Powhatan's allies about the time of the founding of Jamestown. Then, too, there was a small Algonquin tribe in the lower valley (the northern end, since the river flows north) called the Senedoes. They were massacred by the Iroquois long before white settlers arrived. Shenandoah is also said to be similar to the Iroquois word meaning "Big Meadow." Take your choice.

Seeing how far south the valley reaches, it's tempting to assume that settlement moved across the mountain passes in some kind of orderly fashion and that the valley was populated from areas as widely separated as Richmond and Roanoke. And if it were as easily reached through the various gaps via paved highways, as it is today, that would certainly be the case.

In the seventeenth and eighteenth centuries, though, things were a bit different. The wall of the Blue Ridge rose in the west like a barrier set up by some devilish god. The thick Appalachian woods were all but impenetrable; the land beyond was unknown. So, after initial exploration in the 1660s and 1670s by a German, John Lederer, who was reputedly the first white to see the river (although Captain John Smith is said to have glimpsed the Blue Ridge in the early 1600s), the rich valley lay undisturbed.

It was left for settlement to come instead from the northeast. The clearest shot to the rich farmland was out of central Pennsylvania, down the Great Valley. It was the German immigrants from there who, in the 1720s, made the trip down the Cumberland Valley, through the Potomac gorge, and up the Shenandoah. They settled into their new homes about halfway into the valley. Once they were established, the way was paved for others to come from the Virginia coast, through the gaps.

The area through which the Trail travels in northern Virginia and bordering West Virginia falls within a land grant made by a grateful Charles II to Lord Fairfax. Fairfax had endeared himself to His Majesty by acting as one of the prime movers in Charles's ascension to the throne of Great Britain after the overthrow of the Cromwells in 1660. The grant included all lands between the Potomac and the Rappahannock rivers. As Virginia at the time had no clearly established western boundary, the grant was huge and went, as far as anybody knew, all the way to the Mississippi.

The typical absentee landlord, Fairfax sold off much of his holdings piecemeal to settlers and allowed squatters beyond number to ensconce themselves on much of the rest. However, in 1736 a Fairfax lord, Thomas by name, decided to take up residence. He surveyed a tract of nearly 120,000 acres between Hedgeman River and Carters Run and established the famous Manor of Leeds. He became one of the first to do this, building his new home, "Greenway Court," across the ridge in what is now Clarke County, Virginia. He established other manors as well: a nameless one between the "Upper Thoroughfare of the Blue Ridge" (now Ashby's Gap) and Williams Gap (now Snickers Gap); and "Gooney Run Manor" between Gooney Run and Happy Creek (now Chester Gap).

Fairfax was a clever man. In 1767, doubtless foreseeing the upcoming Revolution, he signed title for his manors over to his nephew, who immediately gave them back under a private title. After the successful War of Independence, his seignorial title from the king no longer valid, he still held the private title he had obtained from his nephew.

After the Revolution, the manor system in Virginia continued. Largely settled by runaway cavaliers during the Puritan commonwealth in the mid-seventeenth century, the colony thrived. One reason was the large slave labor force, which equaled the white population in numbers. In spite of the fact that the African slave trade was abolished in Virginia in 1778, the existing slave population was enough to keep renewing the number.

Still, when the North-South tensions grew to a fever pitch in the 1850s and 1860s, Virginia nearly did not secede, doing so only after Lincoln called upon the state for volunteers to fight the upcoming war.

Virginia's secession was a blessing beyond measure for the South. Not only did it get the rich Shenandoah Valley and a base from which to threaten the North, but it also got the Virginia gentry and their trained soldiery—men like Robert E. Lee, a skilled army officer and son of famous Revolutionary War hero "Light-Horse Harry" Lee, and Thomas J. "Stonewall" Jackson, whose lightning movements and diversionary tactics in the valley during the opening years of the war are legend.

After being completely baffled by Jackson in the first months of the war, it wasn't until after Gettysburg that the Union turned its attention on the valley in earnest. By mid-1864 Jubal Early, one of the slickest operators on either side, had repulsed all Northern efforts to penetrate the Shenandoah, and in turn had driven to within sight of Washington, D.C. U. S. Grant responded by sending Phil Sheridan down to settle Early's hash once and for all. Grant's choice was not auspicious for the valley. Sheridan was a ruthless warrior whose best-known legacy is a comment he made during the western Indian wars: "There is only one good Indian, and that is a dead one."

Grant's orders were perfectly suited to the Sheridan character. Not only did he want Sheridan to take possession of the valley; he wanted him to lay it waste—to "eat out Virginia clear and clean as far as they go, so that crows flying over it for the balance of this season will have to carry their provender with them. . . . We want the Shenandoah Valley to remain a barren waste."

Badly outnumbered, Early and his men fought valiantly against this new threat. Narrowly beaten at Winchester and driven from his stand on Fisher's Hill, Early watched as Sheridan put the torch to the northern end of the valley. Taking advantage of Sheridan's absence at a conference in Washington, Early attacked the Union army again south of Winchester. In a famous incident Sheridan arrived back just in time, making a celebrated ride from Winchester to rally his men and finally defeating Early. He then completed scorching the earth of the Shenandoah Valley, which spent the rest of the war as a burnt-over wasteland. Early continued to resist, going down to his last defeat at Waynesboro in March of 1865. For years thereafter, the view west from the Blue Ridge was not a pleasant one.

THE TRAIL IN MARYLAND

The trip through the Free State is without doubt the most straightforward route of the entire AT. For a length of just under 40 miles it stays within hooting distance of the crest of South Mountain from Pennsylvania to the Potomac.

Crossing the line at Pen-Mar State Park, the Trail continues along the western side of the ridge at about the 1300-foot level until it turns east to ascend to its highest point in Maryland—2000-foot Quirauk Mountain, the first 2000-plus-foot spot since northern Connecticut. It then turns south again, passing by a place called "Devil's Racecourse" due to its large boulders.

After passing, in rapid succession, three breaks in the ridge line at Raven Rock Hollow, Warner Gap, and Harman Gap, it again ascends the ridge, which runs unbroken for over 13 miles to Turner's Gap, after passing by the Washington Monument on the crest of the ridge.

Next stop, after a moderate spate of ridge-running, is Crampton Gap, site of the heaviest fighting during the Civil War battle of South Mountain (there are earthworks still preserved). Also of interest is the elaborate gate to the now-defunct Gathland, now Gathland State Park. Former estate of war correspondent George Alfred "Gath" Townsend, Gathland sports an arch, which is said to be the only war correspondent's memorial in the world. It's a study in nineteenth-century neoclassical allegory. Three smaller arches symbolize "Depiction," "Description," and "Photography." Above two shields labeled "Speed," and "Heed," were carved the heads of "Electricity" and "Poetry." Can't you just picture the hard-bitten newshounds assembled in a battleside tavern, discussing in poetic terms the sublime merits of "Depiction?"

After Crampton Gap the Trail ascends steeply once again to the ridge. Six miles down the way it passes Weverton Cliffs, for which the hard conglomerate quartzite of the ridge tops of South Mountain is named. At about the 1100-foot level the Trail makes a beeline for the Potomac. There, it switch-backs down into the gorge and heads up the canal and over the bridge to Harpers Ferry.

The C & O Canal (Chesapeake and Ohio) runs up the Potomac River from Washington, D.C., to Cumberland, Maryland, a distance of 185 miles. Begun in 1829, the building of the canal wasn't completed until 1850. As the Trail nears the Potomac, coming down from South Mountain at last, it crosses the canal and heads west to Harpers Ferry along the towpath, with the Potomac on the left and the abandoned canal on the right (it was put out of service permanently by a storm in 1924).

The C & O's status as a National Historic Park is due in part to a publicity walk taken by Supreme Court Justice William O. Douglas. Always the outdoorsman, Douglas enlisted in the efforts to save the abandoned towpath from development back in the 1950s. The plan was to put a superhighway along the route. His celebrated walk from Cumberland to Washington, D.C., in March of 1954 is credited with raising public attention about the canal, thereby causing its preservation. There were thirty-six other people in his party, including Olaus Murie, the renowned environmentalist. The little group was met on their route by delegations of local people offering support.

Harpers Ferry

Harpers Ferry, situated on a narrow tongue of land at the confluence of the Shenandoah and Potomac rivers, presents a spectacular view. Tucked down beneath towering bluffs on all sides, it was described by Thomas Jefferson as "perhaps one of the most stupendous scenes in nature . . . wild and tremendous . . . worth a voyage across the Atlantic . . ."

Before U. S. Grant's war of attrition ground the Southern armies down into a more defensive posture, Harpers Ferry was at the crossroads of the Civil War. Situated at a major river and canal junction near the Great Appalachian Valley, and site of a major military depot placed by George Washington himself, the ferry was critical in more ways than one.

From the Southern point of view the site was both a danger and an opportunity. A danger it certainly was. In Federal hands it lay too close for comfort to the Shenandoah Valley, which the Confederacy hoped to preserve as a safe food source for the war effort.

But effectively neutralized, the Great Valley system behind Harpers Ferry offered a road to the North. In 1862 Robert E. Lee used the route in an attempt to attack Washington, D.C., taking Harpers Ferry to protect the operation before coming to grief at Antietam. The following year, Harpers Ferry again in Northern hands, Lee had to race up the Great Valley from a point west. He went deep into Pennsylvania, almost to Harrisburg. The Union army, commanded by George Meade, didn't catch up with him until a place called Gettysburg. In his retreat, Lee had to cross the Potomac at Williamsport, far to the west.

If Harpers Ferry is known for anything, though, it is for abolitionist attempts in 1859 to use the Federal arsenal there as a staging point for a slave uprising. John Brown's name is inscribed deeply in the town to this day.

Also in Harpers Ferry is the national headquarters of the Appalachian Trail Conference. In a building on Washington Avenue, a small band of dedicated people handle virtually all the business of the national organization, and much of the work needed to support the various local clubs.

In addition to being the nerve center for the volunteer and professional efforts to maintain the Trail, the ATC also runs a service center/bookstore on the ground floor. Here you can find just about any trail guide or map you might want, both to the AT and to many of the major side trails.

The staff of the ATC share a real love for the Trail and for the people who hike it. If you get the impression that they're genuinely glad to see you when you walk in the door, you're right. They get much of the information they need to improve and maintain the Trail from simple hikers, so don't be surprised if they listen with interest as you tell of your experiences on the Trail.

If you're not a member already, you might consider joining the ATC. It's a great group to be part of.

THE TRAIL IN VIRGINIA

As the Trail winds up out of Harpers Ferry and across the Shenandoah River, it again takes a position astride the great ridge. This is the same Blue Ridge that went all the way through Maryland.

It was this first 18-mile section from Harpers Ferry toward

the south that the fledgling Potomac Appalachian Trail Club blazed in 1927 as their first effort on behalf of the AT. Standing atop Loudoun Heights, the hiker can readily see why Harpers Ferry changed hands so often during the Civil War: It is a veritable sitting duck for anybody who can control Loudoun and Maryland Heights across the Potomac. You'll also find evidence of the Union's recognition of this fact in the form of stone redoubts constructed to aid in the (as it turned out) futile defense of the arsenal.

The Loudoun Heights section is a popular walk. After a brisk 600-foot ascent from the bridge to the Heights, the walking along the ridge is easy and pleasant, running along the Virginia/West Virginia border. There is a short blue-blazed side trail down to the point of Loudoun Heights, which branches off from the AT when it first reaches the crest of the ridge, or an orange-blazed route that enters farther down the hill. The two, which have short spurs to good views at Chimney or Split Rocks, can easily be linked up into a pleasant loop.

The initial section of the AT between the Shenandoah River Bridge and Snickers Gap is a pretty straightforward run along the ridge. Although the route itself is secure from development, it runs a fairly narrow line between the settled and developed lands below. For that reason, except for a number of side trails coming in on either side, the trail system is somewhat limited. To hike sections, you'll have to leave a car at the opposite end of your planned route. This is only a minor inconvenience, and the fairly easygoing section of Trail, with occasional views, makes it worthwhile.

Twelve miles down, though, you'll run into the PATC's Blackburn Trail Center, down a quarter-mile spur. Not only does it have a number of fine side routes, but it's also the beginning of a more rugged part of the Blue Ridge, which will soon enter Shenandoah National Park at Front Royal. Used by the PATC as a work and recreational center, the Blackburn Center was named for longtime PATC stalwarts Ruth and Fred Blackburn. Fred, among other things, was the first chief of the Big Blue/Tuscarora Trail project. Ruth was a president of the PATC, and once received a conservation award from James Watt—a case of the bestower of the award being more honored by the company of the recipient than the other way around.

The Blackburn Center also offers campsites (for PATC members only) and water in season, and it sits at the northern end of a section of the ridge that has several trail loops available. Another 4 miles south and the Trail passes through the Raven Rocks area, in the farthest southeast corner of West Virginia. There are more lookouts here, including the third (or is it the fourth?) spot so far bearing the name "Devil's Racecourse."

South of Snickers Gap the Trail moves off the ridge line to the west to avoid a string of military installations on the crest. The continuous zigging and zagging into and out of the hollows and gullies prompts the PATC to declare this to be more strenuous than any other section in northern Virginia.

After the Trail passes Ashby's Gap (first known as the "Upper Thoroughfare of the Blue Ridge" and later as "Ashby's Bent," after Thomas Ashby, a contemporary of Thomas, Lord Fairfax), it once again sneaks up to near the ridge line. As it does, it comes into the first of two tracts of public land that it will pass in rapid succession. First, it reaches Meadows State Park and then leads into the G. Richard Thompson Wildlife Management Area, which is part of the Virginia Commission of Game and Inland Fisheries. Although the Trail route is not particularly spectacular (there is an unpaved road that runs right along the ridge line, reason enough for the Trail to zigzag around on the side slopes), these two parcels of state land do offer access, campsites (at Meadows, for a fee), and a system of trails suitable for creating nice day-hike loops.

As a last point of interest in the northern Virginia section, the Trail skirts through the small gap between High Knob and Ravensden Rock. It is here, a few yards down the little valley from the Trail, that the mighty Rappahannock trickles out from among the rocks and roots.

The Trail then crosses Route 55 and heads for the entrance to Shenandoah National Park over some pleasant unpaved lanes.

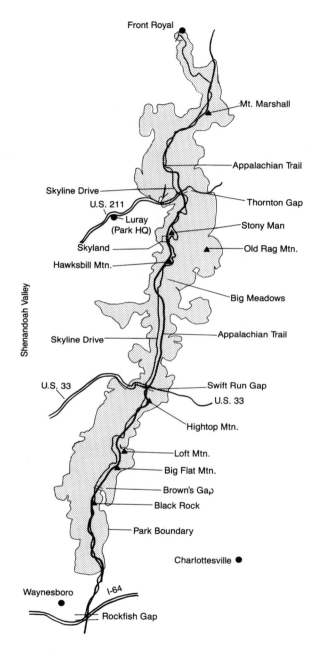

Front Royal

Mt. Marshall

Appalachian Trail

Skyline Drive

U.S. 211

Thornton Gap

Luray
(Park HQ)

Stony Man

Skyland

Old Rag Mtn.

Hawksbill Mtn.

Big Meadows

Shenandoah Valley

Skyline Drive

Appalachian Trail

U.S. 33

Swift Run Gap

U.S. 33

Hightop Mtn.

Loft Mtn.

Big Flat Mtn.

Brown's Gap

Black Rock

Park Boundary

Charlottesville

Waynesboro

I-64

Rockfish Gap

Shenandoah National Park

10

Shenandoah National Park, Virginia

Trail Distance:

> *Front Royal, Virginia, to Rockfish Gap . . . . . 106.6 miles*

Maintaining Club:

> *The Potomac Appalachian Trail Club, in cooperation with the National Park Service*

INTRODUCTION

SHENANDOAH NATIONAL Park is the first of several tracts of federal land along the Appalachian ridge line in the South that protect the largest part of the route all the way to Springer Mountain. Together, these lands form the heart of the southern Appalachians and do much to give the Trail the feel and spirit it has today.

Shenandoah Park is where the Blue Ridge really becomes the Blue Ridge. It's the first time since Killington Peak in Vermont that the trail ascends a ridge that stands over 4000 feet (and the first trip over 3000 feet since Greylock in Massachusetts), and because of its protection in the national park system, it's far more than just a narrow ridge-line strip of green between housing subdivisions.

The park today has the mixed blessing of the Skyline

Drive running at or near the crest of the ridge all the way from end to end. This thirty-five-miles-per-hour two-lane highway does give hikers easy access to some of the finest hiking trails in the East. Though the five-dollar, seven-day park pass is the best deal in town, there is another price. You can never truly get away from the road, and it is often somewhat obtrusive.

But the park is large—almost 200,000 acres. Plan right, and you can get a good long way off the highway. But since the drive and the Trail often follow much the same route, you'll probably want to consider the excellent system of side trails.

GEOLOGY ALONG THE TRAIL

It's an indication of the violence of the uplift that created the Appalachians that the rocks along the crest of the Blue Ridge are among the oldest in the area. The characteristic greenstone is the metamorphosed basalt that was laid down as layer upon layer of lava in the distant Precambrian era. The granodiorite at Mary's Rock and Stony Man, and the granite on Old Rag, are both far older.

Let's start a billion years or so ago. This was the age of the Grenville Event, that imperfectly understood uplift of the original Appalachians, which were eroded away before the current ones were formed. At the time—1.1 billion years ago, to be precise—the area of Shenandoah Park was being subjected to pluton activity. Huge masses of molten rock were bubbling up from underneath, forming hills and highlands. How high these hills rose is a matter of conjecture. We do know that by the time the volcanic activity that followed started burying the hills, nearly half a billion years later, they were still up to 1000 feet tall, so they must originally have been impressive.

The volcanic activity that accompanied the breakup of the Grenville supercontinent, 700 million years ago, was prolonged and considerable. Oozing up to the surface through dikes in the existing rock (these are clearly visible on the trail to Old Rag, where greenstone dikes have eroded away, leaving narrow corridors in the granite), the lava laid layer upon layer of basalt around the hills. There are perhaps seven major layers of basalt in many places.

When the volcanism ended it left an enormously thick

layer of banded basalt. Interspersed between layers was a kind of shale—now metamorphosed into slate—that was the result of volcanic ash, mud, and erosion between the volcanic episodes. This is clearly visible as the dark gray to purple slate that is so easily recognized beneath the greenstone. It's easy to see in such places as the south side of Compton Peak, Swift Run Gap, Smith Roach Gap, and on Bearfence Mountain.

Now remember, this volcanic activity took place on a coastal plain very much like the one to the east of the park today. The lava layer was soon covered by a thin layer of sand that probably eroded off the basalt and granite hilltops. Then the water rose.

As the ancient Cambrian sea rose, the coastal plain became a beach. The sediment from the disappearing hills to the west formed a deep layer (up to 1000 feet deep) of clean white sand, which kept accumulating. Mud and silt built up in some places from ocean deposits and in other places from rivers flowing in. Eventually a layer of limestone may have capped the entire sequence. The resulting limestone is absent from the Blue Ridge but can be seen farther west (it forms the floor of the Shenandoah Valley). But it may easily have been present at one time, only to erode away completely.

Then all hell broke loose. As plates migrated and continents collided, this enormously thick sequence of layers was crushed together like an accordion, tilted, cracked, and eventually thrust over itself like a rug being pushed along a floor. The layers present in the park have been tilted up and over maybe as much as 110 degrees from where they started. The younger, later rocks are exposed to the west; the older Precambrian granites are exposed to the east.

Since the uplift ended (perhaps 250 million years ago), erosion has been the name of the game. Where the rocks were tough, mountains remained; the durable granite left Old Rag Mountain, for example. The erosion-resistant greenstone and granodiorite form the main ridge in most places. The softer and more water-soluble limestones eroded away.

In places the Blue Ridge is flanked by boulder fields similar to those throughout Pennsylvania, and they all formed for the same reasons. The freeze/thaw that resulted from having a 1000-foot-thick blanket of ice just 200 miles to the north cracked and split off huge boulders. Those of resistant rock types, like the quartzites, have remained.

Another major influence on the present-day shape of the Blue Ridge is water action. The gaps especially have been formed by streams and rivers coursing through them. In some gaps, where other streams have pirated the watershed away to one side or the other, "wind gaps" have formed—notches in the ridge line with no stream. Manassas Gap to the north of the park is a good example.

HISTORY ALONG THE TRAIL

Like the sections of the Trail to the north of the park, this part overlooks the rich Shenandoah Valley. It is through the four major gaps in the park that much of the western expansion of the eighteenth century took place.

First Settlers

When the first German settlers arrived from Pennsylvania in the 1720s, the valley was relatively uninhabited by native peoples. No one knows the reason why for sure, but the region had been populated prior to then. Perhaps the repeated raids and massacres by the Iroquois Nations from the north had suc-ceeded in exterminating some groups and discouraging others from living out in the open. The Iroquois, who were known locally as the Massawomek, regularly used the ridge and the valley as a route when sending war parties against their favorite enemies, the Catawbas of North Carolina.

The original settlers appeared to be mainly Algonquins, who were in turn harried by raiding tribes from all sides—not just Iroquois but also Lenni Lenapes, Cherokees, and Sus-quehannocks. Even when the valley wasn't inhabited it was used as a key route between places, just as it is today. There was a major trade route along what is now Interstate 81 and a ridge-top war route that roughly followed the current route of the AT.

After Lederer's initial explorations in 1669 to 1670, others followed. Some went to trade furs, others to explore as Lederer had done. One expedition, organized by the governor of Virginia, dandy Alexander Spotswood, crossed the ridge at Swift Run Gap and went down into the valley below. There they drank a toast, fired a salute, and claimed it all for their king, George I. Then they drank quite a few more toasts. Real estate matters were simpler then.

Settlement followed quickly. Before the eighteenth century was very much older the Great Wagon Road had been established (again, along the route of the Native American trading trails). In addition to the Germans who followed Lederer's lead came Scots-Irish and Swiss. Part of the reason for the speed of the settlement was, no doubt, the fact that unlike other desirable regions, there were no native populations to be dispossessed somehow.

Though the French and Indian War of the early 1760s forced many settlers back across the ridge, everybody returned once things were settled. Perhaps unsure of British support for their welfare in light of their vulnerability to French and Indian attack, and definitely annoyed by Crown interference with westward expansion (the royal edict of 1763 prohibiting settlement west of the Appalachian ridge was a very sore point), the valley (and indeed, the rest of Virginia) supported the Revolution with vigor.

The Ridge and the Revolution

The Blue Ridge in the park was to figure in the Revolution in at least one quirky way. In 1781, with the bulk of the fighting moved to the coastal plains of Virginia, the British were threatening the state capital at Williamsburg. Then-governor Thomas Jefferson decided to remove the state archives and seal to prevent their capture or destruction. He entrusted one Bernis Brown with their safety.

Brown was one of the Browns of Brown's Gap, in the southern section of the park. At first he brought the items to his home below the gap, but when the British started inching closer he decided to hide them better still.

Loading his cargo onto the backs of mules, Brown and an unidentified "mountaineer" (someone residing in the mountains) headed up to the height of Brown's Gap. Then, they turned south toward Black Rocks. There, they hid the Virginia state archives and official seal in a cave until the war was over—to this day, no one knows exactly where.

Mary's Rock

Many of the streams and gaps got their names from the families that settled near them. Often, there would be a planta-tion below, and the features on the ridge above would bear some name bestowed by the owners. The manors were established early on. Gooney Manor, for example, was one of Thomas, Lord Fairfax's plantations, which he established in the 1740s. It passed into the hands of the Marshall family, one of whom (John) became chief justice of the Supreme Court.

One example of an early family's name enduring is Thorn-ton Gap, which is named for Francis Thornton. He was given a parcel of land by his father that stretched up from the piedmont into the Blue Ridge. This was in the early eighteenth century.

Thornton and his wife, Mary, set up housekeeping at his plantation in "F.T. Valley," which runs from near Sperryville south to the foot of Old Rag Mountain. Shortly after they moved there the two went on a camping trip up into Thornton Gap. They camped at a spring just below the summit of Great Pass Mountain. The next day, Thornton took Mary to the top, where he presented the mountain to her as a wedding gift. Each year thereafter, they would return to the rock and camp at the spring, which became known as "Mary's Spring."

When Francis died, Mary moved up to a cabin in Thornton Gap, from which she could see Mary's Rock. The entire section of the gap became known as "Madame Thornton's Quarter."

The rock and spring became, in the early- to mid-nine-teenth century, a popular courting spot for local couples. An invitation to a private picnic on the rock was usually followed by a proposal of marriage.

According to AT historian Jean Stephenson, writing in 1945, the site of the spring was lost sometime in the latter half of the nineteenth century. Perhaps, she speculated, it petered out, or the "roan oak," under whose roots the spring was said to emerge, had died and fallen. Those interested in locating the spring should find the old path that leads uphill from Meadow

Spring. Mary's Spring was said to lie between a half- and a quarter-mile below Mary's Rock, at the spot where the climbing became steep.

The Civil War

The Blue Ridge at Shenandoah Park was witness to much of the same Civil War action already described. These hills must have provided shelter and a lookout for Jubal Early's men as they desperately tried to hold on in the waning days of the war. One can almost picture groups of lean hungry Confederates posted on the rocks on the western slopes of the ridge, watching ugly columns of black smoke in the valley below, and imagine their sadness as the land they tried so valiantly to defend was consumed by flames. They met their final defeat a month before Appomattox, at Waynesboro at the southern end of the park.

The Coming of the Park

After the war the land surrounding the ridge remained rural. Since the farmers of the Shenandoah Valley had never been large slaveholders, little changed in their way of life. They continued to farm and send their products—corn, flour, leather, fruit, and lime they mined from the bedrock and purified in a kiln—down to market via the C & O Canal at Harpers Ferry. To get their goods that far, they loaded them onto "gundalows," barges up to 9 feet wide and 75 feet long, which were poled down the treacherous bends and shallows of the Shenandoah by fifteen or more men. These would be taken to the canal head, unloaded, and broken up and sold for timber. The crew would then walk home. This trade went on from 1798, when the fleet was established, on into the 1890s.

As the nineteenth century closed and the notion of the romantic wilderness seized the spirits of urbanites, the Blue Ridge caught the attention of people from the lowlands bent on more than exploration and farming. Perhaps the most important of these, from the park's point of view, was George Freeman Pollock, the founder of an elaborate camp/resort he named Skyland. In the early 1890s he began scouting out the territory in what is now the central section of the park, looking to establish his resort.

The ridge at the time was inhabited by "mountaineers." These poor, simple folk were the forerunners of the next generation that had such trouble with the prohibition enforcement officers of the Treasury Department. In those days they also had a sizable cottage distilling operation going. It wasn't illegal then.

Pollock's activities were met with a variety of responses by the locals. In general, they regarded him as somewhat strange— much the way country people have always regarded city people. On occasion, though, they took exception to his altering of the hills and their way of life.

This led to at least one incident. In 1893, Pollock and a group of friends were hiking around in the area when they ran into one of Pollock's neighbors, a mountaineer named Fletcher. Relations between the two had never been friendly, but on this occasion Fletcher took them one step further. While his son held the group at gunpoint, Fletcher proceeded to thrash Pollock, warning him to leave the hills and not to come back upon threat of murder. Pollock, of course, ignored the warning, taking care to avoid running into Fletcher unarmed in the future. He later had friendly relations with the mountaineer's son Johnny.

Once established, Skyland became a jumping-off point into the Blue Ridge, and especially to Old Rag Mountain, which is one of the most popular hikes even to this day. Pollock became instrumental in the establishment of the park and the Trail through it. There are newspaper accounts of his entertaining highly placed National Park Service (NPS) managers as early as 1926, as well as hosting a young man by the name of Myron Avery, recently moved down from Connecticut.

Pollock's dealings with the Park Service were all part of the beginnings of the Shenandoah National Park. In an effort that began in 1923 with the NPS recommendation of a park in the southern Appalachians, by 1926 nearly $3 million had been raised and the land purchase begun.

Some of the mountaineers had no desire to move, and had to be wheedled and cajoled out. Many were relocated in the valleys and hollows to the west, bordering the park. The effort took nearly ten years. In the end, the NPS succeeded in obtaining, through purchase and trade, 176,430 acres. Once the park was dedicated in 1936, the Civilian Conservation Corps (CCC) moved in with their axes and shovels and began building. They would later figure prominently in the history of the Trail in the park.

It was by then apparent what Myron Avery had been doing at Skyland. Since the formation of the Potomac Appalachian Trail Club, the Trail had been blazed over the ridge in what would soon be the national park. No sooner was it finished, though, than it had to be moved.

This was due to the construction of the Skyline Drive, begun in 1931 and completed in 1939. Since the drive followed the AT route closely (AT trailblazers have always been such skilled route finders that they have had this problem wherever they go), the park had to build the relocation. This was done in grand style by the CCC.

The Shenandoah National Park section has long reigned as the crown jewel of the Potomac Appalachian Trail Club section of the AT. Right from the very beginning in 1927 their annual get-together (the famous "Midsummer Frolic") has been held at Skyland. Skyland still exists and is operated today by the Park Service.

Use of the park has slowly increased since the 1950s, with attendance taking quantum leaps in the late 1960s. One problem that arose in those days was abuse of park facilities by unskilled back-to-the-landers who would take up residence in the shelters and create untold havoc. Current rules against short-term use of shelters except in emergencies and by thru-hikers were prompted by a desire to solve this problem.

THE TRAIL IN THE SHENANDOAH NATIONAL PARK

Except for a 3.5-mile section in the north and 8 miles in the south, the Trail in this section runs entirely through park land. It quickly ascends to the ridge at Compton Gap at about 2400 feet and heads in a generally southwesterly direction, staying very close to the ridge line all the way to Rockfish Gap.

Two things conspire to make the park a superb site for day hiking and short-term tripping. First is the access made possible by the Skyline Drive. With the Trail never more than a few hundred yards from the drive and parking areas every few miles, it is relatively easy to gain access to just about any point within the park.

Then there is the system of blue-blazed side trails, yellow-blazed horse/foot trails, and assorted nature trails that crisscross everywhere. There are over 500 miles of these, all maintained by the Potomac Appalachian Trail Club and the Park Service. They seem to hit just about every peak, lookout, meadow, and water-fall—of which there are dozens. These side trails offer unparalleled opportunities for side hikes and loops, and are too numerous to be covered in detail here. A book called *Circuit Hikes in the Shenandoah National Park* is available from the PATC.

Of note, though, is the Big Blue Trail, which strikes off to the west from a point just north of Elkwallow Gap in the northern section. This is more than just a side trail. It is the end of the Tuscarora/Big Blue Trail that branched off back in Pennsylvania. Because it was blazed with the typical blue blazes denoting a side trail, the PATC members involved began referring to it affectionately as Big Blue. The name stuck.

Unlike Pennsylvania, where the Trail sticks onto the 1400-foot level like glue, in the Shenandoah Park it goes up and down from peak to valley to knob to gap. In the northern section, for example, it goes, in just a 3-mile space, from Hogback Mountain to Elkwallow Gap: 3400 feet all the way down to around 2400 feet; then, from nearby Thornton Gap, it's immediately back up to 3500 feet on Mary's Rock.

On the other hand, the general condition of the Trail is evidence of the care the Park Service takes of its property. The grading and foot bed of the Trail have eliminated most of the rough edges and you could practically wheel a shopping cart up most sections. If it can be strenuous going up the many hills, it cannot be said to be rough.

Side hikes in the park are often unique in that they usually start at the high point, dip down into the lowlands, and then have to go back up to get back to the car. This is especially true of hikes to see the many waterfalls within the park. Several stand out.

Big Falls (northern section), at 93 feet the tallest of the cascades in the park, lies about 3.5 miles down the Big Blue Trail. It's in the Elkwallow area, which has many side trails even by park standards. You can take the swing down the Big Falls and keep right on going, returning by any of several interesting loops.

Perhaps the best cascade hike, though, is down White Oak Run (central section). Over a distance of about a mile are a half-dozen falls ranging in height from 35 to 86 feet. They can be reached from Skyland on the White Oak Canyon Trail, which you might want to consider as an alternate route (albeit a lengthy one) either to or from Old Rag Mountain. White Oak Canyon also makes an excellent loop when combined with the Cedar Run Trail, which has falls of its own. They are, however, exceedingly popular day hikes, so expect to run into people unless you're there way out of season.

In the southern section the best cascades are on Doyles River, just east of Brown's Gap. At 28 and 63 feet tall, these are quite worth the trip, and have the added advantage of being closer to the road than many other falls. One can imagine Bernis Brown and his mountaineer companion passing by in 1781 on their way to stash the state archives at Black Rocks.

The Popular Central Section

Since the establishment of Skyland late in the last century, the middle portion of the area covered by the park has been by far the best liked. Not only does it have the best waterfalls, but it also has the highest, ruggedest, most spectacular peaks, and some of the most interesting terrain.

Hawksbill Mountain, of course, is at 4050 feet the highest point in the park. Like most of the other high points it is made of greenstone, the remains of the lava flows of 700 million years ago. Just beneath the summit knob the AT reaches the highest point yet achieved in the park at around 3600 feet. This will be topped just south of Big Meadows on Hazeltop, over 3800 feet.

Old Rag Mountain lies just off the main ridge to the east of Skyland. Unlike the main summits, it is constructed of the old granite left over from the plutons of 1.1 billion years ago. Especially sought after on this most popular of peaks within the park is the Ridge Trail, which is picked up on the northern approach to the mountain from either the small parking area near the hamlet of Nethers or via the Corbin Hollow or Nicholson Hollow trails. On this route the Trail passes up through narrow rock-walled corridors that are actually the remains of the dikes through which lava flowed 700 million years ago to form the thick layer of greenstone. The somewhat softer basalt has eroded out of the dike, leaving just the harder granite side walls.

Big Meadows are interesting in another way. Composed of plant communities that would be more naturally found several hundred miles to the north, these wide fields are, like the famous balds to the south, most likely the last remains of more boreal ecosystems left over from the retreat of the last ice age. If that's the case, then the more typical southern Appalachian forests are slowly encroaching on the meadows. They may only last a few thousand more years, so see them while you can.

The Wild Southern Section

Much of the southern part of the park is designated as Federal Wilderness Area. That's not just a paper title. Only areas that qualify can be so named, and once given Wilderness designation, the land has just about as powerful a protection as it can get.

This section of the park is much less developed—and much less visited—than the other two. It is also much wider than some other sections, offering the hiker and backpacker a chance to get a fair piece away from the crowds.

It might surprise some people that the AT doesn't actually pass through the tracts of Wilderness Area, but there's good reason for that. Running as it does along the crest of the Blue Ridge, and accompanied every step of the way by the Skyline Drive, the Trail is disqualified by default from being in a Wilderness area: such lands must be roadless. For that reason, hikers wanting solitude must take to the blue blazes. As elsewhere in the park, the side trails in the southern section go just about everywhere.

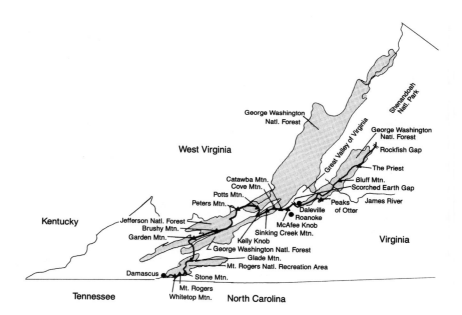

George Washington
Natl. Forest

Shenandoah
Natl. Park

West Virginia

Great Valley of Virginia

George Washington
Natl. Forest

Rockfish Gap

The Priest

Catawba Mtn.
Cove Mtn.

Bluff Mtn.
Scorched Earth Gap

Potts Mtn.

Peters Mtn.

James River

Peaks
of Otter

Daleville

Kentucky

Roanoke

Jefferson Natl. Forest
Brushy Mtn.

McAfee Knob

Sinking Creek Mtn.

Garden Mtn.

Virginia

Kelly Knob

George Washington Natl. Forest

Glade Mtn.

Mt. Rogers Natl. Recreation Area

Damascus

Stone Mtn.

Mt. Rogers

Tennessee

Whitetop Mtn.

North Carolina

Central and Southern Virginia

11

The Central/ Southwest Virginia Section

Trail Distance:

> *Rockfish Gap to Damascus, Virginia . . . . . . 380.2 miles*

Section Maintenance:

> *Old Dominion Appalachian Trail Club: Rockfish Gap to Reeds Gap . . . . 15.4 miles*
>
> *Tidewater Appalachian Trail Club: Reeds Gap to Tye River . . . . 9.9 miles*
>
> *Natural Bridge Appalachian Trail Club: Tye River to Black Horse Gap . . . . 87.9 miles*
>
> *Roanoke Appalachian Trail Club: Black Horse Gap to Stony Creek Valley/New River to Virginia Route 608 (Brushy Mountain) . . . . 108.2 miles*
>
> *Kanawha Trail Club: Stony Creek Valley to New River . . . . 20.7 miles*
>
> *Virginia Tech Outing Club: Virginia Route 608 (Brushy Mountain) to Virginia Route 623 (Garden Mountain) . . . . 29.6 miles*

Piedmont Appalachian Trail Hikers: Virginia Route 623 (Brushy Mountain) to Virginia Highway 16 (Brushy Mountain) . . . . *40.8 miles*

Mt. Rogers Appalachian Trail Club: Virginia Route 16 to Damascus . . . . *50.7 miles*

INTRODUCTION

"It cannot be said to be finished—and a completely finished trail would be one to avoid."
                    THE ROANOKE APPALACHIAN TRAIL CLUB

IT IS in this section of the Old Dominion that the AT had some of its greatest challenges. Once so remote and wild that it was one of the hardest sections to blaze, the route here was threatened several times by a variety of things, ranging from federal road-building to simple development. The unbroken Trail has in the past been difficult—and at times actually impossible—to maintain. That it passes through an uninterrupted—and by now largely protected—right-of-way is tribute to countless hours on the part of volunteers and professionals alike.

Southwest Virginia is where the arrow-straight ridges over which the Trail has passed since near the New York/New Jersey border become much more complicated. They split up and in places disappear into the flatlands below, only to reappear farther south. The Trail in this section leaves the Blue Ridge, crosses the Great Valley, and passes for a time over the westernmost ranges of the Appalachian system, the Alleghenies.

As the Appalachian Trail heads for Tennessee and North Carolina and the home stretch toward Springer, it climbs into increasingly tall mountains and passes through more and more federally protected land. By the time it reaches Damascus and the Tennessee border, it will have climbed above 4000 and even 5000 feet, staying once again along the crest of a ridge easily as impressive as the Green and White mountains far to the north. The narrow corridors through which it must pass in the more developed places to the north give way to acres and acres of national forest and Wilderness area—fabulous, beautiful, and wild lands that offer in full measure the re-creation of the spirit that Benton MacKaye intended his Trail to offer to civilization-weary hikers.

GEOLOGY ALONG THE TRAIL

As in any part of the Appalachian chain, the ridges and side peaks south of Rockfish Gap are a continuation of trends that started far to the north and that will continue far to the south. Various rock layers have been shoved up along a line of overthrust faults—sidewise breakages in the rock strata in which layers are shoved up over other layers like playing cards scooped into a pile. The resulting mountains frequently feature older layers lying *above* younger ones.

Rockfish Gap has given its name to a fault, which marks the thrust of one rock formation, the Lovington Formation, over another, the Pedlar. The Lovington terrane is composed of Precambrian gneisses and granites—the ancient granites that bubbled up through the earth's crust toward the surface. The Pedlar Formation it climbed over is composed of granodiorites and the greenstone (metamorphosed basalt) and various sedimentary/metamorphic strata that remain from the inland sea of half an eon ago.

The Rockfish Valley Fault is a scissors-type fault, starting small just south of Old Rag Mountain in Shenandoah National Park and increasing in displacement over the 100 or so miles it travels to the south. It's as though the southern reaches were swung over each other with the northern point near Old Rag acting as a pivot.

The Trail soon comes down off the Blue Ridge and heads over the Valley of Virginia toward the western ranges of the Appalachians: the Alleghenies. The valley is a continuation of the enormous valley system that travels through the Shenandoah River drainage, through Pennsylvania to central New York state, where it passes Albany before heading up to form the Great Valley of Vermont. It is mostly underlain by limestones, indicating its origin in shoreline carbonate banks of the shallow Cambrian and Ordovician inland sea. These were left from before the sea was uplifted by the onrushing European and African plates, nearly 300 million years ago. Down the center of the valley is a sandstone syncline, a continuation of Massanutten

Mountain, the prowed parallel ridge so prominent just to the west of Shenandoah National Park. This runs as mountain down to about Harrisonburg, halfway down Shenandoah Park, but continues as a poorly defined syncline all the way to below Waynesboro.

The valley floor is undercut by many caverns that have dissolved their way into the carbonate rock strata beneath. Natural Bridge, to the west of the AT route, is a former cavern that has eroded away except for one part of the roof that remains as a span.

South of Roanoke the Blue Ridge peters out down to the level of the piedmont to the east. It will pick up again farther south. At that point it also splits, forming a huge elliptical formation with the Blue Ridge proper to the east, and a series of other, generally higher ranges, such as the Unakas and the Great Smokies, to the west. There is in some places as much as 50 miles between the two ranges.

As the Trail moves farther to the west, toward its route in the Alleghenies, it enters the zone of rocks formed in the ancient inland seas of 400 million years ago. These rocks consist of the sandstones, graywackes, and shales that accumulated until they were finally uplifted less than 300 million years ago in the Alleghany Orogeny. This was the final, and heaviest, crunch of all, when all of Africa collided with North America, buckling the continent all the way to the borders of the Midwest.

West of the Allegheny Mountains lies the Allegheny Plateau, an uplifted area that was too far inland to be folded and faulted, but was raised up just the same. It forms much of the land in central and western New York and Pennsylvania and southward toward the Ohio Valley. Glacial gouges in the Allegheny Plateau, once hundreds and even thousands of feet deep, survive today as the Finger Lakes of New York.

HISTORY OF THE APPALACHIAN TRAIL IN CENTRAL AND SOUTHERN VIRGINIA

When the Trail was first blazed in the late 1920s and early 1930s, it continued southward along the crest of the Blue Ridge as it had done since Pennsylvania. At the time, Roanoke was a trail town and the Peaks of Otter section was among the most popular routes.

In the mid-1930s, though, trouble brewed for the section of the Trail south of Shenandoah National Park. In 1935 the Park Service was proposing the extension of the Skyline Drive farther down the Blue Ridge, all the way into North Carolina and Tennessee. It was a controversial move and, as you'd expect, sides were chosen up very quickly.

Therein lies one of the great tragedies of the AT, because the two luminaries of the Trail movement, Benton MacKaye, the spiritual head, and Myron Avery, the administrative one, took opposite sides. Avery favored the extension of the drive; Mac-Kaye opposed it.

It was probably inevitable. The two men, though equally passionate in their desire to see the Trail completed, were of necessity opposite in their reasoning and methods. It has long been an axiom of movements that the idea people tend not to be the best organizers. So, while the original idea of the Trail and its accompanying parkland were MacKaye's, he never really attempted to be the one who coordinated the realization of the dream.

Avery, on the other hand, was a goal-oriented man who would let nothing stand in the way once he had decided on a course of action. Energetic beyond belief, inspiring, occasionally abrasive, and psychologically incapable of taking no for an answer, he was the perfect choice to head up the Appalachian Trail Conference.

Avery's point of view was simple: The extension of Skyline Drive (which would be called the Blue Ridge Parkway) would make the new Trail through the southern reaches of the Blue Ridge more accessible. Just as the Park Service had done in Shenandoah National Park, so would they here: The Trail could be moved away from the route.

It would have to be. The proposed route of the drive's extension was virtually identical to that of the Trail for a distance of 202 miles. Avery's response was predictable: "It is perhaps a great tribute to the original route of The Appalachian Trail that so much of the Blue Ridge Parkway connecting the Shenandoah National Park to the Great Smokies, is almost superimposed on the Appalachian Trail in Southern Virginia." He went on to say that the nearness of the highway would help solve another chronic problem of the Trail: maintenance in remote sections.

MacKaye, for his part, felt that the highway would inevitably interfere with the wilderness feel of the ridge. That, in his mind, was paramount.

Anyway, the two exchanged letters. They were said to be heated communications. MacKaye accused Avery of destroying the purpose of the Trail along the Blue Ridge. Avery accused MacKaye of insensitivity to a local problem of access. MacKaye withdrew from most ATC activities. (ATC members can console themselves in the thought that all the time he was outside the Conference, MacKaye was spending his energy on the founding of The Wilderness Society.) It would be years before the father of the Appalachian Trail would once again be a close part of the movement he inspired.

The route ran into a time of troubles. Development began encroaching on the wildlands through which it passed even while the ATC and the Park Service were trying to complete the rerouting made necessary by the building of the Blue Ridge Parkway. In a region where just a decade before, trail-blazing efforts were hampered by remoteness and even by lack of maps, the AT was rapidly reaching the point at which it would have to be put onto roads. When World War II hit right in the middle of the effort, what would today be considered unthinkable happened: Gaps appeared in the Trail, and the continuous 2000-mile route was broken. It wasn't until the last 9.5-mile section between The Priest and Three Ridges was completed in 1951 that the route through central Virginia was made whole again.

That wasn't the end of the trouble, though. As I mentioned, in the years that followed the completion of the rerouting around the new Blue Ridge Parkway, the land south of the James River became increasingly developed. The footpaths over which the Trail passed became roads; roads became highways. By the early 1940s it was conceded—even by Myron Avery—that something had to be done about it.

Enter the Roanoke Appalachian Trail Club. Under the guidance of the club's president, Jim Denton, an opportunity was found. The federal government had just purchased more land for the Jefferson National Forest to the west of the existing route, offering a new avenue over the Alleghenies. Denton proposed the change to Myron Avery, still president of the ATC, and

Avery reluctantly agreed. (First, though, Avery insisted that they blaze the entire section along the old route—even if most of it had to be on paved roads, which it in fact did: Priority number one was to reestablish the complete 2000 miles. Denton and company complied.)

The new section was blazed between 1952 and 1954, with the first blaze made on Sinking Creek Mountain on April 20, 1952. When it was dedicated in May of 1954, the relocation was presented to the ATC by the Roanoke Appalachian Trail Club, saying, "We, the Roanoke Appalachian Trail Club . . . proudly present to the Appalachian Trail Conference the consummation of a 20-year dream. It cannot be said to be finished—and a completely finished trail would be one to avoid." It is possibly as eloquent a recognition as there has been in the history of the AT that the Trail is a living, growing thing, constantly changing and improving.

THE TRAIL IN CENTRAL AND
SOUTHWEST VIRGINIA

One thing to do right off the bat, once you've gotten your trail guide, is figure which map follows which in order, and then mark them clearly. There's no indication on the maps as to their proper order.

The Trail continues south from Rockfish Gap once it leaves Shenandoah National Park and immediately climbs again to the crest of the Blue Ridge. For the first several miles the trailway is within a narrow corridor provided by the Blue Ridge Parkway, which the AT crosses several times. The Trail quickly ascends to over 3000 feet and stays there most of the way down the ridge.

After paralleling the Blue Ridge Parkway for about 16 miles, the Trail branches off to the south, following the Three Ridges (3970 feet) up into the "Religious Range." Here, on "The Priest" (other peaks are named Little Priest, The Cardinal, and The Friar), it actually crosses over 4000 feet for the first time since Killington in Vermont. The area, which alternated between George Washington National Forest and private land, is criss-crossed by trails and unimproved roads offering access from the roads below.

You will run across remnants of the record-breaking rain-storm that hit here in August of 1969. In places, nearly a yard of rain was said to have fallen in under six hours. There are slides everywhere. Meteorologists theorize that such rainstorms may hit only once in a century—or in a millennium. This one was the result of Hurricane Camille, downgraded into a tropical storm, coming over the ridge and bumping smack into another air mass.

Staying close to the side ridge along which the route takes it, the AT repeatedly crosses over 4000 feet at Maintop Mountain (4040 feet), Rocky Mountain (4072 feet), Cole Mountain (4022 feet), and Bald Knob (4059 feet), before finally crossing Brown Mountain Creek valley and heading back up to the Blue Ridge Parkway at Little Irish Creek. It immediately leaves the highway, continuing across it to the west. At Fuller Rocks, over-looking the James River, it offers one of the finest views any-where on the whole trailway: hikers can see from the Alle-ghenies to the west all the way across the piedmont to the east.

After crossing the James on the Route 501 bridge (at 660 feet, the lowest point on the AT in central Virginia), the Trail quickly climbs into the James River Face Wilderness, topping out on Highcock Knob at around 3000 feet. This large roadless area offers acres and acres of wildland, with many trails radiat-ing down into the valleys around it, offering good day hiking from all directions. The Wilderness Area and its contiguous partner, the Thunder Ridge Wilderness Area, make for a 5-mile section of Trail that is as primeval and solitary as any in this part of Virginia.

As you'd expect, though, it isn't long before the Trail meets up with the Blue Ridge Parkway again, which it does at Petites Gap. It stays with the road closely for about 10 miles, where it again branches off into the Buzzard Ridge/Cove Moun-tain area. Here again there are numerous side trails and unim-proved roads, giving the day hiker and weekend camper lots to work with.

As the AT winds down off Cove Mountain (the second of that name on the route so far), it meets up with the parkway again at Bearwallow Gap. For the next 7.5 miles, all the way to Black Horse Gap, you could practically stand on the Trail and spit across the highway. This runs through a section of Jefferson

National Forest that is, at its widest, a mere mile and a half across. When the Trail finally leaves the parkway, it is to head downhill into the Valley of Virginia in the Daleville-Cloverdale area as it makes its move to the ranges to the west.

The AT Leaves the Blue Ridge

Situated in the Great Valley of the Appalachians that runs all the way down from Vermont in its various permutations (such as the Cumberland Valley in Pennsylvania and the Shenandoah Valley of Virginia), Daleville is popular with thru-hikers in search of mail and ice cream. But for day hikers and short-term campers, it serves mainly as a trailhead to the sections to the east and west.

Heading south (actually west at this particular point), the Trail enters a Trail Corridor, which is just another friendly service of your national parks and the National Scenic Trails Act of 1968. It consists of a narrow ribbon of protected land over which the Trail passes.

This section of Trail was as recently as 1978 moved off its traditional route on Catawba Mountain due to landowner troubles. For the better part of a decade the AT passed instead over the less-desirable North Mountain, visible just to the north over the Catawba Creek. So, the Park Service purchased the land and the Trail came back. Once again, the route crosses Tinker Cliffs and popular (and photogenic) McAfee Knob, with their heart-stopping precipices and splendid views of the Catawba Valley, Carvins Cove, Tinker Mountain, Peaks of Otter, and—on a clear day—Roanoke.

Out of the valley just south of Daleville the Trail quickly ascends Tinker Mountain—actually a long ridge—which it follows to the northwest. From there it descends into Scorched Earth Gap—named for an incident in which a hike leader inadvertently led his group through dense thickets. According to another Roanoke ATC luminary, Tom Campbell, and dutifully reported to the *Appalachian Trailway News,* Jim Denton was leading the hike, and led the group on a bushwhack off the side of Tinker Mountain. One woman took exception to the routing.

"No one had suspected the wealth of vituperative epithets contained in the vocabulary of one of the women of the group,"

Campbell reported, "but this soon came to light as the brush thickened. Backlashes from numerous branches encountered her anatomy, and a flow of words directed at our expert increased as we descended.

"By the time the gap was reached, this flow had reached flood stage, and our expert beat a strategic and hasty retreat. It was averred by a number of those present that the very ground was seen to smoke beneath the force of her imprecations.

"Hence the name 'Scorched Earth Gap,' which has lasted to this day." (Reported in the Appalachian Trail Conference's *Appalachian Trailway News*, July/August 1982.) Campbell, ever the gentleman, failed to include the name of Denton's antagonist.

Campbell's own service with the Roanoke ATC wasn't without incident. Once, when he and Jim Denton were hard at negotiations with a landowner as part of the efforts to relocate the Trail farther west, he and Denton stood talking for a long while. When the deal was struck, he and Denton left. Only then did he show Denton the bloody wound where the landowner's dog had bitten his leg. Not wanting to spoil the promising business, Tom had decided not to mention that there was a dog taking a piece out of him.

At Scorched Earth Gap, Tinker Mountain turns abruptly southward. It probably avoids being named Cove Mountain by the nearness of the *next* ridge of that name just a few miles down the Trail. At the southwestern end of Tinker Mountain the Trail climbs up about 500 feet to McAfee Knob, long famous in AT literature for the spectacular photos hikers take there of their companions perched on the jutting rocks of the knob. The Trail then descends to the lower ridge of Catawba Mountain, where it runs for about 4 miles or so.

Once the Trail has traversed its hard-won route (politically, at least) along Catawba Mountain, it descends into Catawba Valley and crosses toward North Mountain. Passing just west of North Mountain, it climbs instead up the eastern flank of— believe it or not—yet another Cove Mountain. Like its Pennsylvania counterpart, this cove is also a U-shaped figure on the surface of the planet. The Trail will ascend to its ridge and take the entire circuit around the top.

As the AT reaches the southern end of the Cove Mountain

ridge, it passes by the impressive standing rock called the Dragon's Tooth. Once called simply Buzzard's Rock, Campbell decided that it needed a better name. So he gave it one. Once around Cove Mountain, the Trail descends into Craig Creek valley.

The trail guide kindly warns hikers that the next section has rocky footing. But except for that, the route is a cakewalk, staying up along the crest of Sinking Creek Mountain around the 3200-foot level. This steep and sometimes narrow ridge offers views into Sinking Creek valley to the north, and Craig Creek valley to the south. There are a number of good lookouts and ledges.

When it reaches the Sinking Creek valley at Huffman, Virginia, the AT crosses its first Gulf-bound stream—that is, the first stream that drains into the Mississippi and the Gulf of Mexico. This is appropriate, since the route is now getting into the Alleghenies, the westernmost range of the Appalachians. From that point it's off into the wilderness—Mountain Lake Wilderness Area, that is. At this point, it's again over 4000 feet at Potts Mountain—including a 2000-foot ascent out of John's Creek valley. Throughout this section, which stays the vast majority of the time over 3000 feet, the hiker must be prepared to make rapid ascents and descents.

West of Sinking Creek Gap are two more Wilderness areas, Mountain Lake Wilderness and Peters Mountain Wilderness, both of which contain peaks over 4000 feet. Each offers side trails, as well as other side routes into the national forest on either side. At its narrowest point in this section, the forest is 2 miles wide.

In Peters Mountain Wilderness the Trail reaches the crest of the Peters Mountain Ridge, which forms the border between Virginia and West Virginia in the area. Staying over 3000 feet for the next 17 miles, it heads down the ridge in a west-southwesterly direction. Between Dickinson Gap and Symms Gap a new access trail, the Groundhog Trail, has been blazed by the Kanawha Trail Association, which splits off to the northeast. It's the only Trail access from the West Virginia side in this section, and it's accessible from near the Full Gospel Assembly Church on West Virginia 219. There is also said to be a blue-blazed trail leading down from Dickinson Gap to Virginia 635 near the former town of Ronk, Virginia.

Coming down off the ridges into the New River Narrows near Narrows, Virginia, and Pearisburg, the Trail meets one of the oldest and most interesting rivers in America. The contrarily named New River was actually formed in the Paleozoic era, before the uplift of much of the Appalachian range. Once a much more forceful stream that has in its history cut through over 4000 feet of rock, it may in its earliest years have emptied into the forerunner of the St. Lawrence River. When the European and African continents were bashed up against the coast, it in all probability had its mouth in the shallow inland sea that formed so much of the rock that it now cuts through. For a time during the last ice age it was blocked from its normal destination in the Ohio River by glacial till, and flowed instead into the Mississippi. It is the only southern river to flow mostly north; it is the only river to traverse the entire Appalachian range—a feat it accomplished simply by being there before the Appalachians were and cutting through them as they were formed.

Once across the New, the Trail climbs steeply for over 2500 feet to Angels Rest, a fine lookout over the narrows. It then resumes its ridge-running ways, through the thick rhododendron and azalea thickets along the hilltops, down the streambed of Dismal Creek (it's not), passing by a side trail to Dismal Creek Falls. It then crests Brushy Mountain, traveling up high again. Still, that's fortunate. The ridge sides are heavily stream-cut, and any route off the height of the land would be brutal.

The section of Brushy Mountain west of routes 77 and 52 makes a nice camping destination. It's fairly remote as things go in this narrow forest and there are lots of camping areas along the rugged ridge top. The Trail travels through the Little Wolf Creek valley just south of the ridge line (there is a trail along the crest, but due to woods, no views in the warm months). The route then ascends the ridge again, goes over the other side to the northward-facing escarpment of Garden Mountain, and follows it all the way to Beartown Wilderness. After crossing 4000-foot Chestnut Knob it valley-hops through Poor Valley, Rich Valley, and Crawfish Valley until it reaches the Mt. Rogers National Recreation Area near Groseclose. This is one of the most popular areas of Trail in Virginia, and it runs almost all the rest of the way to Damascus and the Tennessee border.

The Mount Rogers National Recreation Area

It is here that, for the first time since New Hampshire, the Trail will climb over 5000 feet, and it's the beginning of more high-elevation hiking to come as the route winds southward. It was named for Dr. William Barton Rogers who, in 1840 as a University of Virginia natural sciences professor, was hired by the state to submit reports on resource potential in the region. He mentions "Balsam" Mountain in his reports, a 5729-foot peak that would be named for him in 1883.

Many of the trails in the area follow old logging roads and the beds of old railroad routes placed there just after the turn of the century to haul the timber out of the area (like most areas in the East, the vast majority of the woodlands are second growth). Where these roadbeds exist, such as in the Iron Mountain area just to the north of Mt. Rogers itself or on the old roadbed of the "Virginia Creeper Railroad" (it's easy to figure *that* name), the walking can be expected to be fairly uniform and pleasant if a bit less challenging than an area that hasn't been smoothed over.

These areas of the Iron Mountains, a spur of the Alleghenies leading to the summits of Mt. Rogers and Whitetop Mountain (the two highest peaks in Virginia and among the highest in the Allegheny range), are covered with alpine-type meadows and rock outcrops, this time made of sedimentary rocks thrust up from the bed of the Paleozoic inland sea. The summit of Mt. Rogers itself is one of the northernmost "balsams," a southern term for a summit covered by balsam or spruce. The stand on Mt. Rogers is of Fraser fir, the only native southeastern fir species. It's also known as "balsam" locally, and the smell of it will remind any northern mountain hiker of home.

The area around Mt. Rogers is laced with fine side trails, including the former route of the AT across Iron Mountain just to the north of its current route over the shoulder of Mt. Rogers. This trail parallels the current route all the way from Chestnut Flats just north of Mt. Rogers almost the entire way to Damascus, Virginia. It can be used as a 50.7-mile circuit hike/backpack either from Damascus or Virginia 603 outside the small town of Trout Dale. Other trails loop around on either side of the AT, such as the many side trails on Stone Mountain that lead to several impressive side peaks.

The Mt. Rogers National Recreation Area is bordered to the south by the Grayson Highland State Park, another area protected from development, which offers campsites and other access routes. Several trails lead from the parking areas at Grayson to the summit of Mt. Rogers and the surrounding area.

Since 1984 there have been two National Wilderness Areas within Mount Rogers National Recreation Area: Lewis Fork Wilderness Area, which covers the immediate surroundings of Mt. Rogers itself, and the Little Wilson Creek Wilderness Area, in the Stone Mountain area. The Trail traverses sections of both.

The ridge line in the Mt. Rogers area, if it could be called a ridge line, is heavily eroded by stream action. This creates a countless number of side valleys and coves, each an environment unto itself. There are many meadows reminiscent of the "balds" so common on the summits to the south, as well as treeless "laurel" areas covered instead by rhododendron and azalea, and others that are simply open meadow. Pine Mountain just east of Mt. Rogers is like that.

Even though they're over 5000 feet high, these summits aren't truly over tree line the way their northern counterparts are. In spite of their occasional subalpine balds, these summits are likely to be wooded. Some of the higher areas are even grazed—a thing that no northeastern farmer would even attempt above 4000 feet.

After passing by Mt. Rogers (the summit is 0.5 miles off the trail on a blue-blazed route), the AT passes directly over Whitetop Mountain, the second highest in Virginia. It then descends gradually, in stages, until it hovers around 3000 feet, finally making the last drop off "The Cuckoo," a knob on Feathercamp Ridge, into Damascus, Virginia.

Damascus, called by some "Trailtown, U.S.A.," is an obligatory stop for thru-hikers. Famous for its hospitality to hikers, it makes a fine jumping-off point for the veritable supermarket of hiking in the Mt. Rogers National Recreation Area.

Virginia
Tennessee

● Damascus

Watauga Lake Dam
Laurel Fork Gorge
Unaka Mtn.

Tennessee
North Carolina

Yellow Mtn. Gap
Roan Mtn.

Shelton Monument

Hot Springs
Snowbird Mtn.
Mt. Cammerer
Mt. Guyot

Max Patch
Mtn.

Pisgah Natl.
Forest

Mt. Kephart
Great Smoky Mtns. Natl. Park
Clingman's Dome
(highest point on the AT)
Thunderhead Mtn.
Shuckstack

● Asheville

Bryson City

North
Carolina

Nantahala Natl. Forest

North Carolina
South Carolina

Georgia

North   Carolina

Tennessee and
North Carolina

12

The Tennessee/ North Carolina Section

Trail Distances:

Damascus, Virginia, to Fontana Dam, North Carolina . . . . .283.9 miles

Maintaining Clubs:

Tennessee Eastman Hiking Club: Damascus, Virginia, to Spivey Gap . . . . 125.6 miles

Carolina Mountain Club: Spivey Gap to Pigeon River . . . . 87.8 miles

Smoky Mountains Hiking Club: Pigeon River to Fontana Dam . . . . 70.5 miles

INTRODUCTION

THE APPALACHIAN Trail in this section succeeds in making the shift from the Alleghenies back to the western branch of the Blue Ridge Mountain complex. As it does, it enters the southern Appalachian forest in earnest. This biological system is noted for its almost endless variety of tree and plant types, and in its more mountainous regions for successive floral types ranging from lowland pine forests to mixed deciduous forests of incredible vigor and variety to the boreal fir-spruce forests that look and smell very much like their northern counterparts.

This is also a region of incredible topographical variety. From the Great Valley of Tennessee to the Great Smoky Mountain summits just a few miles to the east, for example, constitutes a rise in elevation of over 5000 feet in places. Summits over 6000 feet will here be the rule rather than the exception, and the 5000-foot level will be reached literally dozens of times before the southern terminus at Springer Mountain, just 450 miles away from Damascus.

The Trail has reached the quarter pole and it's heading into the stretch.

GEOLOGY ALONG THE TRAIL

The western reaches of the Blue Ridge complex are largely characterized by a move to younger, more sedimentary, less metamorphosed bedrock. These are the sediments laid down on what was originally the continental shelf of the pre-Appalachian North America of 600 million years ago, in the vast inland sea that was formed when the approach of eastern continents uplifted the present coastal areas.

This is a region characterized by parallel folds and thrust faults—great thick slabs of bedrock broken off on low angles and slid to the west over neighboring slabs. Frequently, older rocks will be thrust over younger ones. Think of this as a patio made of flagstones that have been scraped into a pile by a bulldozer. In places the slabs will be piled up onto one another; in others they will be jumbled in different directions.

But don't take the analogy *too* far. Here, because we're dealing with rock strata and not stiff, brittle flagstones, and with compression that took place over millions of years, not a few moments with an earth-moving machine, the story is a bit different. Some strata will bend before they break; rocks to the east will in general be thrust over rocks to the west, never under, and erosion has had as much to do with the present appearance as the original uplift did. But the principle is much the same.

In the more eastern areas the sediments will be more clastic, like the sandstones and siltstones that eroded out of the old Grenville mountains and, later, from the new mountains formed just to the east by the earlier stages of the Appalachian Revolution. As you travel west, into the Great Valley regions, the bedrock will be still younger limestones, formed farther from the shore of the inland sea. In the final episodes of the Appalachian Revolution, 250 to 350 million years ago, the older rocks were pushed up and over the younger, thrusting to the west. In the eastern Blue Ridge, which the Trail left north of Roanoke, it is the ancient Grenville gneisses and plutonic granites that have been uplifted. Here, to the west, it is the more recent sediments: the later Precambrian sandstones and siltstones of the Grenville continental shelf, and still farther west the Cambrian, Ordovician, and—west of the Great Valley—carboniferous deposits. As you travel farther and farther away from the coast, the younger and younger the rocks become.

Along the ridges of the Unakas and the Smokies the Trail passes largely over the late Precambrian, Cambrian, and Ordovician bedrocks, occasionally (depending on how far east or west the route travels) dropping down to exposed rocks of either earlier or later eras. It is in these erosion-formed "windows" that we can see the configuration of the faults and folds in a given area. Wautauga Lake, just south of Damascus, is in such a window to an area of younger rocks. Many of the coves in the various ranges will also offer views of what lies beneath.

NATURAL HISTORY ALONG THE TRAIL

Traveling from the lowlands to the peaks in the southern Appalachians is much like traveling along the coastline from Richmond, Virginia, to somewhere up in Nova Scotia. You traverse approximately the same life zones.

Even here, the ice ages had a profound effect. Since the great ice sheets did not come this far south to scrape away topsoil and sculpt the bedrock, it is in the ecological makeup of this region that their effects are felt. For example, the incredible variety of plant species in the mixed deciduous forests at mid-elevations has been attributed to the climatic swings caused by the massive glaciers just to the north. In the relatively short warming periods, species from farther south would take hold; the colder times would be sufficient to keep them from taking over from the more boreal species.

Some experts theorize that the balds on southern summits (there are said to be somewhere in the neighborhood of eighty of them) are a remnant of a time when these peaks were above the tree line. Just what has kept them clear (they are at present being taken over by the surrounding forests) is a matter of conjecture. Many have been grazed by farmers' livestock for the past several hundred years; they may have been burned off by Native Americans for various reasons. And many may endure; the Forest and Park services are keeping several clear to preserve the balds for posterity.

On the summits and in the areas immediately below, the spruce-fir forest is king. Left there by the retreating glaciers, the conifer-clad highlands form islands of a more northern ecosystem. Holding sway as the dominant species down to the 5000-foot level (boundaries are never distinct in this mild climate), they are also found mixed in at lower levels and still contain some of the mighty monarchs that made this such a paradise for loggers—huge, straight giants that three people can't gird with their arms fingertip to fingertip. Southern fir is still written into the beams and studs of northern building codes.

Unfortunately, what the Forest Service and the Park Service now protect from logging may fall to other threats. The ridge lines in the Great Smokies are crested with the dead trunks of trees killed by the balsam woolly aphid, a parasite that bores into the bark and breeds in the delicate cambium layer. Then, too, there is the as-yet-unmeasured damage caused by acid rain. As the political argument plods on, otherwise healthy trees—especially red spruce—wither and die.

On a pleasanter note, the deciduous forests in the middle elevations thrive. These woodlands contain not only the species that New Englanders would recognize, but also countless others. In one cove you may find yourself walking through a southern variety of maple-beech forest; on a nearby ridge line it may be oak-hickory. Then there are the sometimes-huge yellow poplars that northerners know mostly from cultivated specimens, and which they call tulip trees. At the borders between deciduous and coniferous forests there will even be the birches so dear to northeasterners.

The southern Appalachians are home to many animals (although the elk is gone and is remembered mostly in place names), most of which would be recognizable to people in the north. There are, however, a few exceptions. Most noticeable is the European wild boar. Brought over early in the twentieth century for a nearby game park, a number of them escaped around 1909 and took hold in the Great Smoky Mountains area. They are ill-tempered and territorial and revel in rooting up ground cover with their noses. They are only beloved by local hunters, which is perhaps just as well.

The wild turkey has remained strong in the southern ranges and hikers will hear them often, if not see them. They are heirs to the gobblers that amazed the eyes and delighted the palates of Spanish and English explorers three and four centuries ago, when there were still birds over fifty pounds in these hills. Although mostly smaller, these turkeys are just as wily as their ancestors.

HISTORY ALONG THE TRAIL

These mountains were once (and in some places still are) the home of the marvelous Cherokee people. This was the nation that—unique among Native American peoples—developed a written language. They formed a government and a society that was as well-organized as that of the Europeans who conquered them.

The term "Cherokee," like so many other tribal names that have endured, was probably not what they called themselves originally. It may have come from a Chocktaw word meaning "Cave People," or perhaps a Creek word meaning "People of a Different Speech." According to one source, they called themselves "Yunwiya."

In any case, the closest relatives of the Cherokees were the various Iroquois nations to the north. The Cherokee language is a very aberrant Iroquois dialect—truly "different speech."

The first European to meet the Cherokee was, of course, de Soto in 1540. Intent as he was on finding riches, he apparently noticed little about them beyond the fact that they didn't seem to have any gold. Their next contact was with Spanish captain Juan Pardo, who sallied west from his base on Parris Island to follow his orders to "discover and conquer territory from there to Mexico." He made it about as far as the Blue Ridge in North Carolina, where he established a fort for a couple of years.

In that area, he probably encountered the "Valley Cherokee," who lived in the eastern foothills of the Blue Ridge. Between there and the Smokies lived the "Middle Cherokee," with the "Overhill Cherokee" located west from the Smokies and Unakas. At the time, there were probably somewhere in the neighborhood of twenty-two thousand Cherokees in the area (they had originally come from the Great Lakes region, but had been forced south by pressure from the Delawares and their own cousins, the Iroquois).

During the Revolution the Cherokees supported the British, mainly because the colonists had their usual track record of taking over Native American lands without paying attention to legal niceties. Their support, however, was not influential: In their two attempts to aid the Crown—raids on Continental forts at Eaton's Station and Ft. Watauga—they failed badly.

After the Revolution, the Cherokees, as was their habit, made the best of the situation. They adopted the colonists' methods of agriculture and architecture. Soon allied with their former enemies, they helped Andrew Jackson in his war against the Creeks.

In fact, the early years of the American republic were a kind of short-lived golden age for the Cherokee. Their culture thrived, as did their fortunes. It was during this time, in 1821, that Sequoyah, a half-Cherokee who had served with Jackson, invented the Cherokee alphabet and writing. So ingenious was this system that virtually the entire tribe became literate, practically within months. In 1828, a Cherokee newspaper was founded, the *Cherokee Phoenix*.

For all these reasons, what was about to happen to this most Europeanized of Native American cultures should have been unthinkable—as if anything that European settlers and their descendants did to the native peoples could be described as "thinkable."

What happened was, however, predictable. Land speculators entered the scene eager to move the Cherokees and not too careful about how they went about it. Their constant anti-Cherokee agitation bore some tragic results: In 1814, for example, as

Chief Junaluska and his warriors fought at Jackson's side against the Creeks, other white soldiers were back in Cherokee villages, raping and pillaging.

Then, in 1827, speculators discovered that there was gold on Cherokee land in northern Georgia. Whipped up by gold fever, the Georgia state government immediately declared all Cherokee lands forfeit—and treaties be damned. It was a neat package: Native Americans were forbidden to dig for gold on their own land; they were forbidden to testify against whites or even to resist in any way the seizure of their lands.

By 1836, efforts by the Cherokees themselves, and by sympathetic whites such as congressmen David Crockett, Henry Clay, Daniel Webster, and Edward Everett, proved to be of no avail. Not even the law could help: Informed of a Supreme Court decision in favor of the Cherokee, President Andrew Jackson quipped, "[Chief Justice] John Marshall has made his decision. Now let him enforce it."

In spite of widespread sympathy for the plight of these people (one general, sent in 1836 to prevent a supposed Cherokee uprising, gathered his men together and pointedly informed them that they would instead protect the Cherokee from harm, and that the whites deserved no such protection), General Winfield Scott was sent south in 1838 to remove them to Oklahoma. Thus came to pass the Trail of Tears.

After gathering seventeen thousand Cherokees, he herded them into what amounted to concentration camps. From there they were marched—as quickly as possible, on starvation rations—all the way to a desolate plain in Oklahoma. Over four thousand died.

Some stayed. Those who wander the Great Smokies and other ranges in Cherokee territory can understand how Winfield Scott couldn't possibly gather them all. Those that remained (some one thousand or so) fought and hid, raided and endured—and somehow survived. They were only allowed to come down from the hilltops years later, when one of their elders, Tsali, agreed to surrender himself with two of his sons. According to the agreement, they would be executed for murder and the hunt for the rest of the Cherokees would stop. Gallant Tsali, whose only sin was killing one of Winfield Scott's men while resisting brutal capture, handed himself over to federal authorities near the present town of Cherokee. The federals, too, kept their part of the bargain, in all its gruesome particulars. Later, the Qualla Indian Reservation was established in the eastern edge of the Great Smokies, largely on land donated by W. H. Thomas, a merchant and philanthropist who had maintained contact with the band during their flight.

One little-known legacy of the Cherokee Nation is their inspiration for the Uncle Remus tales. Apparently great story-tellers, they also told of a race of little people who lived in the hills—about the size of children, very pretty, and with long hair down to their ankles. They were said to lead lost children home, and, on occasion, to come in the night to do work for good people.

Strange that the people the settlers forced from the land should view the wilderness as such a friendly place.

At Hot Springs on the French Broad River, the Trail crosses the route of Hernando de Soto, who, in 1540, came up out of Asheville (Chimney Rock, where he found an Indian village) via Hickory Nut Pass until he crossed over the mountains at Hot Springs on his way to the Knoxville area. From there he continued to his fateful crossing of the Mississippi, which, promising lots of mud and not much gold, he passed by as though it were of little consequence.

De Soto's must have been a bizarre entourage. He had begun the previous year in Florida with a train of some six hundred iron-clad conquistadors and a herd of a few hundred pigs. These animals were intended for consumption by his men, but for the first year he refused to allow any to be slaughtered.

De Soto was typical of most Spanish military leaders in the New World. Greedy, sadistic, and violent, he regarded the native peoples as something less than human. Torturing a native to death for news he did not wish to hear was as natural to him as eating and sleeping. Small wonder that the native chiefs learned quickly to tell him exactly what would please him.

News of gold, of course, was what he longed to find. Unfortunately, there really was no gold to be had in the area (even the modest Georgia lodes that would come to haunt the Cherokees three centuries hence were unknown then). So the chiefs devised a method of dealing with their rude, overbearing, overeating, and generally undesirable guest.

"No, sorry," they would say, "No gold here. But our neighbors, just west of here—they have lots of gold. Just head up through that pass and ask them. They'll be glad to give you a bunch of it."

They might then provide him with a guide, who would stay with de Soto just long enough to see him over the border and would then vanish. De Soto, who doubtless caught wise to what was being done to him, really had no choice in the matter. "Oh, sure," he would say. "Well, men, let's go. It's over the next hill for us."

What a sight he must have made—clanking and oinking down the narrow valleys, followed by his men and his swine. The latter had, of course, bred in the interim. There he went, de Soto the conquistador, followed by six hundred disgruntled men and literally thousands of grunting, squealing pigs.

De Soto's legacy, though, remains. Upon sighting the high mountains ahead he promptly named them the Appalachians, after the Appalache tribe he encountered along the Gulf Coast. But lest this explorer's name be forever besmirched by the fact that he named the great range after the wrong tribe, it should also be mentioned that his estate contained another interesting item: When he died on the banks of the Mississippi the next year, his share of the expedition's pork consisted of over two thousand pigs. And in local terms, that's making good, indeed!

Like the rest of the Appalachians, the southern parts of the range presented a formidable barrier to western expansion. For that reason, the lion's share of settlement came not from the east, but from the north, as immigrants from Pennsylvania made their way down the Great Valley along the New and Holston rivers.

It really wasn't until the latter part of the eighteenth century that overland routes were found from the east. This was the era of Daniel Boone, who established several routes to eastern Tennessee and Kentucky. Too footloose to stay still for long, ol' Dan would keep moving west, finally hanging up his long rifle near Defiance, Missouri, on the Missouri River.

It might be noted that Boone and his compadres pushed west in defiance of the British edict of 1763 against western expansion. The Tennesseans and Kentuckians paid even less attention (if that is possible) to the prohibition than did their counterparts in Pennsylvania and Virginia.

Those who did settle in the coves and valleys were of necessity an independent breed. Sequestered by geography from their more accessible neighbors, they developed ways of their own. Largely too poor to own slaves, the sympathies of these "mountaineers" lay largely with the Union during the Civil War, to whom they sent more volunteer soldiers than they did to the South.

This mountain way of life has been slow to disappear. Famous in literature (especially in the *Foxfire* series, which I recommend highly), it is also preserved within the Great Smoky Mountains National Park, with a reconstructed mountaineer homestead at the Oconaluftee Ranger Station on the south border of the park and a more extensive museum of mountain lore and crafts at Cades Cove to the north.

THE TRAIL IN TENNESSEE AND NORTH CAROLINA

Leaving the center of Damascus, Virginia, and crossing into Tennessee, the AT immediately climbs back up to around 4000 feet. (The trail maps list elevations in meters, at a contour interval of 50 meters. You can convert back to feet by multiplying the meters by 3.2808. Appropriately, the latest item on an AT hiker's equipment list is a calculator.) The Trail heads off in a generally southwesterly direction, along the ridge crest of Holston Mountain.

Holston Mountain and its neighboring ridge, the Iron Mountains, look too similar, too parallel, to be together by mere coincidence. They are, as a matter of fact, the two rims of a very regular syncline. The sandstone from which they are constructed has resisted erosion on either side. To the west, Holston is bordered by the Great Appalachian Valley, over which its sandstone was thrust; to the east of Iron Mountain lies a window down to the younger shales and limestones that lie underneath the overthrust.

The Trail in this area, like most Forest Service trail, is well graded and protected from erosion.

This area is full of side-trail opportunities. When the Trail leaves Holston Mountain at Double Springs, an old route of the AT (abandoned in 1954) continues south along the ridge of Holston Mountain for another 13.1 miles, to Holston High Knob. Another blue blazer runs from near the site of the AT's reaching of the crest of Iron Mountain after it leaves Holston Mountain. This route starts about 3 miles down a narrow road from there, and then runs 16 miles back northeast, almost all the way to Damascus. A short side trail hooks it up to the AT again. In addition, there are numerous side trails to both the AT and the Iron Mountains route from the Shady Valley area along Beaverdam Creek.

Once on Iron Mountain, the Trail again heads in the same general direction it followed on Holston Mountain. Soon after joining Iron Mountain it passes near the grave and monument to hermit "Uncle Nick" Grindstaff (the trail guide will tell you exactly where). It then follows the narrow, at times double, ridge of Iron Mountains for 15 miles until it descends again to Watauga Lake.

This lake, a 1949 Tennesee Valley Authority project, is near the site of Fort Watauga, raided unsuccessfully by the Cherokees in their efforts to aid the British during the Revolution. It is also on the line of the Iron Mountain Fault, the fracture between rock strata over which the sandstone of Iron and Holston mountains slid over the limestones and shales of the lower valleys. The fault is visible on the eastern end of the dam, with the older sandstones clearly visible above the younger limestones.

This next section is especially nice. The Trail crosses Watauga Dam and, after passing by a couple of Forest Service recreation areas, heads up onto Pond Mountain, just to the south of Watauga Lake. Once up on the ridge, it travels through some rugged country and by a 1.1-mile side trail to the summit of Pond Mountain. In this area it passes over a succession of knobs. There are campsites on top, at The Pond Flats, and many side trails in the highlands.

West of the Watauga Lake geologic window, the Trail passes up onto older, more metamorphosed quartzite formations. On top of the Pond Mountain Ridge, the quartzite contains a common AT feature—the *Skolithus* wormholes left by some of the earliest forms of life to exist on earth. These have remained, even though the rocks that formed from the beach sands in which they lived have been crushed into hard quartzite.

The hardness of the rock is also responsible for Laurel Fork Gorge, the narrow cliff-lined defile through which the Trail passes after descending from the Pond Mountain Ridge. This exceedingly rugged stretch of trail covers 2.7 miles, passes by some fine 40-foot-high waterfalls, and contains a stone shelter. Laurel Fork is a vigorous stream, draining high mountain valleys.

After leaving Laurel Fork Gorge, the AT enters Dennis Cove (another geologic window), which is home of yet another recreation area. This one has campsites.

Leaving Dennis Cove, the AT once again enters the woods, climbing up onto White Rocks Mountain (named, naturally enough, for the white quartzite of which it is composed). Passing by Coon Den Falls (small), it quickly ascends to the White Rocks Mountain lookout tower. Perched as it is over 4000 feet, the tower is said to offer great views.

At the end of the White Rocks Mountain section the AT meets up once again with several side trails that it either crossed, or which connect with it by other side trails, back on Pond Mountain. These routes, lined up with the various small roads and jeep trails, offer fine access to this rugged little section of national forest.

After passing by civilization again at U.S. Route 19E, the AT enters North Carolina and ascends Hump Mountain. From here, it sawtooths over a few knobs until it descends slightly into Yellow Mountain Gap. Since the state border runs along the ridge line in this area, the Trail will cross back and forth from North Carolina to Tennessee.

It was at Yellow Mountain Gap, in October of 1780, that a strange army passed. The story is no less a curious one.

Up until that time, the mountaineers had had all they could do to withstand the constant barrage of attacks by the Cherokees, who were allied with the British. That they succeeded in forming a barrier for the struggling Republic against these attacks is a tribute to their fortitude.

This standoff might have remained until the end if it weren't for the arrogance of one Colonel Patrick Ferguson, a British officer at the head of a force of Tories. He sent word over that unless the mountaineers declared allegiance to George III, he would "march [his] army over the mountains, hang [their] leaders, and lay [their] country waste with fire and sword."

This message wasn't received in quite the way Ferguson had in mind. Feeling that they had been insulted, the "Overmountain" men gathered at Sycamore Shoals (Elizabethton, Tennessee), and decided to teach Ferguson a lesson.

Gathering 1000 men, they set out along Bright's Trace through Yellow Mountain Gap to where they heard the British could be found, over in North Carolina. Their little force expanding to over 1800 (the figure has been estimated as low as around 800) as they marched, they caught Ferguson and his 1125 Tories at Kings Mountain on October 7, 1780. Ninety minutes later Ferguson lay dead, his men either killed or captured. Nobody escaped. It was a turning point of the Revolution, opening for Cornwallis another front to his south.

Then, their work done and their honor satisfied, the Overmountain boys hurried back home to take up the fight against the Cherokee once again.

The section near Yellow Mountain Gap, traveling along the Tennessee/North Carolina border, lies above Roan Mountain State Park. Day hikers can find several access points from the park.

Passing down the ridge to Roan Mountain, the AT enters the first groves of Fraser fir (the trail guide says there is an isolated grove in Shenandoah National Park). This is the aromatic tree that will cover the summits of even the highest mountains for the rest of the way to Springer Mountain. Even a northerner like me can sit beside a grove of these trees, close his eyes, take a deep breath, and imagine he's in the White Mountains of New Hampshire.

It's appropriate. Roan Mountain is the first time since the Whites that the Trail has climbed above 6000 feet.

Roan Mountain is also known for its "Cloudland Rhododendron Gardens." Not actually cultivated, the name refers to the profusion of pink catawba rhododendrons that bloom there in mid to late June. There are also patches of Scotch heather, probably transplanted by a homesick Scotsman. There are several balds along the ridge followed by the Trail.

After descending Roan Mountain the Trail crosses Iron

Mountain, still following the state line, and enters Iron Mountain Gap. This passage, along with Bright's Trace through Yellow Mountain Gap, offered the most popular overland routes to the west in this part of the Appalachians.

Iron Mountain Gap also marks the beginning of the Unaka Mountains, one of the western ranges of this split of the Blue Ridge, along with the Great Smokies to the south.

This ridge is one of those mountains that have a road across the top. While it might detract from the wild feel of the area, it does make a nice area easily accessible. There are several balds and open summits, and the views are quite good.

After descending the Unaka ridge, the Trail crosses the Nolichucky at the northern end of that river's spectacular gorge.

Once on the other side, the Trail climbs rapidly to the crest of Cliff Ridge, where there are fine views of the Nolichucky Gorge. The road builders have yet to find a way through the gorge; maybe they never will. The AT then proceeds over Temple Ridge and No Business Knob (said by the guidebook to be named for an unidentified hiker who got hung up in the thickets and decided that he had "No business" being there in the first place).

This is an area of laurel, rhododendron, hardwood, and pine. The Trail does a fair amount of zigzagging about to stay on the crest of the ridge at around the 3500-foot level and to avoid descending into any of the numerous valleys. When it comes down into Spivey Gap on U.S. 19W, it reaches the end of the Tennessee Eastman Hiking Club Section, and enters the Carolina Mountain Club's area of responsibility.

On the southern side of Spivey Gap the Trail climbs very steeply up to High Rocks (a vertical grunt of over 1000 feet), goes over 5185-foot Little Bald (which isn't a bald), and 5516-foot Big Bald (which is—it's a rather nice one, as a matter of fact). By the time hikers get there, though, they have ascended over 2200 feet in 5.1 miles. Ouch!

Big Bald, by the way, is owned on its south side by a development company that has put in a network of roads and summer homes. The roads are for the most part out of sight of the Trail.

Habitation is not new to Big Bald, though. In the early

nineteenth century it hosted a hermit, David Greer, or "Old Hog Greer." He seems mainly to have chosen the solitary life because of a violent temper that rendered him unfit for the company of humans. He was said to live in a hole he dug under Greer Rock, near the summit of Big Bald, though no trace of his den is to be seen today.

Once down from Big Bald, the Trail leaves the Cherokee National Forest for a time, traveling over private land, some of which is open country suitable for farming. This goes on for about 10 miles as the AT travels along the ridge of the Bald Mountains, keeping close to the boundary of small tracts of the forest. It eventually reenters federal land, this time the Pisgah National Forest, as it crosses deeper into North Carolina east of Hot Springs.

In the Pisgah National Forest the Trail stays along the Bald Mountains, ascending to around 4200 feet for several miles. It's really getting into rhododendron country here, and for those unfamiliar with the frustration of a rhododendron thicket, a quick trip off to the side of the AT in this section will cure their curiosity.

The Pisgah forest is also fairly wide in places, offering day hikers a number of side trails from which to mount loop routes. This is especially true in the long section east of Route 208 in Allen Gap, which has two shelters and a handful of trails leading off to the north. It's noted for its open crests and pleasant campgrounds.

It is in this section that hikers may find the famous twin tombstones just southeast of Big Butt Mountain, familiar to many around the country from the pictures of them in magazines. These mark the grave of William and David Shelton, a nephew and uncle who, like so many around these parts, enlisted with the Union during the Civil War. Returning to attend a family gathering, they were caught and killed by a Confederate force nearby.

South of Allen Gap the Trail again follows the Bald Mountains ridge. The best views are at the Rich Mountain fire tower, but Lover's Leap has fine views of the scenic French Broad River valley, 500 feet below. Throughout these sections, backpackers can find good campsites and there are shelters located at convenient intervals.

Coming down off Bald Mountains ridge, the Trail crosses the road that goes into Hot Springs. It's typical of many of the routes in this part of North Carolina: It's windy enough to twist a mule. Fortunately, the Trail crosses it and makes the scenic climb up Lover's Leap before descending into Hot Springs.

Lover's Leap, according to the trail guide, was named by the Cherokees for a young Cherokee woman said to have hurled herself off it after her lover was killed in a triangle rivalry. It is not known who translated the name.

Hot Springs has a long history. As the name suggests, it is the former home of a famous spa that grew around the waters of the warm springs on the site. It is also where de Soto passed through in 1540. It seems impossible for him to have been disappointed with the magnificent valley of the French Broad, but he was. Who knows what he saw, but perhaps Benton MacKaye could have straightened him out: To walk, to see, and to *see* what you see.

South of Hot Springs, the Trail starts heading south again, in a leisurely fashion at first. It passes right through town (the Trail Register is in the lobby of the post office), past the Jesuit monastery (which offers a hostel to thru-hikers), and up into the hills again.

Don't be fooled. This easy stuff won't last long. Seven miles out of Hot Springs, the Trail only having climbed 700 or 800 feet, it's nosebleed time again. You reach the base of Bluff Mountain and the AT climbs 2000 feet in about 3 miles.

This entire section goes up and down a lot after that. It eventually climbs Max Patch Mountain, listed in the trail guide as "the southernmost point on the AT being retained as a typical, open, grassy bald." This, as far as I know, is no longer true. Siler Bald in the Nantahalas is being cleared by the Forest Service and several side peaks in the Smokies are kept clear by the Park Service as well. Chances are, though, that the Max Patch experience had a lot to do with the decision to clear Siler Bald.

In any case, Max Patch makes a fine destination because of its excellent views all the way to Mt. Mitchell to the east.

This part of the Trail is in a relatively narrow corridor, making access generally available only along the AT and from narrow roads at two points: Lemon Gap and Garenflo Gap.

There is also a dirt road just below Max Patch Mountain.

The last territory before the AT reaches Great Smoky Mountains National Park crosses Snowbird Mountain, a 4000-foot-high hump in the southernmost reaches of the Pisgah National Forest. Snowbird has given its name to the Snowbird Formation, a group of sandstones and quartzites that make up the oldest rocks of those that form the Smokies. The kinship with its neighbors to the south is appropriate: The views of the Smokies from the Snowbird fire tower are among the finest to be had.

THE GREAT SMOKY MOUNTAINS NATIONAL PARK

The section of the Appalachian Trail that traverses the Park is one of the crown jewels of the entire system. Located as it is in a popular, heavily attended national park, the layout of the park nevertheless allows hikers to get away from civilization at most times of year.

The Great Smoky Mountains National Park, unlike some other parks, like the Shenandoah, is not a linear ridge-line affair. The highest mountains are along a cordillera that runs, like the Trail in the area, generally east to west; but, unlike the Shenandoah, there is an average of 12 to 15 miles to the edge of the park on either side. Also, unlike other federal lands, there are simply no roads in most sections. Except for the major route through the park at Newfound Gap and a few others that head part way inland at a few points, you really have to work to get to the Trail in most places.

As you'd expect in a national park, camping in the backcountry requires a backcountry permit. And as is the case in other parks, these are free and may be obtained at ranger stations and at self-service stands at several entry points. There are a number of restrictions, mostly intended to lessen the impact on the land and to spread out human activity in order to lessen crowding and, more important, the *feeling* of being crowded.

Also like other trails in other national parks, the Trail through the Great Smokies was built by the Park Service and is maintained in cooperation with the local Appalachian Trail club—in this case the Smoky Mountains Hiking Club. Like all

Park Service trails, the trails in the Smokies were put in with a lot of Civilian Conservation Corps effort in the 1930s.

Geologically, the mountains of the Great Smokies are mostly formed of late Precambrian sediments, rocks laid down on the continental shelf of pre-Appalachian North America. These are mainly sandstones, with some siltstones and shales mixed in.

Again, the farther you go toward the western edge of the ridges—in this case, toward the north—the younger the rocks become. In the southern Smokies there are several earlier Precambrian granitic domes reminiscent of Old Rag Mountain in the Shenandoahs, as well as stream-cut windows (Big Cove is an example) down to the older rocks. In the north, on the other hand, are windows down to younger Ordovician limestones and dolomites—examples are Cades Cove and Wear Cove.

These heavily folded and faulted mountains are, then, the result of a monumental shove from, in all probability, the southeast, which both pushed up the older basement rocks under the middle-aged sandstones and pushed the plates of sandstone over the younger rocks to the north and northeast. Erosion did the rest.

The flora and fauna of the park are what you'd expect from an ecosystem that has been carefully protected since 1930: healthy and diverse. With the exception of the balsam woolly aphid problem among the fir trees at high elevation, the tree and plant life can best be described as vigorous.

The park maintains a staff of experts on all aspects of the wilderness to be found in the park. They can be contacted at Park Headquarters on the Gatlinburg end of the Newfound Gap Road.

The Trail through the Great Smoky Mountains

The park deserves its status as a popular destination for hikers and backpackers. Not only does the AT run along the highest ridges, through some of the wildest sections, but there are side trails aplenty in literally all parts of the Smokies—mostly of the even foot-bedded, erosion-protected, National Park Service variety. To enumerate all the loops, side trips, base-camp-and-day-hike venues, and nature walks would take a volume in itself. Get hold of a copy of *Hiking in the Great Smokies* from the Smoky Mountains Hiking Club. It's also available from Appalachian Trail Conference headquarters.

The names of land features in the park are much more logically designated than in most areas. In 1929, as the Park Service was preparing to issue the first maps of the soon-to-be national park, they formed a commission of knowledgeable people to go through the various (and often contradictory or redundant) names and to straighten out any problems. What resulted was the elimination of many of the duplications—there were, for example, a dozen "Mill Creeks," since every body of water with a mill on it was so named. There were also numerous "Indian Creeks" and "Fork Ridges." Sometimes a peak or gap would be known as one thing in North Carolina and another in Tennessee.

One member of the commission even tried to delve into the origin of the term "Smoky Mountains," discovering that the expression was already in use in 1789, when the state of North Carolina ceded its western land to the federal government. It was, coincidentally, similar to the designation used by the Cherokees, which was said to be *Sha-cona-ga,* which meant "blue, like smoke."

Many of the names are merely taken from the people who used to live in the area. Mt. Mingus, for example, comes from the same Mingus family who ran a mill near the present-day site of the Oconaluftee Ranger Station.

Another result of the name survey was that where duplications were eliminated, certain land forms were left without names and could be dedicated to the memory of things—and usually people—of the Park Service's choice. One such is the first peak that the AT crosses once within the park boundary: Mt. Cammerer, named for onetime National Park Service Director Arno B. Cammerer.

It's an ascent you'll pay for. In approximately 4 miles the Trail climbs about 3000 feet. There are several rewards: a magnificent view from the lookout tower on Cammerer, and the fact that you've just done the lion's share of the gruntwork for access to the nearly 6000-foot ridge that leads to Newfound Gap.

First, though, you have to dip down into Low Gap, just the other side of the 5000-foot Mt. Cammerer/Sunset Knob hump. Down the northern slope from the gap is the valley of Cosby's

Creek. Near the source of the creek is the place called "Cryin' Creek," named when one brother accidentally shot and killed another while the two were bear hunting. After Low Gap, and once over the top of 5145-foot Cosby Knob, the Trail finally makes its way to the 5600- to 5800-foot level that will be its normal elevation in the Smokies.

First stop is the Mt. Guyot area. After crossing 6356-foot Old Black, the AT traverses near the summit of the 6621-foot peak named after Arnold Guyot, the Swiss-born scientist/explorer who did so much of the early work in the Appalachians. He spent time in the Smokies before 1860, making maps and noting elevations of the mountains. Mt. Guyot is the second highest peak in the Smokies (and the second Mt. Guyot on the AT).

After crossing Mt. Chapman (named for Colonel David C. Chapman, who was instrumental in the creation of the park), and Mt. Sequoyah (named, of course, for the great inventor of the Cherokee syllabary) through virgin fir-spruce forest, the Trail starts down the long winding ridge of Peck's Corner and Laurel Top, staying within a few feet of the 5800-foot level for 5 miles. There are fine views from fairly frequent overlooks.

Once over Laurel Top, the route descends slightly before climbing sharply up 6150-foot Mt. Kephart (named for the author of *Our Southern Highlanders,* considered one of the most authoritative volumes ever written on the southern mountaineers). A 0.8-mile side trail leads to the summit and The Jumpoff a few feet below. The best views are from The Jumpoff. From there, it's a short trip down to Newfound Gap at 5045 feet.

From Newfound Gap the Trail parallels the Park Service road to the top of Clingmans Dome, a distance of 7.5 miles. After passing the "obscure trail to right to summit of Mt. Mingus, 5802 ft.," it reaches Indian Gap, site of the old Cherokee trail from the lowlands to the south and east to the Great War Trail through the Great Valley on the other side of Gatlinburg, Tennessee.

After crossing the wooded summit of Mt. Collins (6188 feet), and dipping into Collins Gap (5886 feet), the AT ascends to its highest point in the entire route from Maine to Georgia: 6643-foot Clingmans Dome. Formerly named Smoky Dome, it was named for General Thomas L. Clingman who, in 1858, first measured the peak. To those familiar with the bare rock summit of Mt. Washington in New Hampshire, over 1000 feet above tree line, it will come as something of a surprise that Clingmans's summit is thickly wooded. Only by climbing up the neo-extra-terrestrial-style lookout tower can the hiker see the surrounding countryside.

In his excellent contribution to "The Naturalist's America" series, *The Appalachians,* Maurice Brooks takes up the interest-ing question: How much higher would these southern Appala-chians have to be in order to top the tree line? Actually referring to 6684-foot Mt. Mitchell in the Black Mountains of the eastern Blue Ridge (though noting that the observation tower on Clingmans Dome might just top Mitchell, making observers there "the highest individuals in eastern North America. It takes very little to make some of us happy."), he concludes that "If fifteen hundred feet were added to Mitchell's summit, the new mountain would, I believe, reach treeline."

Be that as it may, you will not find solitude on the AT's highest point. A road leads to a parking lot within about a half-mile of the spot, and the trail uphill, though a moderately stiff climb, is paved over with macadam. Still, if you close your eyes, the smell of the Fraser fir and spruce could make you think you were in New Hampshire, and, as always, it's perfectly permis-sible to park the car and hike away from the crowds.

One side trail of note leads south from the Forney Ridge parking lot near the summit of Clingmans to Andrew Bald, 2.5 miles away. It's said to be one of the finest balds in the Appalachians.

The Trail, though, strikes out in another direction, still heading west along the North Carolina/Tennessee border. First stop is 6582-foot Mt. Buckley, named for S. B. Buckley, who climbed with Clingman. On this end of the park the Trail is graded carefully less often. It also travels more through typical mixed hardwood forest and less in the fir-spruce that typifies the eastern end of the park.

From Buckley, the route crosses the narrow ridge called The Narrows, leaving the crest only to avoid ledges. It then ascends 5607-foot Silers Bald.

The bald is interesting for two reasons. First, it was through the early years of AT planning (pre-1930) a bone of contention between the Georgia Appalachian Trail Club and the Smoky Mountains Hiking Club. The former wanted the AT to end in the Mt. Oglethorpe/Springer Mountain area; the latter was just as anxious to have it traverse the entire length of the Smoky Mountains. In order for the Trail to reach Springer, rather than heading for the more westerly (and, to the Georgians' minds, inferior) terminus in the Cohuttas, the plan called for the AT to leave the Smokies at Silers Bald and head down into the Nantahalas. A compromise brought the Trail down farther west, first at Cheoah Dam and later, once it was constructed, at Fontana Dam. It would then head back east for a while into the Nantahalas.

The second point of interest surrounding Silers Bald is in its name. Named for the Siler family who once grazed cattle on the summit (names like "Sweat Heifer Trail," near Newfound Gap, begin to make sense in that context), it stands as a reminder of what Maurice Brooks called the lifestyle "from cove to bald." The necessity to find lands for grazing drove the lowland cove dwellers far into the hills in search of the precious open land of the balds. Had the balds not existed, the hills people would, Brooks opines, have been more the stay-at-home lowlanders and not the kind of people they were (and are): isolated, rugged, and independent.

From Silers Bald the AT passes Buckeye Gap on its way to the junction with Miry Ridge Trail. Miry Ridge's name is pretty self-explanatory, especially for hikers who have wandered off the trail into the black muck that has accumulated in the concave depression along its height over the years.

Once past yet another Sams Gap (the last gap of this name lies a 125-mile walk to the north), the AT enters a 17-mile stretch—almost the rest of the way in the Smokies—of strenuous up-and-down hiking. Perhaps the steepest section (going south) is the short hop up from Beechnut Gap to Thunderhead.

At 5527 feet, Thunderhead has given its name to the late Precambrian sandstone out of which much of the Great Smoky range is made. It offers fantastic views as well.

Running north from the Thunderhead/Rocky Top massif is Defeat Ridge. This isn't named for any dire battle, but rather after an exercise in democracy on the part of some old-time

Cherokee trail builders, which took place just before the Civil War.

Faced with a choice of routes for the Anderson Road, proposed to run from Cades Cove to the north to other settlements on the Tuckasegee Creek to the south, the Cherokees put it to a vote. Not having the "vee" sound in their language, they designated the ridge that won the vote as "Bote Ridge," and ever after referred to the rejected route as "Defeat Ridge." A mile down the Trail from 5441-foot Rocky Top, on the western end of Thunderhead Mountain, you'll pass the head of Bote Ridge. Traces of the old road can be seen down the ridge near Bote Ridge Trail.

Once down off Thunderhead, past Spence Field and Russell Field shelters, the Trail comes down to Big Abrams Gap and Little Abrams Gap, with a rugged knob in between. Old Abram was the Cherokee chief who led the last war parties against the Watauga settlements during the American Revolution. His wife, called Kate by the white settlers, was also immortalized by having her name affixed (after being changed) to Cades Cove.

Above Little Abrams Gap the AT runs for a half-mile or so along a grassy ridge line, crossing Devils Tater Patch. It then descends into Ekaneetlee Gap, formerly Egwanulti Gap, site of an old Cherokee footpath between the Middle Cherokee towns and the Overhills.

Another mile or so down the ridge the Trail reaches Doe Knob, the place where it turns south toward Fontana Dam and the Nantahala Mountains. It descends into the valley surrounding 4020-foot Shuckstack, a singular knob with spectacular views of the entire Clingmans-to-Gregory-Bald ridge line, much of which the Trail has just covered. This view is said to be one of the best in the southern Appalachians.

From Shuckstack it's an easy downhill to Fontana Dam, where the Trail officially leaves the Great Smokies.

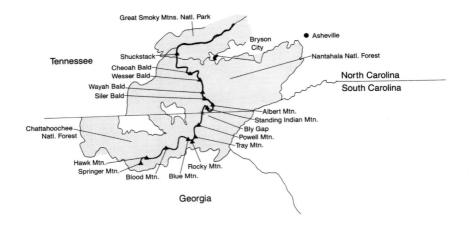

Great Smoky Mtns. Natl. Park

Bryson
City

● Asheville

Tennessee

Shuckstack

Nantahala Natl. Forest

Cheoah Bald
Wesser Bald

North Carolina

Wayah Bald

South Carolina

Siler Bald

Albert Mtn.
Standing Indian Mtn.

Chattahoochee
Natl. Forest

Bly Gap
Powell Mtn.
Tray Mtn.

Hawk Mtn.

Rocky Mtn.

Springer Mtn.

Blood Mtn.   Blue Mtn.

Georgia

Southern North Carolina and Georgia

13

The North Carolina/ Georgia Section

Trail Distances:

> *Fontana Dam, North Carolina, to North Carolina/Georgia state line* . . . . *86.6 miles*
>
> *North Carolina/Georgia state line to Springer Mountain, Georgia* . . . . *77.5 miles*
>
> > *Total Distance* . . . . *166.1 miles*

Maintaining Clubs:

> *Smoky Mountains Hiking Club: Fontana Dam to the Nantahala River*
>
> *Nantahala Appalachian Trail Club: Nantahala River to Bly Gap on the North Carolina/Georgia state line*
>
> *Georgia Appalachian Trail Club: Bly Gap on the North Carolina/Georgia state line to Springer Mountain, Georgia*

INTRODUCTION

THIS ENTIRE section of the Trail was almost bypassed when the original route was penciled out. For it was here, in the Nantaha-las, that the final compromise was made to route the Trail to

219

Mt. Oglethorpe via Springer Mountain back in the early days of 1929–30.

And what they would have missed! The Nantahala Mountain section has long been touted as the rip-roaringest in the South. In fact, only the Mahoosucs in New Hampshire and Maine claim anywhere near the ruggedness found in this short range between the Great Smokies and the Georgia finale of the Blue Ridge.

This whole area of the South has been undergoing impressive recreational development in recent years. Long famous for white-water paddling and rafting, there is now a growing community of rock climbers and other outdoors-types assembling in the region.

GEOLOGY ALONG THE TRAIL

This section of the Appalachian cordillera is a continuation of the mountain-building that we have been following all along— especially from southern Pennsylvania and the formation of the Blue Ridge. The forking of the Blue Ridge south of Roanoke, Virginia, was cause of much of the debate in the late 1920s about what route south the Trail would take. Would it opt for the eastern branch through the Blue Ridge proper (and over Mt. Mitchell, at 6684 feet the tallest in the East), or would it take the westerly route through the Great Smokies? The decision to include the Smokies created further challenges.

As was discussed in the chapter on history, when the verdict to take the AT through the Smokies was reached, it complicated the selection of the southern terminus. The logical point was in the area of Mt. Oglethorpe and Springer Mountain, which are the accepted joining points of the divergent branches of the Appalachian range. But due to complications in the range, a route had to be found to get there.

Enter the Nantahalas. They are not really part of either branch but are, rather, a transverse range that crosses between the two. Born of the approach and massive impact of the African plate over 250 million years ago, the Appalachians in the south seemed not to fold and fracture quite as neatly as they did to the north.

If you want an example of how this happens, lay a few

heavy blankets on something slippery, like a sheet of plastic. Then push the blankets across the plastic and watch how they fold. Push them from a slightly different direction. Rather than pushing perpendicular to the edge of the blanket, push at an angle. What you'll end up with is not a set of parallel accordion folds, but rather a wrinkled surface comprised of any number of complicated pleats. Somehow, through a quirk of folding no doubt aided by differences in rock strata, volcanism, and later erosion, the Nantahalas (and other transverse ranges) were formed along with the other escarpments.

Once back onto the Blue Ridge, as the Nantahalas approach Georgia the Trail enters onto the same ridge line it left near Peaks of Otter, north of Roanoke, Virginia. The eastern edge of the Appalachian ranges, the Blue Ridge is all along its length composed of the older metamorphics and occasional plutons and volcanics that we saw back in the Shenandoah National Park. As it moves south it is eroded into a rugged series of balds and knobs by the vigorous stream action of this moist region. The southernmost section, the first part of the Trail covered by the majority of thru-hikers, is a test of strength and fortitude that many do not pass.

HISTORY ALONG THE TRAIL

When the Europeans arrived, the Nantahalas were a kind of border area. Mainly within the Cherokee sphere, there were other tribes in the neighborhood. The Catawbas, who were bounced around by their neighbors quite a bit, occasionally lived in some of the valleys to the east, over by Asheville, North Carolina, and the Cheraws hunted to the eastern borders of the Nantahalas.

Like the mountain areas immediately to the north, the ranges of northern Georgia and adjacent North Carolina were settled fairly late. Early attempts to settle the coastal areas of North Carolina came to grief; the British settlement on Roanoke Island simply disappeared. Recent archaeological evidence suggests a massacre by local tribes.

When settlement finally did come in the mid-to-late eighteenth century, it followed the age-old pattern of centering on the coastal areas, spreading out over the piedmont agricultural areas, and moving slowly up into the mountain valleys and coves.

Like the areas around the Smokies, the hills of Georgia and the Nantahalas were populated by independent mountain people. The culture, renowned for its folkways, craftsmanship, and music, is the object of vigorous efforts at preservation. The *Foxfire* series of books was the result of information-gathering efforts by local students in northern Georgia.

Much of the settlement in Georgia and North Carolina was by Irish settlers as well as poor English. This fact is perhaps best known to music historians who, for years, have traced the Celtic origins of traditional mountain music.

HISTORY OF THE APPALACHIAN TRAIL IN NORTH CAROLINA AND GEORGIA

In the early days of the trail-blazing efforts of the Appalachian Trail Conference, if mountain lore was rich in this area, mountain hiking was virtually unknown. This would prove to be a problem.

In those days the ATC hadn't even decided upon the actual southern terminus of the Trail. Largely through the efforts of the established (in 1924) Smoky Mountains Hiking Club, it had been decided to route the Trail through the Great Smokies. But from there, nobody seemed able to agree on anything.

Enter Roy Ozmer. In 1929 the ATC asked him to scout out sections of the Trail. He started in the south, intending to walk all the way north. A back injury in Virginia prevented him from becoming the first thru-hiker.

According to sources within the Georgia Appalachian Trail Club (GATC), Ozmer was not given much to go on and probably felt that the choice of route was up to him. The route he chose started at Mt. Oglethorpe and headed northeast over Springer, Blood, and Tray mountains, over the Nantahalas, and across to Silers Bald near Clingmans Dome in the Smokies. With the exception of the compromise that routed the Trail's exit from the Great Smokies farther west to Doe Knob, this is basically the route that the AT follows today.

The trouble was, the ATC had in reality decided on a more western terminus, at Cohutta Mountain in the northwest corner of Georgia. The influential Smoky Mountains club much preferred that course, since it would allow the Trail to traverse the Smokies in their entirety.

In his efforts, Ozmer was assisted by two Forest Service men: Everett "Eddy" Stone and his assistant Charlie Elliott. They were both passionately devoted to the AT idea.

Ozmer reported his suggestions for routing to the ATC and found a supporter in Myron Avery. It was that fact, along with a compromise with the wishes of the Smoky Mountains Hiking Club that brought the Trail farther west in the Smokies and established the present route of the AT. The original southern terminus at Mt. Oglethorpe was abandoned in the late 1950s, due to heavy development of the summit area for chicken farming, in favor of the current site at Springer Mountain.

It was Everett Stone who realized that the Georgia bargaining position against the desires of the existing Smoky Mountains club weren't too compelling without a similar Georgia club to carry out the plans. No matter how often they proposed the eastern route, other clubs kept suggesting changes. And that was the main disadvantage the Trail had in this part of the South. Unlike New England, where things had gone so easily, there were no hiking clubs in Georgia; there were no blazed hiking trails. They would have to start from scratch.

So Stone simply ordered Charlie Elliott to start the Georgia Appalachian Trail Club. Elliott, in his own fashion, complained vehemently—and comically—about being told to recruit a mountain club among people who had never seen a mountain. Charlie would have made the perfect movie sidekick—ever the Sancho Panza to Stone's Quixote.

After several false starts Elliott finally succeeded, in the fall of 1930, in getting enough people together to form a club, with Eddy Stone as its first president. From the start they tried to keep the GATC as a club for active people—no "dead wood." It's pretty much that way today.

The following year Myron Avery came south to hike the recently decided upon southernmost section. Taking the trek with him was Warner Hall, soon to replace Stone as president of the GATC and to gain immortality as the hiker whose image appears on the plaque that marks the southern terminus on

Springer Mountain.

The existing route actually became a reality when the Smoky Mountains club got their compromise. Continuing the route through the Great Smokies past Silers Bald to Doe Knob before descending into the valley of the Little Tennessee River, the Smoky Mountains club trail crews pushed the route across the river, then back east along Yellow Creek Mountain until it hit the main line of the Nantahalas at the Nantahala River near Wesser Bald.

The rest of the North Carolina part of this section was and is the responsibility of the Nantahala Appalachian Trail Club. Its most famous founding father and guiding light for most of its first fifty years was the Reverend A. Rufus Morgan, a local minister and longtime resident of the area (he was a descendant of the Siler family, after whom Siler Bald, not to be confused with Silers Bald in the Smokies, is named). A man of immense personal energy, he would single-handedly (footedly?) walk the Trail in his club's section with great regularity on into his later years. He ranks with the major luminaries in Trail history.

THE TRAIL IN NORTH CAROLINA

Once, the AT did not cross the Little Tennessee at Fontana Dam. It traveled instead practically the entire length of the Great Smokies, crossing at Tapoco, North Carolina, before coming all the way back east to where the Trail passes today. But that was in the very early, pre-Trail-completion days.

Once 1930–31 had rolled around and the Tennessee Valley Authority had put in the Fontana Dam (at 480 feet, the biggest in the East), the Smoky Mountains Hiking Club quickly took advantage of the occasion to divert the Trail to it to make use of the more direct crossing to the Nantahalas.

The Nantahalas aren't nearly as tall as the Smokies—in the entire section the Trail will top 5000 feet only a few times, and it won't come near 6000 again. But they are rugged and wild. It's hard to recommend destinations in this section because in its entirety it makes such a great place to go.

Like many national forests, the Nantahala and Chattahoochee national forests, through which much of the AT in this section passes, are laced with gravel and dirt fire-and-service roads. Many of these are open to the public, but some may not exactly be a great avenue for the family's Honda Civic. Check with the ranger stations about road conditions. They'll be glad to tell you which roads are best to use—especially since it'll probably be them you call to pull you out if you go wrong. They can also tell you good spots to leave the car when you set off on the Trail and they'll help you steer clear of areas where active logging is going on. That doesn't mean you have to worry about them clear-cutting the Trail route (but a log truck *can* make a mess of your car if you block the logging road even a little bit when you park).

After leaving Fontana Dam the Trail goes along a road for almost a mile, but it then gets serious in a hurry. In a little over 2.5 miles it climbs over 1600 feet to the ridge crest in the Yellow Creek and Cheoah mountains. This is not a ridge line like the ones in Pennsylvania, and more than one hiker has lamented the absence of those steady, trustworthy Pennsylvanian walks for mile after mile at 1400 feet. Here, it's up to 3500 feet, and then the yo-yo routine. First you're up onto Yellow Creek Mountain, then down 800 feet into Yellow Creek Gap. Then back up, dipping down into Cody Gap, Brown Fork Gap, and the knee-busting (or gut-busting, depending on which way you're going) dip into Sweetwater Gap. After a few more drops it's the big grunt up onto Cheoah Bald, at 5062 feet one of the big ones. Then it's a few more knobs and the big drop to the Nantahala River. And I mean a big, *big* drop—from 5000 feet to 1700 feet in less than 8 miles. That's what I'd call in polite society an inexorable descent. Hikers traveling this section in either direction are welcome to use less restrictive language.

The AT crosses the Nantahala at Wesser, North Carolina. This is the home of the Nantahala Outdoor Center (NOC), which has its headquarters in nearby Bryson City and outposts on the Chattooga down on the South Carolina border and on the French Broad up at Hot Springs. The NOC is famous as a whitewater outfitter and offers one of the best training courses in the country on all methods of travel on moving water. I took my first kayaking lesson at their Chattooga outpost and couldn't wait to do it again. Considering the danger of these pot-holed undercut rivers, I wouldn't paddle one of them without getting the straight story from the NOC gang.

Once across the Nantahala, the Trail again gains altitude that was lost in the descent into the valley (passing by Rufus Morgan Shelter, named for the founder and guiding light of the Nantahala Appalachian Trail Club). This time, it's up to Wesser Bald—an ascent of nearly 3000 feet in 5.7 miles. It's in this section that the Nantahalas get their reputation as one of the ruggedest sections—if not *the* ruggedest—on the entire AT. The Nantahala club has in recent years routed this part of the route away from a wooded hike on the east side of the ridge to the ridge itself, providing the hiker with great views from time to time all the way to the summit of Wesser Bald. The route to the top is steep and frequently switchbacked. There used to be a fire tower on Wesser Bald but all that remains are the concrete footings and an old fire road leading down to the highway near Beechertown.

And, once again, it's downward. In 2 miles of walking it's down a mere 800 feet to Tellico Gap before ascending once again, this time to Copper Ridge Bald—another 5000-footer. This is a fun section to walk: It never dips below 4000 feet and there are several campsites on the shoulder of Wayah Bald (the peak also sports a restored observation tower with views to just about everywhere). Tellico Gap is accessible by car on some gravel roads linking U.S. 19 and U.S. 64, as is Wayah Bald itself, but they don't show up very prominently on the guidebook maps. Get the USFS map of the Nantahala National Forest instead, from: United States Forest Service, Nantahala National Forest, P.O. Box 2750, Asheville, North Carolina 28802. They charge a couple of bucks for postage and handling.

The section around Wayah Bald and south goes mostly over Forest Service trails. These are carefully constructed and well graded, making for less rugged—though just as strenuous—hiking.

After descending off Wayah Bald, the AT drops another 1000 feet or so into Wayah Gap, which is accessible on North Carolina Route 1310, which runs between U.S. 19 and U.S. 64 and past Nantahala Lake. It was here, during the Revolution, that a detachment of North Carolina irregulars, tired of the British-aroused Cherokees raiding their settlements, fought a fierce, though brief, encounter with a group of Cherokee warriors, defeating them. The Trail then moves back onto the ridge line and heads toward Wallace Gap, ascending a few hundred feet to top 5000 feet again on Siler Bald.

Siler Bald is currently undergoing reclamation. In recent years the "bald" part has dwindled down to a space about 100 feet long and 75 feet wide (crossed by the Trail just below the summit). After much discussion the Forest Service decided to clear the top of Siler Bald and make it a true bald again. When last I saw it, work had progressed to the point where practically the whole north side above the AT crossing was cleared. Whether it stays that way or not is another matter: The tree stumps on the upper slopes had already sprouted again. But if it can be maintained as a bald, it should offer splendid views of the whole range toward Fontana Lake and down into Georgia. You already have a great view of Wayah Bald and Nantahala Lake.

From Siler Bald it's down a heavily switchbacked trail (several good campsites) to Winding Stair Gap and U.S. 64. There's a parking area a few hundred feet down the road. Another couple miles or so bring you to Wallace Gap.

After leaving Route 64 and Wallace Gap, the AT heads up over the last section in the Nantahalas. Unlike most sections of the AT through these rugged hills, the route here sports plenty of side trails to the west of Albert Mountain. There is a National Forest Service Campground, the Standing Indian site, about 1.5 miles south of Wallace Gap via a branch off Forest Service Road 67, at the headwaters of the Nantahala.

The Trail heads once again steeply uphill. *Please don't cut across the switchbacks.* This area, with 5250-foot Albert Mountain down the trail, and the side trails cutting across the AT in a half-dozen locations between Wallace Gap and Standing Indian, makes a great short-hop destination. There are many popular campsites in many of the high gaps, like Mooney Gap, Carter Gap, and Betty's Creek Gap.

After Betty's Creek Gap the Trail heads up a long ridge, Little Ridgepole Mountain, at the 4800-foot level. As it hits its southernmost spot on Ridgepole Mountain, look to the northward along the ridge you've just joined and tip your hat. On the spot where you're standing, the AT rejoins the Blue Ridge proper, the long line that it had been forced to leave up near Peaks of Otter so many miles ago.

In the meantime, head north again—or, more accurately,

northwest. The Trail, after coming within about a half-mile of the Georgia border, is looping back again for the specific purpose of crossing near the summit of 5498-foot Standing Indian Mountain. You'll pay a bit to get there: From Beech Gap, you'll climb around 1000 feet in about 3 miles. From Deep Gap on the west side it's even steeper.

The view from Standing Indian, like that from so many peaks around here, is worth the effort. The Talulah River Gorge, running out of the southern slopes of Standing Indian itself, is impressive, as are the views of the mountains of southern Georgia. For a northerner, there are few better views of the hills of the south as you look down toward Rabun and Neels gaps in Georgia and Foxfire country.

Which brings us to an important point. Many northerners tend to hold a rather comic-strip view of southern people. We've been fed in recent years the idea that they're somehow threatening. Movies like *Easy Rider* and *Deliverance* (filmed a few miles to the south of where you're standing) presented us with the whole myth, all nicely wrapped in a slick Hollywood package.

The truth is different. Nicer, more helpful folks have never been born. And think of this: At northern trailheads you hide your stuff and lock your car for very good reason; in the South, you do it mainly from force of habit.

The Trail comes down off Standing Indian along the Blue Ridge. There are a few ups and downs, and you'll pass the Chunky Gal Mountain Trail (now *there's* a name to be reckoned with!), which branches off to the northwest. Then it's a quick roller-coaster descent to Bly Gap (3840 feet), and you're in Georgia.

THE TRAIL IN GEORGIA

"We are sincere in the belief that we have a very desirable section of the Trail down here and dare say that a great many ideas about Georgia will be changed on a hike through its mountainous portion."

—CHARLIE ELLIOTT, 1931

Georgia ranks as the only state along the entire length of the AT wherein the Trail is completely protected. The whole thing is within the enormous Chattahoochee National Forest.

Bly Gap, where the Georgia Section starts (it's actually a few yards within North Carolina) is a great destination all by itself, especially for overnight campers. Remote and consisting of a pleasant clearing, it's perfect for a weekend getaway. From Bly Gap you can make day hikes up into the Standing Indian Range or back down the lower Blue Ridge in Georgia, with its terrific views of the Nantahalas and the surrounding Georgia peaks.

The trouble is, Bly Gap is a bit difficult to get to. It can be reached from the north either by coming in by the Chunky Gal Trail from U.S. Route 64, 7 miles west of Wallace Gap, or by heading straight to Deep Gap on Forest Service Road #71. From Deep Gap it's 7.1 miles; via the Chunky Gal and the AT it's more like 9.5 miles. From the south it's a bit more complicated. USFS Road #72 goes through Blue Ridge Gap, 3.1 miles south of Bly Gap, but normally a car can't get through the narrow, rough track. There are some trails up from 72 on either side of the gap on which the Forest Service may be able to give you some information. Some years, though (depending on road conditions), you may be able to get within a mile or so of the gap. Ask the Forest Service for road conditions and parking possibilities. Four-wheel-drive might help.

The 8.7 mile stretch of the AT from Bly Gap to U.S. Route 76 at Dick's Gap will give you an idea of the character of the Trail in Georgia. Situated as it is in the Chattahoochee, it's wild and remote. It's not a case of paralleling highways as far off as possible to preserve at least the illusion of wilderness; the Trail here actually cuts across the wildlands. When it cuts across roads the intersection is usually perpendicular.

Leaving Route 76, the Trail begins to cross the last miles blazed in this region. It was put through in the spring of 1931 by the GATC.

Although this section traverses over 16 miles of Wilderness, it travels much of that distance over abandoned Forest Service road. These are pleasant to walk because they have been graded. However, even road builders can't totally overcome these mountains' tendency to go up and down.

But the magnitude of the ascent/descent isn't *too* extreme. In this stretch the peaks are around 4000 feet, and the gaps in the 3500-foot range. You won't hear your ears popping the way you did in the Nantahalas.

Forest Service road approaches are available at Addis Gap, Tray Gap, and Indian Grave Gap. Some of these, especially the Addis Gap road, are rough and not passable to all vehicles. For details, contact the Forest Service at: Chattahoochee National Forest, 508 Oak Street NW, Gainesville, Georgia 30501. They also have a number of good maps that generally go for a dollar apiece.

From Addis Gap the route heads up along "The Swag of the Blue Ridge," a stretch along a ridge crest where the Trail changes elevation very little, staying at around 3400 feet. The best views in the area are to be found on Tray Mountain (4430 feet), between the Blue Ridge Swag and Indian Grave Gap. After Indian Grave Gap, the Trail descends into Unicoi Gap, where it crosses Georgia 75. Like so many highways in America, Route 75 follows where an old, popular Native American trail once ran.

At Unicoi Gap the Blue Ridge makes a semicircular swing to the northwest as it loops around the large cove that contains the headwaters of the Chattahoochee River. There is a short side trail leading downhill from Chattahoochee Gap, 4.5 miles from Unicoi Gap to Chattahoochee Spring, the official source of the river from which the national forest gets its name. There is also a 5.3-mile blue-blazed side trail that leads north to Brasstown Bald, the highest point in Georgia.

The Trail in this area generally stays level on the ridge line, going around 4045-foot Horsetrough Mountain until two knobs are reached just shy of Tesnatee Gap. Both Poplar Stamp and Sheep Rock Top are in the 3300- to 3600-foot range, and constitute fast climbs of about 500 feet from the ridge line below.

Tesnatee Gap is the site of the Richard B. Russell Scenic Highway, another such route that members of the local hiking clubs tried in vain to prevent. Until the highway was completed in 1966, this was the longest section in Georgia without a major road crossing.

The ridge line west of Tesnatee Gap becomes a bit more saw-toothed, crossing Cowrock Mountain (3842 feet), Levelland Mountain (3942 feet), and after crossing Neels (Frogtown) Gap finally topping out on Blood Mountain (4461 feet). It was supposedly named that because of a battle between the Cherokees and Creeks that took place there.

Just south of Blood Mountain is de Soto Falls, a series of

cascades along Frogtown Creek that might be worth a visit. It can be reached from U.S. 19 a few miles south of Neels Gap. Blood Mountain itself has a number of rocks and ledges from which hikers can get splendid views of the surrounding terrain. There is a stone shelter on the summit, refurbished in 1981.

Descending from Blood Mountain, the AT will remain at around the 3000-foot level all the way to Springer Mountain. As it crosses the peaks of Big Cedar, Justus, Sassafras, and Hawk mountains, it continues through the gentle rolling ridges and valleys of the Chattahoochee National Forest. The ridges here are generally laid out on an east/west axis.

The terrain through which the last miles of the AT travel is characterized by the lush, healthy southern Appalachian forest that has been so prevalent since up by Virginia. But all is not always as it seems.

In the last miles, between Hightower Gap and Springer Mountain, the army from nearby Fort Benning is in the habit of running complicated maneuvers. It may sound like World War III, and you need to be careful of things like booby traps, mines, and the like. This is all simulated, but it can be somewhat disconcerting just the same. The Army, however, knows full well that the Appalachian Trail passes nearby and their personnel have a reputation for being generally polite and helpful to hikers.

Springer Mountain (3782 feet) has been the southern terminus since 1958, when the ATC and the GATC finally rerouted the Trail from its former ending (or beginning) amid the chicken farms and desolation of Mt. Oglethorpe. As a terminus, Springer is far superior. Standing amid a protected wilderness, an 8.7-mile hike from the road, it offers views of the surrounding territory from ledges near the summit. The bronze plaque of the hiker (Warner Hall) that is set into the rock at its summit is a fitting marker. It bears the legend:

APPALACHIAN TRAIL
GEORGIA TO MAINE

A Footpath for Those who seek
Fellowship with the Wilderness

THE GEORGIA APPALACHIAN TRAIL CLUB

The plaque pleased Benton MacKaye so much that he wrote to the GATC: "It is seldom that I've been hit between the eyes with utter and instantaneous delight as I was on viewing [a picture of] this real work of art. Here in vigorous embodiment is (to my mind) the spirit of the Appalachian Trail. . . . 'A footpath for those who seek fellowship with the wilderness.' This (to my mind) is a masterful definition of the Appalachian Trail. . . .

"Your words keep coming back to me: 'fellowship with the wilderness [part of the motto of the GATC].' The last word cannot too often be repeated—*wilderness, Wilderness, WILDERNESS!* Not man but nature; man's relation not to man but to nature. And thereby—incidentally—the man-to-man relation finds its place."

To those of us who hike this Trail today, this serves as a reminder. The idea of Benton MacKaye, so simple, yet so pervasive, caught on for one inexorable reason: People immediately understood it, in a unique way. Perhaps not on an intellectual level, but in their hearts. Just as the folks in Georgia, in their unpretentious inscription at the southern terminus, defined the concept to the delight of its creator, so did the people of Maine—and of every place in between. They were all struck by the simple *rightness* of it.

And rightness never dies.

Appendices

LOCALISMS

RUNNING AS the Trail does through several different geo-graphic and demographic regions of the United States, the hiker may become confused with some of the terminology used. Truth to tell, what is called one thing in Maine may be another in North Carolina.

A narrow mountain valley that is called a notch, pass, or even col in the Northeast will be called a gap by the time the Trail reaches Pennsylvania. Where northeasterners tend to re-gard a summit as a summit, the farther one travels south, the more differentiation there is, depending on what the summit is like. Beyond the general southern terms for a peak (top, knob, high top, high knob), a rocky summit will be known as a *dome.* A mountain topped with meadows is a *bald,* while one topped with heath is a *slick.* A predominance of balsam or spruce earns the title of *balsam,* while mountain laurel and rhododendron will sit atop a *laurel.*

This only occasionally gets confusing, as it does on Clingmans Dome, which is actually a balsam. Formerly known as "Balsam Mountain," the "Dome" designation may prove pro-phetic because the balsam woolly aphid and acid rain are con-spiring to kill all the trees on the highest summit on the AT.

On the other hand, in his 1943 book, *The Great Smokies and the Blue Ridge,* Roderick Peattie said: "A hogback vividly if inelegantly describes a type of mountain so characteristic that it might almost be called an appalachian as one speaks of an alp." He was speaking, of course, of the long humpbacked ridgelike mountains so common in all parts of the Appalachians.

In the south, valleys also have specific designations: A big valley may just be called a *valley,* while a smaller one might be a *hollow.* A small valley leading up into the mountains is a *cove,* while true bottomland is called a *bottom.*

Streams, too, get special consideration. In Maine, a small stream will be a *stream.* By the time the Trail reaches New Hampshire it will be a *brook.* That term will continue through Vermont and upper New England, only to give way (though not entirely) to *creek* in lower New England and New York.

Once down to Pennsylvania, however, use of the term brook peters out until it is totally out of use. In the south, the normal usage is *river* for a large stream and *creek* for a smaller one. It's pronounced "creek," too, not "crick," the way they do in the Midwest. The only other aberration is the use of the term *run* for creek. This happens only in Virginia.

According to a 1941 article in the Potomac Appalachian Trail Club Bulletin, the seemingly incomprehensible system of what trailside shelters are called can be ironed out as follows:

In Maine, they are *lean-tos.*

South of Grafton Notch, they are *shelters.* Closed shelters are *huts,* except those maintained by the Dartmouth Outing Club, which are *cabins.*

In New York, shelters are called *Adirondack lean-tos* (the original inspiration for the design).

On the Blue Ridge closed shelters are called *shelters,* while open ones are called *lean-tos.* In the Great Smokies, lean-tos are *shelter-cabins.*

Over the years, as the society moves about, names evolve, but for the most part, the regional designations have remained. Fortunately, a tent is still called a *tent.*

USEFUL ADDRESSES

Appalachian Trail Conference National Offices

Appalachian Trail Conference
PO Box 807
Harpers Ferry, West Virginia 25425

Appalachian Trail Conference Regional Offices

New England

Appalachian Trail Conference
PO Box 122
Norwich, Vermont 05055

Mid-Atlantic

Appalachian Trail Conference
PO Box 381
Boiling Springs, Pennsylvania 17007

Southern

Appalachian Trail Conference
PO Box 738
Blacksburg, Virginia 24060

Appalachian Trail Conference
100 Otis Street, Box 2750
Asheville, North Carolina 28802

Member Organizations

Maine Appalachian Trail Club
PO Box 283
Augusta, Maine 04330

Appalachian Mountain Club
5 Joy Street
Boston, Massachusetts 02108

Dartmouth Outing Club
PO Box 9
Hanover, New Hampshire 03755

Green Mountain Club
PO Box 889
Montpelier, Vermont 05602

New York-New Jersey Trail Conference
232 Madison Avenue, Room 908
New York, New York 10016

Keystone Trails Association
PO Box 251
Cogan Station, Pennsylvania 17728

Potomac Appalachian Trail Club
1718 N Street, N.W.
Washington, D.C. 20036

Old Dominion Appalachian Trail Club
PO Box 25283
Richmond, Virginia 23260

Tidewater Appalachian Trail Club
PO Box 8246
Norfolk, Virginia 23503

Natural Bridge Appalachian Trail Club
PO Box 3012
Lynchburg, Virginia 24503

Piedmont Appalachian Trail Hikers
PO Box 945
Greensboro, North Carolina 27402

Tennessee Eastman Hiking Club
PO Box 511
Kingsport, Tennessee 37662

All other member organizations may be reached through the Appalachian Trail Conference's national offices in Harpers Ferry.

Useful Addresses and Phone Numbers

Baxter State Park
64 Balsam Drive
Millinocket, Maine 04462
(207) 723-5140

Great Northern Paper Company (major landowner in Maine)
Millinocket, Maine 04462

Scott Paper Company (major landowner in Maine)
Winslow, Maine 04902

White Mountains National Forest
PO Box 638, 719 Main Street
Laconia, New Hampshire 03246
(603) 524-6450

Green Mountain National Forest
Federal Building
Rutland, Vermont 05701
(802) 775-2579

Pennsylvania Dept. of Environmental Resources
Bureau of Forestry
PO Box 1467
Harrisburg, Pennsylvania 17120

Swatara State Park
R.D. 1, Box 410
Pine Grove, Pennsylvania 17963
(717) 865-5722

Pine Grove State Park
RD 2, Box 399
Gardners, Pennsylvania 17324
(717) 486-7174

Caledonia State Park
40 Rocky Mountain Road
Fayetteville, Pennsylvania 17222
(717) 352-8419

George Washington National Forest
PO Box 233
Harrisonburg, Virginia 22801
(703) 433-2491

Jefferson National Forest
210 Franklin Road
SW Roanoke, Virginia 24001
(703) 982-6270

Blue Ridge Parkway Headquarters
700 Northwestern Bank Building
Asheville, North Carolina 28801

Cherokee National Forest Headquarters
PO Box 2010
Cleveland, Tennessee 37311
(615) 476-9700

Great Smoky Mountains National Park
Gatlinburg, Tennessee 37738
(615) 436-5615

Nantahala National Forest
Wayah Ranger District
8 Sloan Road
Franklin, North Carolina 28734
(704) 524-6441

Cheoah Ranger District
PO Box 16-A, Rt. 1
Robbinsville, North Carolina 28771
(704) 479-6431

Tusquitee Ranger District
201 Woodland Drive
Murphy, North Carolina 28906
(704) 837-5152

Pisgah National Forest
Pisgah Ranger District
PO Box 8
Pisgah Forest, North Carolina 28768
(704) 877-3350

Toecane Ranger District
PO Box 128
Burnsville, North Carolina 28714

French Broad Ranger District
PO Box 128
Hot Springs, North Carolina 28743
(704) 622-3202

Chattahoochee National Forest
601 Broad Street
Gainesville, Georgia 30501
(404) 536-0541

Index